IMAGES
of America

FREEPORT

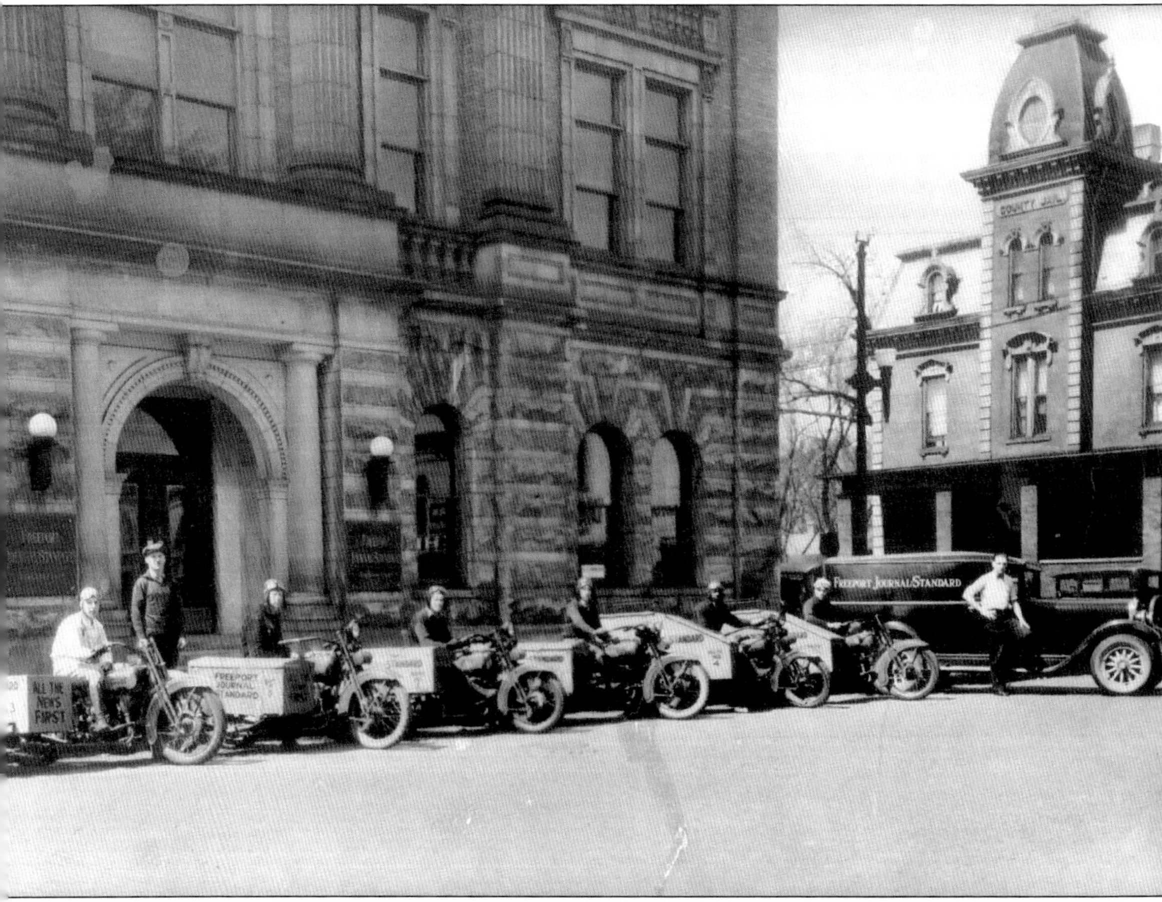

READY TO ROLL. Carriers for the *Freeport Journal-Standard* rode motorbikes with sidecars in the 1930s while the newspaper was in this large stone and brick building on downtown Galena Avenue between 1930 and 1960. The building on the right served as the Stephenson County jail from the late 1870s until 1962 when it was destroyed by fire. (The Journal-Standard archives.)

On the cover: **PEOPLE FLOCK TO GRUPE GROCERY.** The A. H. Grupe Grocery, typical of neighborhood stores in the 1920s, held an advantageous location at the corner of West Galena and North Foley Avenues. It was considered safe in those days for folks to send their children down the street for that loaf of bread. Note the men wearing hats and the boys wearing everything from knickers to bib overalls. (Courtesy of the Stephenson County Historical Society.)

IMAGES
of America

FREEPORT

The Journal-Standard

ARCADIA
PUBLISHING

ISBN 978-0-7385-6013-7

Published by Arcadia Publishing
Charleston, South Carolina

Printed in the United States of America

Library of Congress Control Number: 2009926699

For all general information contact Arcadia Publishing at:
Telephone 843-853-2070
Fax 843-853-0044
E-mail sales@arcadiapublishing.com
For customer service and orders:
Toll-Free 1-888-313-2665

Visit us on the Internet at www.arcadiapublishing.com

*This book is dedicated to the youth of this community,
hoping it may ignite in them a reverence for those who have gone before*

Contents

ACKNOWLEDGMENTS

This book would not have been possible without the generous support and assistance of a number of people.

The book's editors are Harriett Gustason and Lori Kilchermann. Members of the *Journal-Standard* staff who assisted include publisher Steve Trosley, managing editor Eric Petermann, Jodie Butler, Marge Collins, Heather Holloway, Dave Manley, Donna Schoch, and Bethany Strunk. Stephenson County Historical Society contributed photographs and assisted in research.

Those who represented the society were director Ed Finch, board president Harvey Wilhelms, and board members Judy Birdsell and Crystal Haddad, who were in charge of special displays.

Freeport Public Library staff members Cheryl Bronkema and Cheryl Gleason and volunteers in the library's Frances Woodhouse Local History Room have helped immeasurably in securing information and photographs.

Lenora Luecke and the Ted Luecke family, Jerry "Kokie" Griffin, and Harvey Wilhelms also provided photographs and information.

Our profound appreciation is extended to all these people.

Unless otherwise noted, all images appear courtesy of the Stephenson County Historical Society.

INTRODUCTION

This book was created by staff of the *Journal-Standard* with you, our loyal following, in mind.

We have seen how you cherish Freeport's historical heritage. In this book, we have sought to approach the main aspects that have influenced this heritage and present photographs illustrative of them.

We do not have to remind you that it is a rich heritage of unique, nationally impacting individuals, events, and industries empowered by ambition and the work ethic. Remarkable individuals shine out from every chapter of Freeport's history. Characteristics of our people also encompass an inherent thirst for the fine arts, including music in all its forms of expression, as evidenced by community choruses and bands, and passion for dancing and community theater.

Victorian mansions retain their elegance on deep lots along tree-lined streets, and middle-class America goes about its business on avenues alive with the goings and comings of family life.

We have seen an appreciation of the diversity and creativity of our people. Crafts of every genre were produced here.

Education has always been a major priority exemplified by our public and private school systems and our community college. Our graduates go on to pursue higher education and careers.

We at the *Journal-Standard* are proud of our city and its place in history. One focus has been on the debate held here in 1858 between Abraham Lincoln and Stephen A. Douglas. We have basked in the glory of that event's resounding Freeport Doctrine, to which history has credited the election of Lincoln to the presidency and the eventual Emancipation Proclamation.

We are all a part of that history.

We have attempted to make this book something that will give readers a sense of what life was like here throughout Freeport's growing pains and a view of the various phases of everyday life.

Freeport was, from its beginning, unique. Its somewhat eccentric founder, Tutty Baker, knew what he was doing in his pioneer land dealings. He was actually an astute businessman. His generosity in feeding and lodging incoming settlers, however, prompted his irate wife, Elizabeth Phoebe Baker, to suggest the city be named Freeport.

It was those settlers and the droves that followed them that have made Freeport a vibrant city with its variant cultures and its passion for living life to the fullest. Freeport was known for its brewing industry and thriving saloon numbers prior to Prohibition. And what goes with beer and ale? Of course there was a pretzel bakery here, hence Freeport's nickname, the "Pretzel City."

The city's exceptional park system has attracted folks from far and wide for family reunions, concerts, rallies, circuses, weddings, baseball, tennis, boating, fishing, hiking, jogging, nature study, and all manner of social events. Freeport once had a popular track for sulky races, a zoo, and an amusement park. Famous evangelist Billy Sunday conducted revivals here. Freeport was on the chautauqua circuit for a number of years. The entertainment and guest speakers performed in Krape Park before mass audiences who traveled there on a streetcar line that led into the park. Families brought picnic lunches and spent the day there. Traveling shows pitched tents in vacant lots.

One of Freeport's proudest landmarks is the Masonic temple with its acoustically designed auditorium, which seats more than 1,200 people and has a ballroom/dining hall that accommodates large crowds for everything from senior proms, wedding receptions, and chamber of commerce annual meetings to large-scale estate auctions and sit-down banquets.

The multitude of churches, charitable and service organizations, and clubs has contributed significantly to the city's betterment and opportunities for enrichment.

Freeport's Andrew Carnegie Library silently served the population for more than a century only to be replaced in December 2003 by a new, state-of-the art facility.

Yes, Freeport has had an eventful, productive past, one chock full of just about every type of human enterprise. We hope you enjoy these glimpses of it and learn from our plucky ancestry what it takes to make a city a good place to live.

—Harriett Gustason

One

Celebrations and Events

Freeport's population is enamored with music, drama, and all the fine arts.

The numbers of community bands and choruses that have played in the parks, school auditoriums, and on the Masonic temple stage are astounding, and with the multilevels of schools here, Freeport audiences have had more than ample opportunity to engage in these pleasures. Many of the local industries fostered bands and choruses that performed at various functions. Freeport Arts Museum features regular exhibits, recitals, and activities to feed all such interests.

Freeport has always loved a parade. In fact, the staging of festivals, celebrations, circuses, entertainment, recreation, and political rallies held here have all been a conspicuous characteristic of its fun-loving people. Taylor Park, being a shaded, flat area located close to railroads, was considered an ideal location for traveling circuses. It was known widely as the circus capital of the Midwest. The world-famous Ringling Brothers Circus once offered $80,000 to buy the park for its winter quarters.

The top historical event held here was the 1858 debate between Abraham Lincoln and Stephen A. Douglas. The outcome of that event, due to the reply Douglas gave to Lincoln's leading question regarding legalities of slavery in the territories, is known historically as the Freeport Doctrine. Lincoln's election to the presidency is generally attributed to the stance Douglas took in his answer to Lincoln's question.

Another giant celebration, held here in 1903, brought Pres. Theodore Roosevelt to Freeport for the dedication of a boulder, which was being placed as a monument for the Lincoln-Douglas debate.

For many years, Freeport hosted an annual festival called Tutty Baker Days, named for the town's founder. Large crowds flocked to the downtown to partake of entertainment on an outdoor stage, food and crafts concessions, street dances, and various relays and contests.

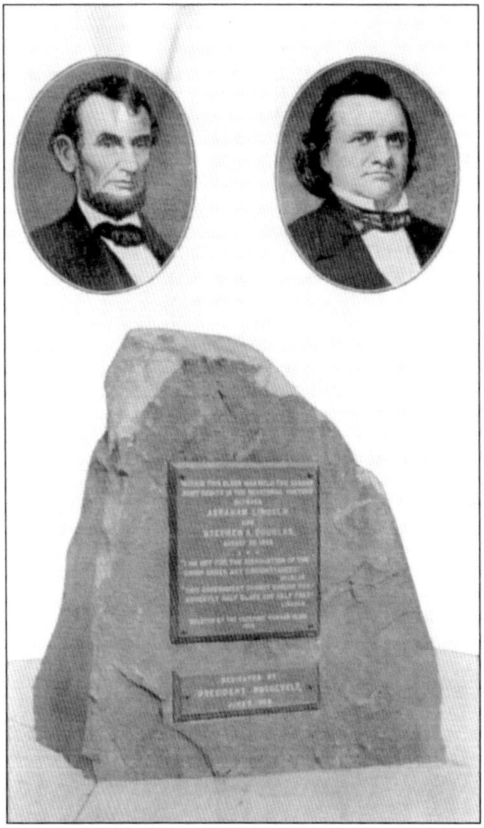

A LASTING MONUMENT. This boulder commemorates Freeport's historic distinction, the Lincoln-Douglas debate of August 27, 1858. Pres. Theodore Roosevelt visited Freeport for the 1903 dedication. The Freeport Woman's Club went to great lengths to bring the boulder here from Wisconsin. After several location changes, it now marks Freeport's beautifully landscaped Debate Square fostered by the local Lincoln-Douglas Society on East Douglas Street.

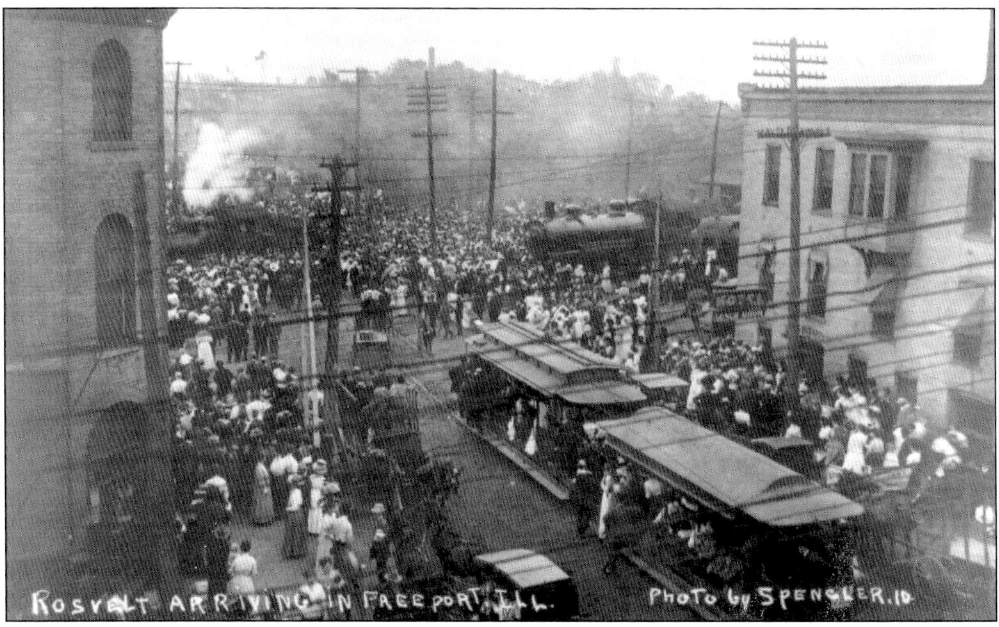

THE PRESIDENT CAME. Theodore Roosevelt drew a huge crowd when he came to Freeport in 1903 for the dedication of the stone monument brought here to mark the site of the 1858 Lincoln-Douglas debate. Hordes waited to meet his arriving train.

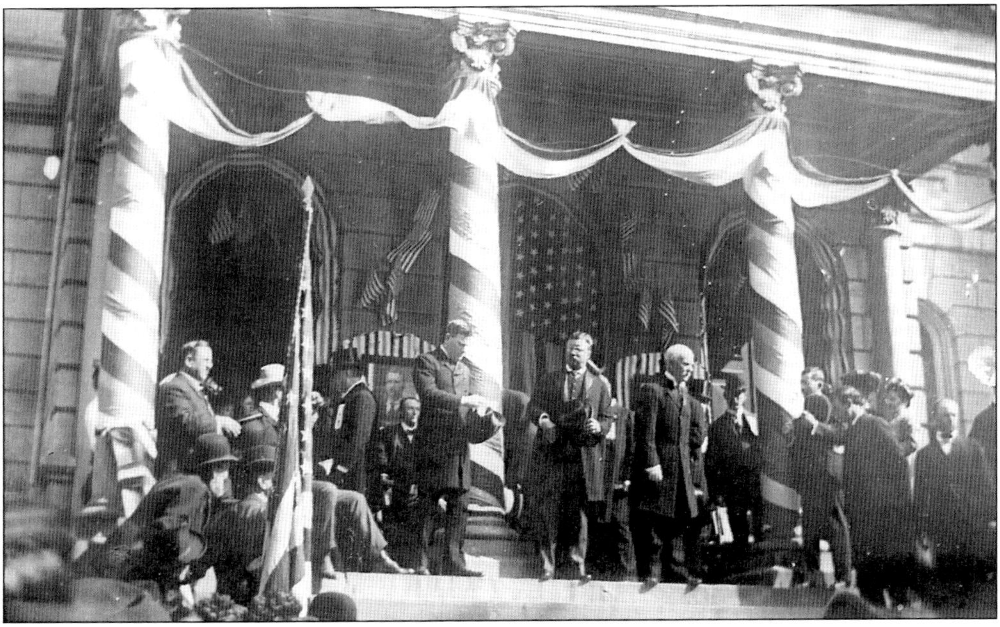

PRESIDENT COMES TO TOWN. Theodore Roosevelt stands at the top of the outdoor stairway at Stephenson County Courthouse. The ceremony moved to the courthouse steps because of the muddy terrain at the site. (Courtesy of the Freeport Public Library.)

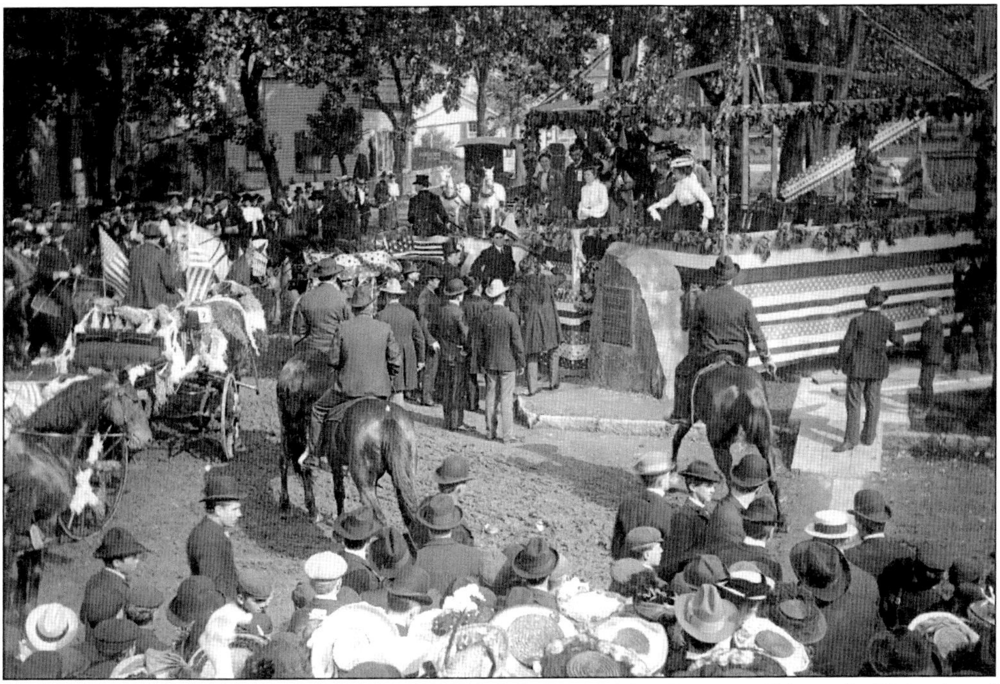

PRESIDENT'S VISIT CAUSE FOR CELEBRATION. In 1903, the Freeport Woman's Club placed a stone monument to mark the site of the nationally famous Lincoln-Douglas debate held in Freeport in 1858. Roosevelt came for the dedication, drawing a huge crowd to the site. Here he stands at the base of the stage, tipping his high silk hat. The stone, moved twice, now heralds the landscaped debate site on East Douglas Street.

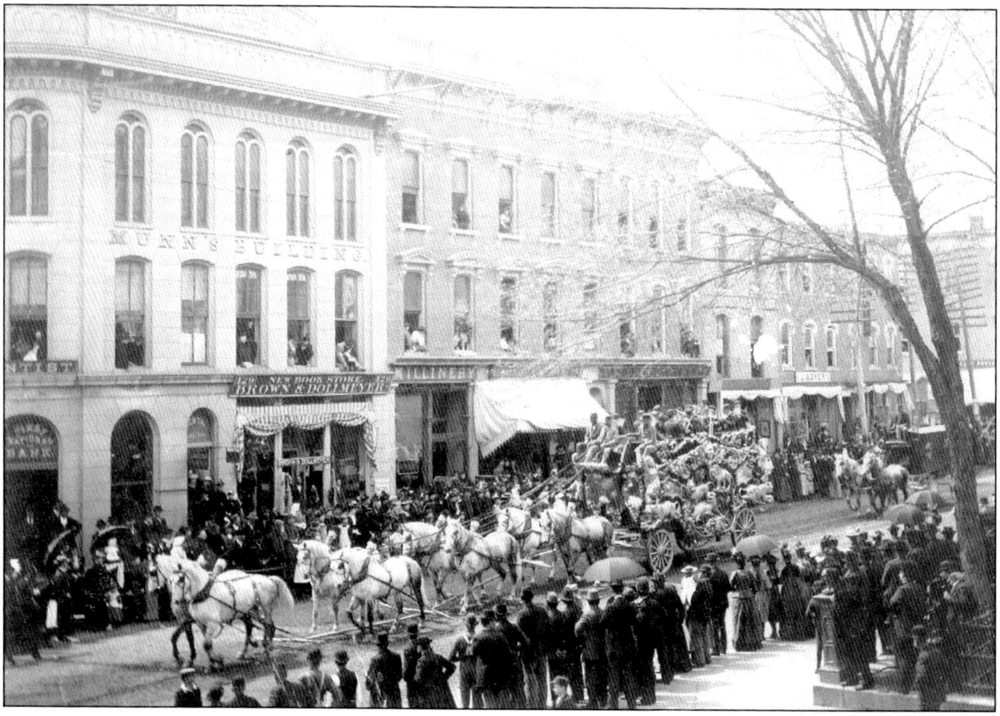

A Circus Came to Town. A circus parade drew crowds to Stephenson Street in 1892. Stephenson County Courthouse was on the right. An eight-horse team pulled the large circus bandwagon. In those days, all circus parades headed west on Main Street and east on Stephenson Street. Circuses were set up on the east side of the Pecatonica River. In the photograph above, First National Bank occupied the building at the far left. (Below, courtesy of the Freeport Public Library.)

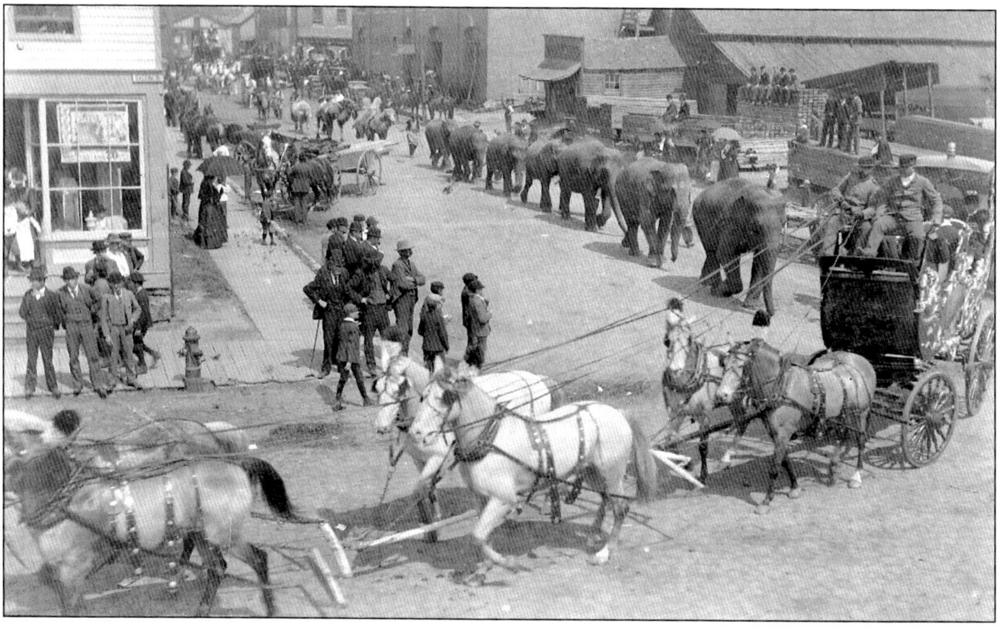

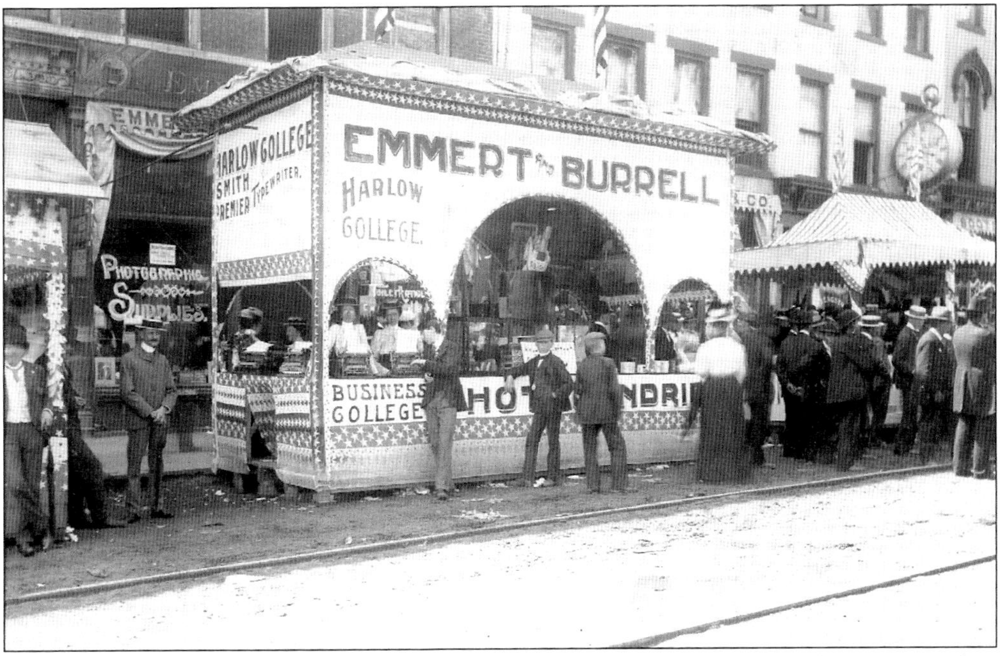

STREET FAIRS DREW CROWDS. Merchants moved their wares to front sidewalks for street fairs during the late 1800s. Emmert and Burrell drugstore had its stall in front of the business. The drugstore later became known as Emmert's and was owned and operated for years as Freeport's oldest business by Art Haas and his son Roscoe Haas. (Courtesy of the Freeport Public Library.)

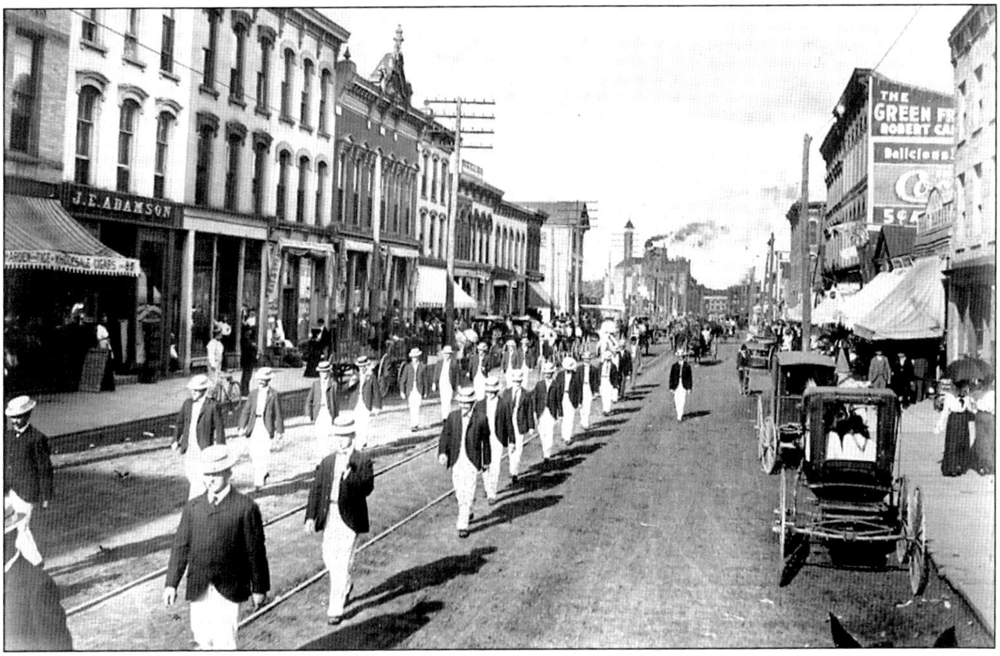

ELKS BROTHERHOOD FOUNDED. In 1900, members of the new Brotherhood of the Paternal Order of Elks, now known as the Benevolent and Protective Order of Elks, celebrated the founding of the lodge by marching through downtown Freeport. The scene is on Stephenson Street, just east of State Avenue. (Courtesy of the Freeport Public Library.)

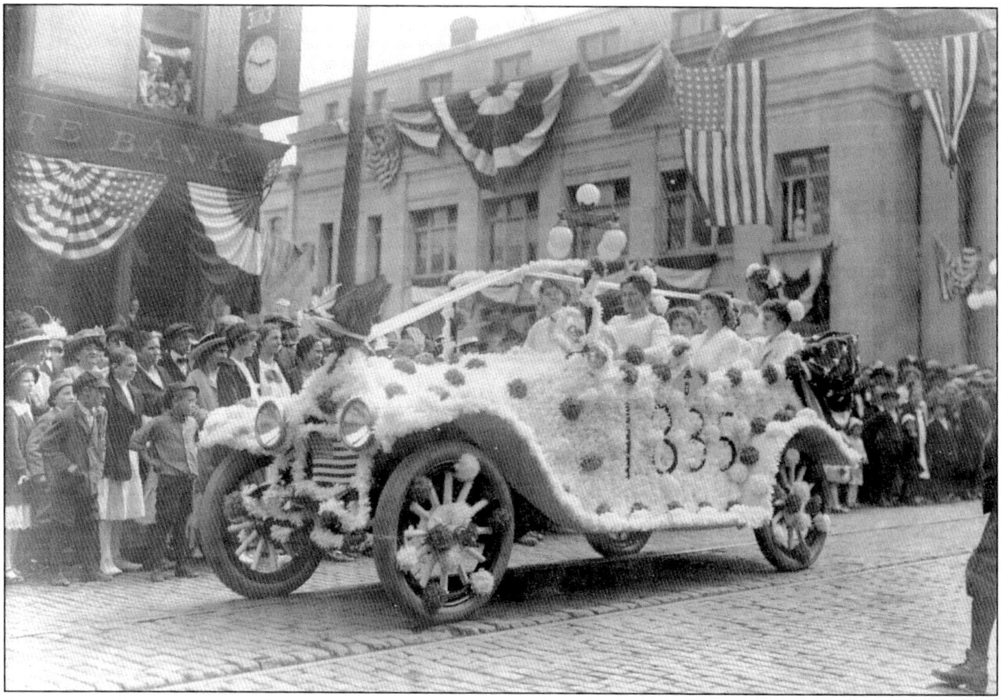

TIME TO CELEBRATE. This posy-decked automobile was a standout at an 1835 parade. The building on the right was an early structure of First National Bank.

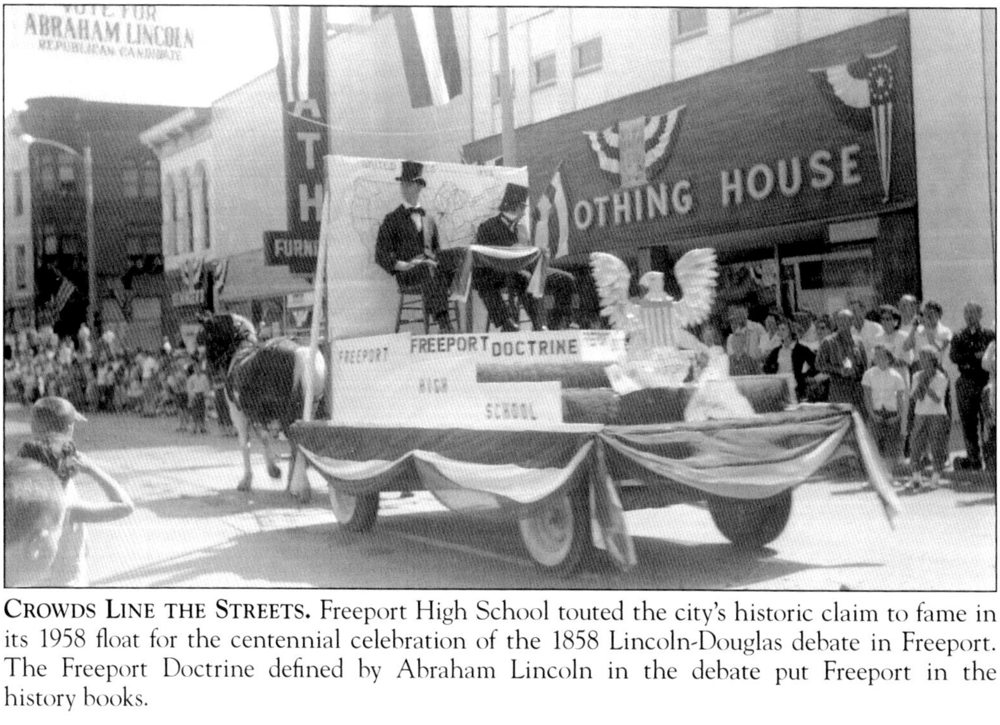

CROWDS LINE THE STREETS. Freeport High School touted the city's historic claim to fame in its 1958 float for the centennial celebration of the 1858 Lincoln-Douglas debate in Freeport. The Freeport Doctrine defined by Abraham Lincoln in the debate put Freeport in the history books.

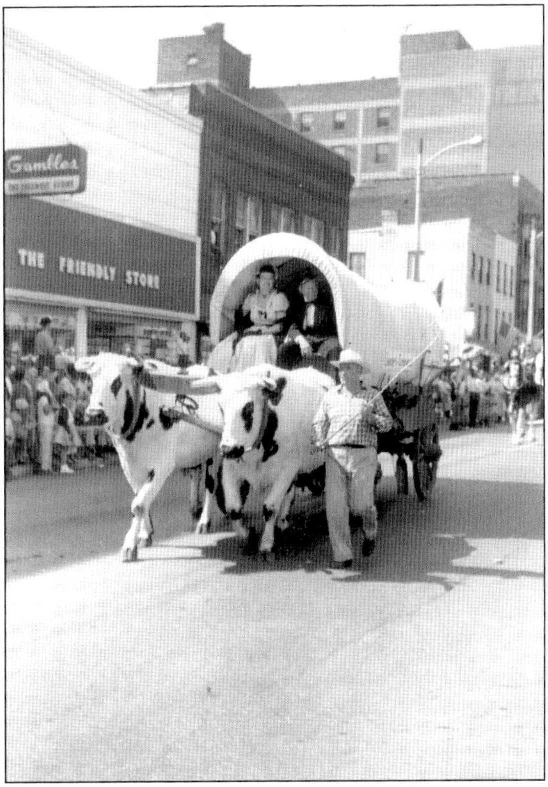

EVERYONE LOVES A PARADE. Freeport outdid itself in 1958 with its weeklong celebration for the Lincoln-Douglas debate centennial. There were activities to suit every taste, including plays, pageants, parades, formal balls, and reenactments. This float shows oxen pulling a covered wagon of yesteryear in the grand parade.

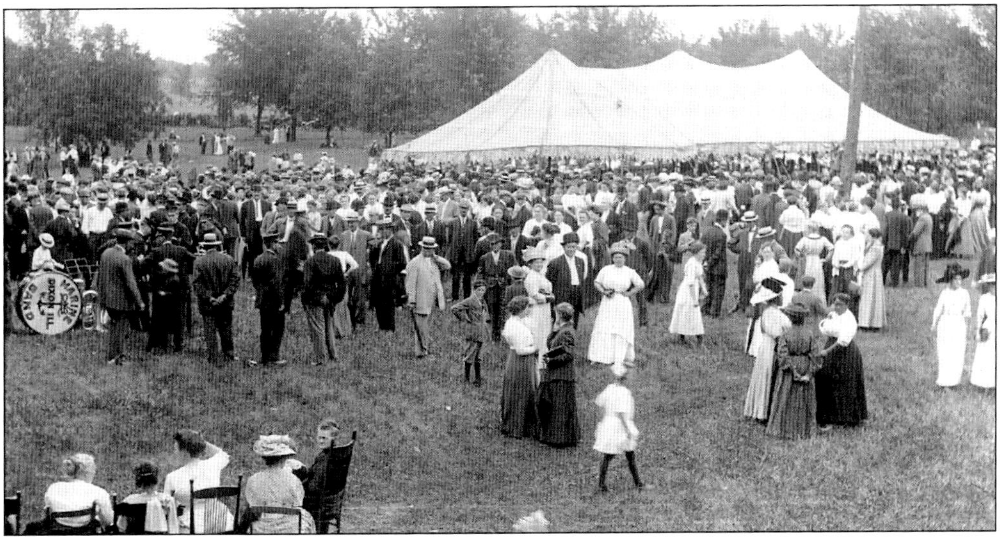

CHAUTAUQUA BROUGHT OUT THE CROWDS. During the first quarter of the 20th century, chautauqua traveling troupes toured the country during the summer months. In Freeport, lectures, plays, musical groups, and other forms of entertainment were featured in Globe Park and Highland Park. On July 4, 1907, there was a reported crowd of 10,000 people at a chautauqua gathering in Krape Park. (Courtesy of the Freeport Public Library.)

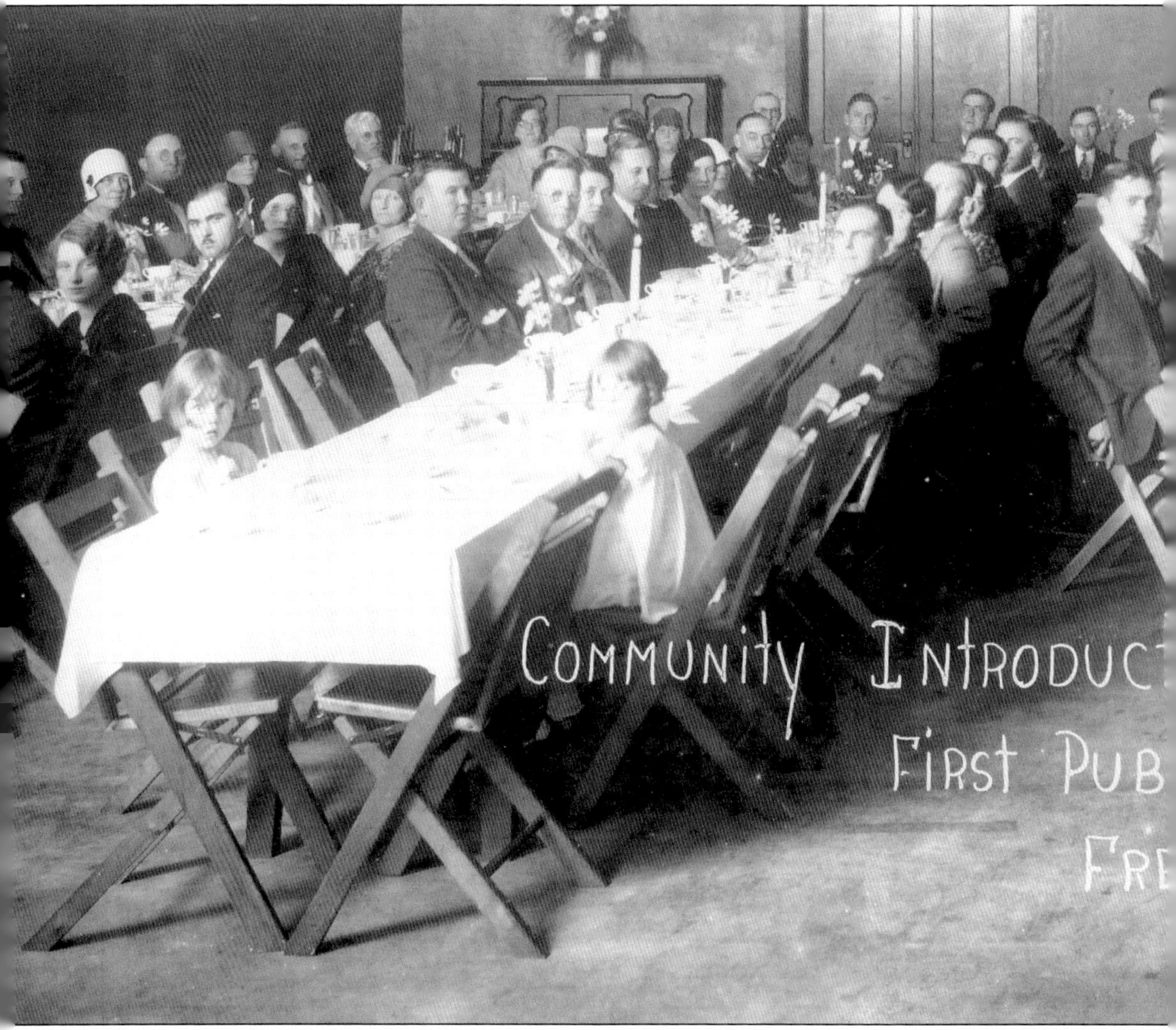

Latest Kitchen Helpers. This photograph from September 27, 1929, shows a wonderful

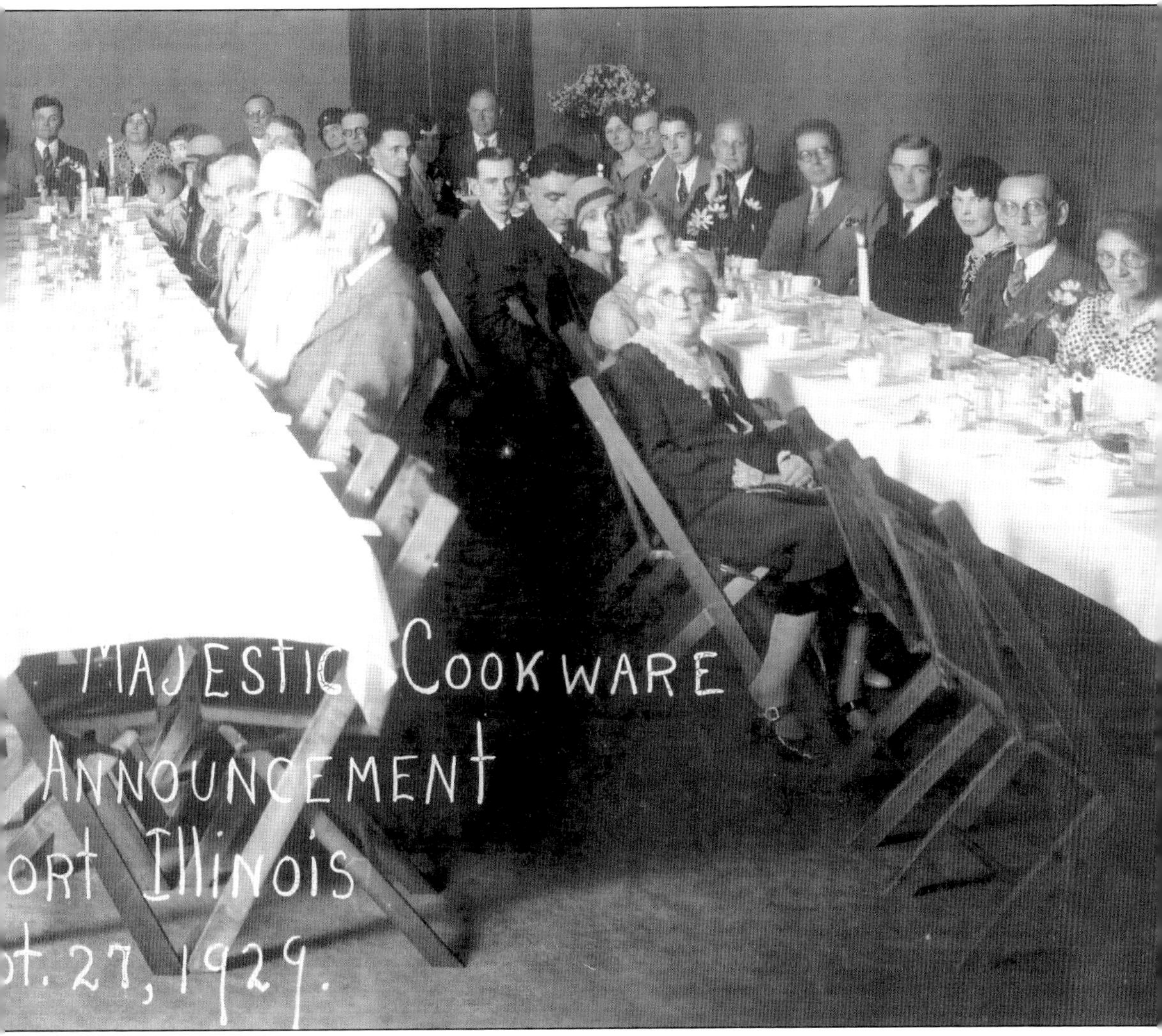

turnout of folks of all ages for the public unveiling of Majestic Cookware.

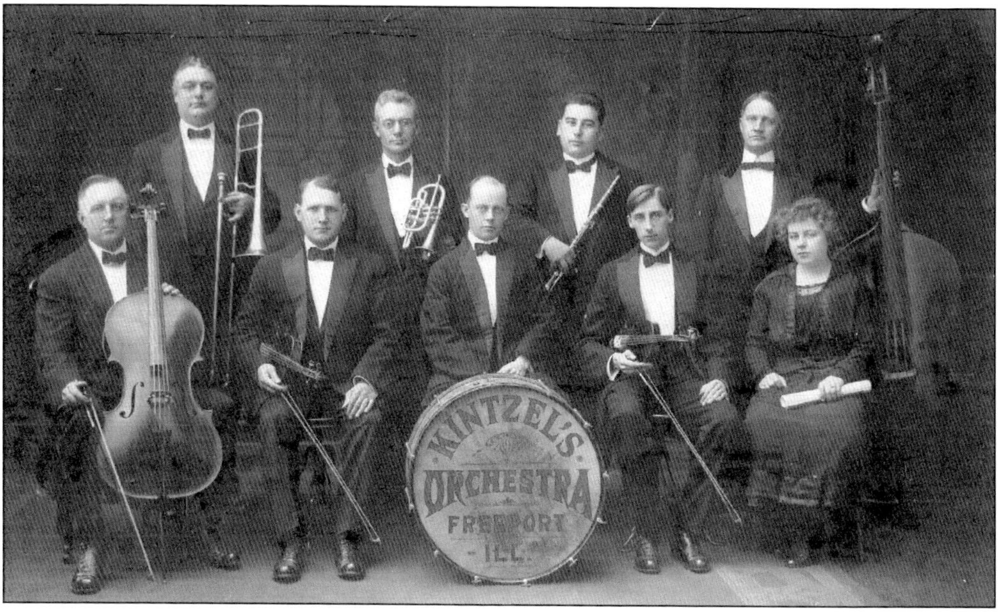

TUXEDO CLAD. This Freeport musical group, Kintzel's Orchestra, played for formal events such as charity balls, proms, and wedding receptions. This may have been an event at the Freeport Masonic Temple, where many such events took place in the city's past.

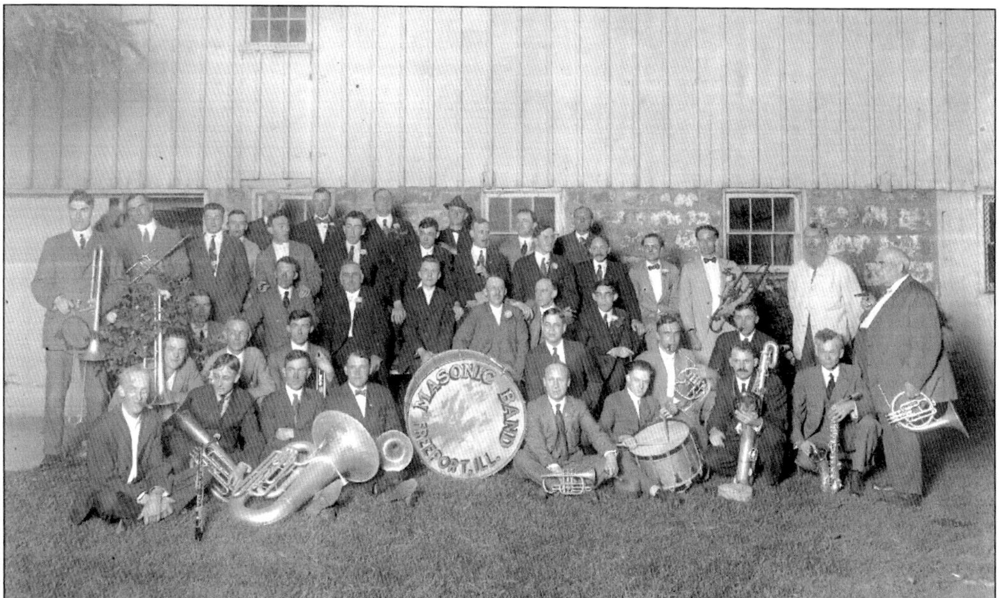

ACTIVE MASONS. Freeport has maintained active Masonic orders since 1851. Its band was made up of young and old alike.

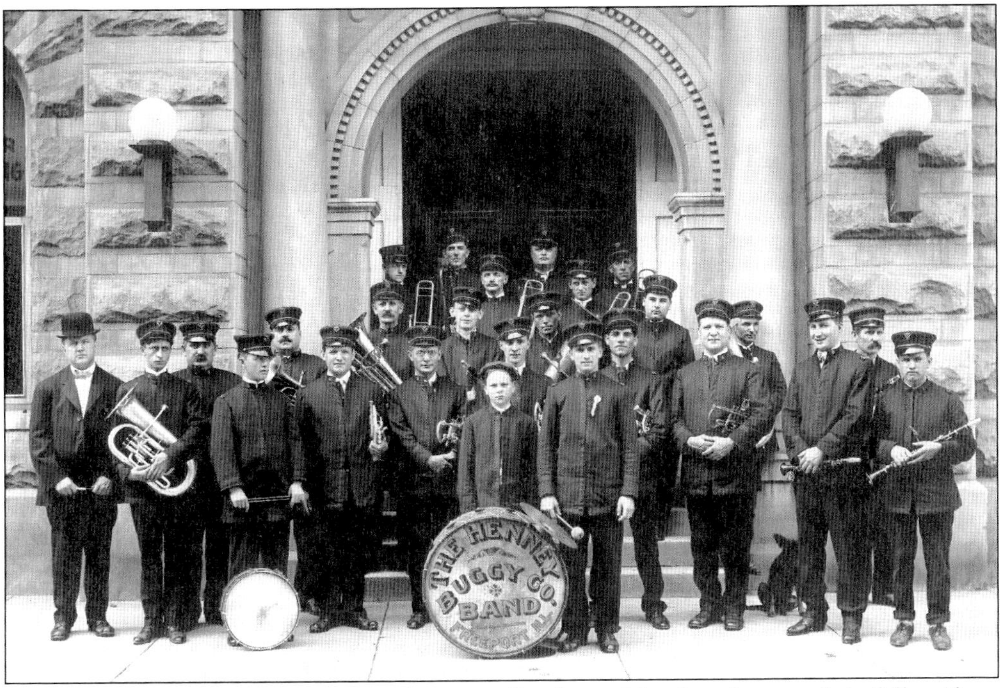

MUSIC MAKERS. The Henney Buggy Company Band posed for this photograph in full uniform in 1910. Freeport was great for music; many bands were formed and played in parades and public festivals. Henney Buggy Company eventually became Henney Motor Company, manufacturer of sleek hearses, limousines, and ambulances.

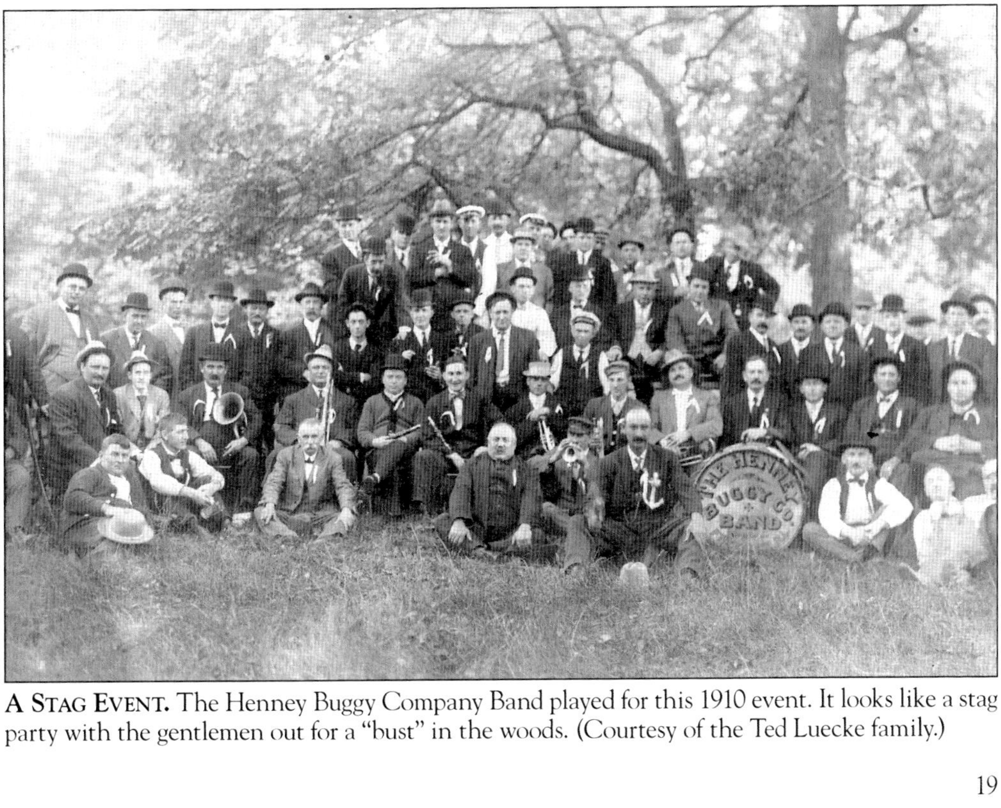

A STAG EVENT. The Henney Buggy Company Band played for this 1910 event. It looks like a stag party with the gentlemen out for a "bust" in the woods. (Courtesy of the Ted Luecke family.)

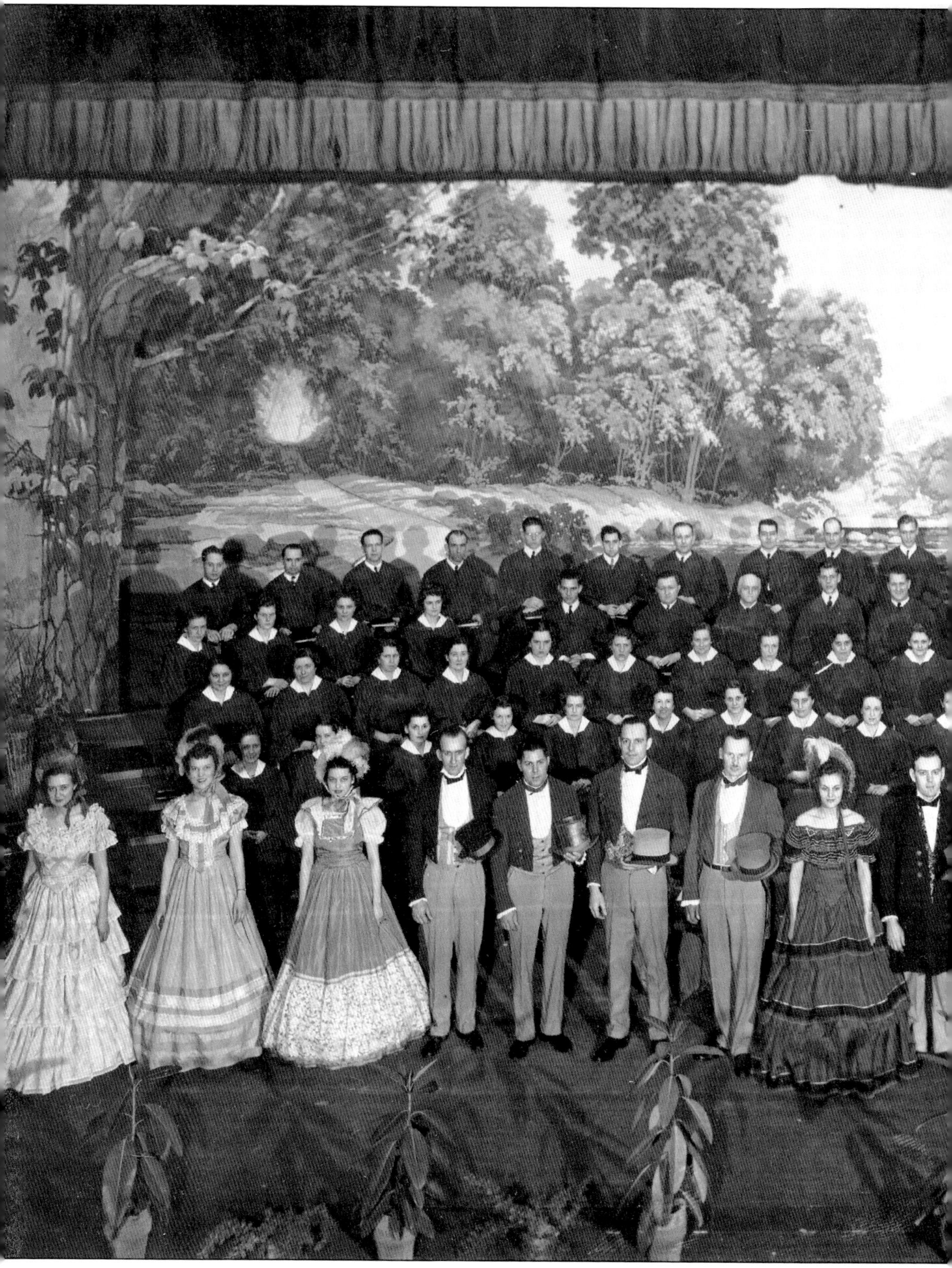

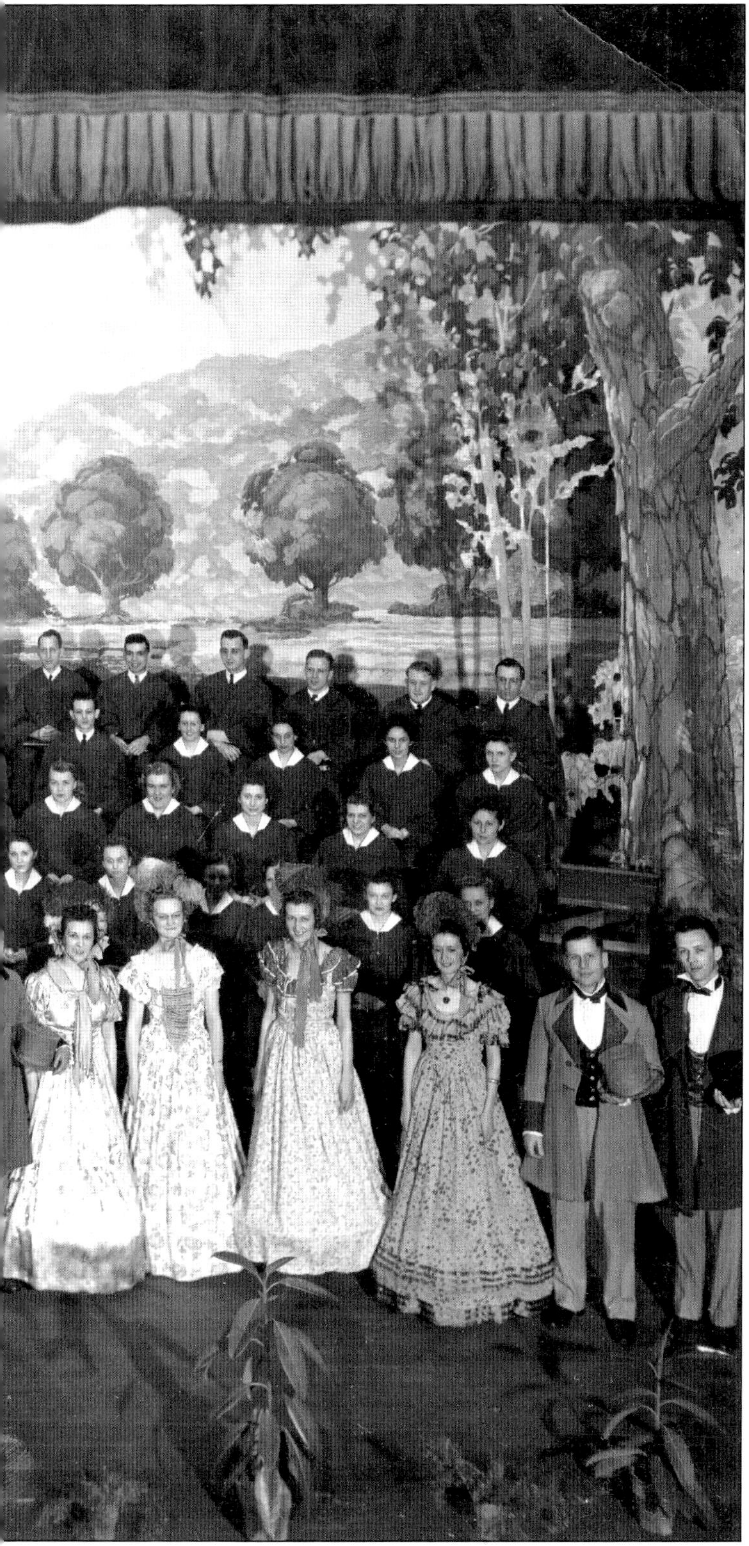

KRAFT CHEESE CHORAL SOCIETY. The Kraft-Phenix Cheese Company, after purchasing a local operation, began manufacturing cheese products in Freeport in 1930. The company sponsored a chorus, which was popularly used for entertainment throughout northern Illinois. This photograph shows a performance in 1942. The company developed into the Kraft Cheese Company, with the largest cheese-processing plant in America. In 1950, the plant discontinued operations here and was moved to Chicago.

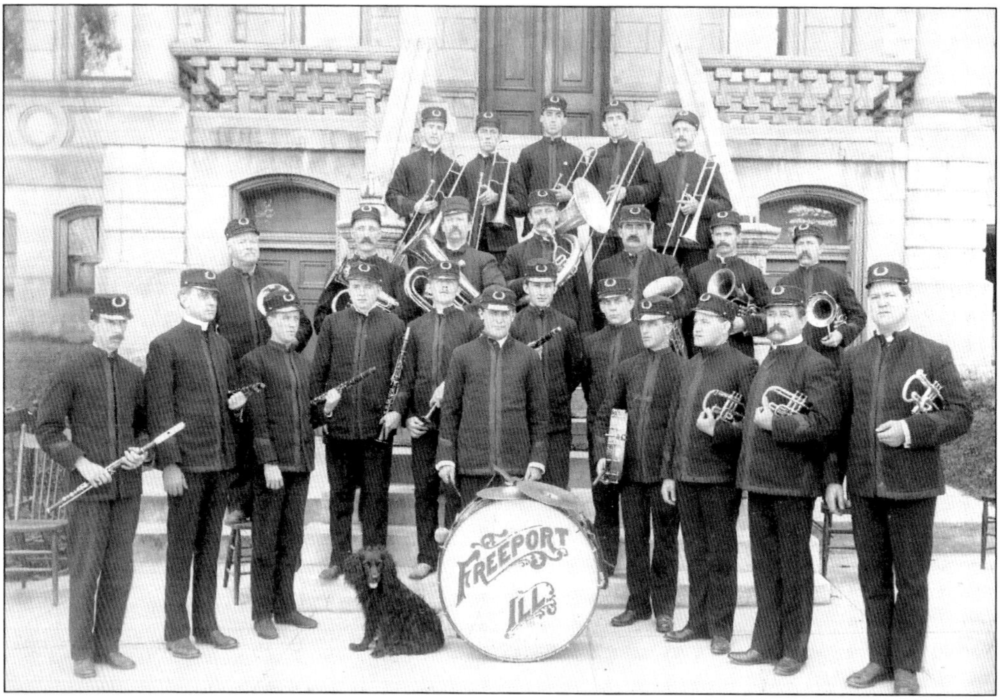

The Globe Band. The Knights of the Globe society sponsored this band, which is pictured in 1906.

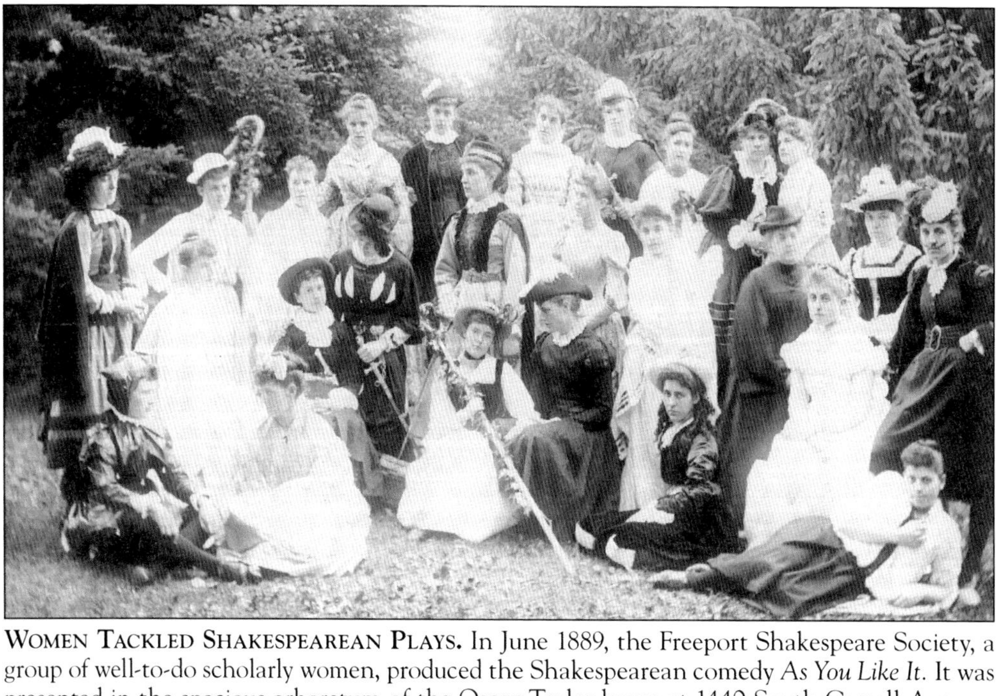

Women Tackled Shakespearean Plays. In June 1889, the Freeport Shakespeare Society, a group of well-to-do scholarly women, produced the Shakespearean comedy *As You Like It*. It was presented in the spacious arboretum of the Oscar Taylor home at 1440 South Carroll Avenue. The home is now the site of the Stephenson County Historical Society. The Taylor women were among the society's founders.

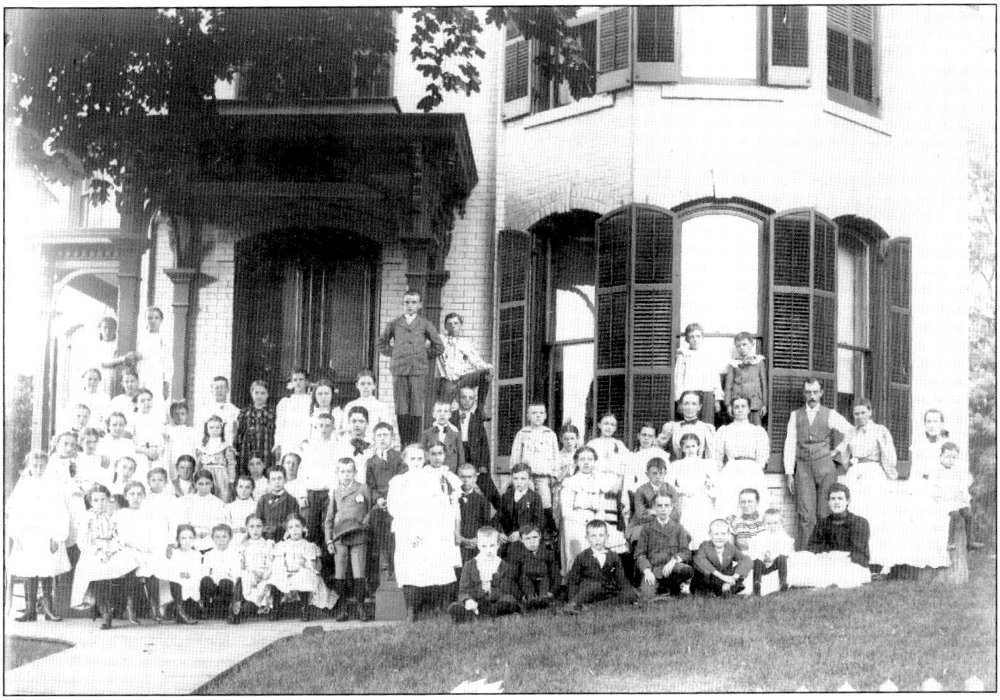

AN 1890S BIRTHDAY BASH. A giant birthday party of both adults and children was given in the early 1890s at the Seyfarth home at the corner of Washington Street on South Adams Avenue.

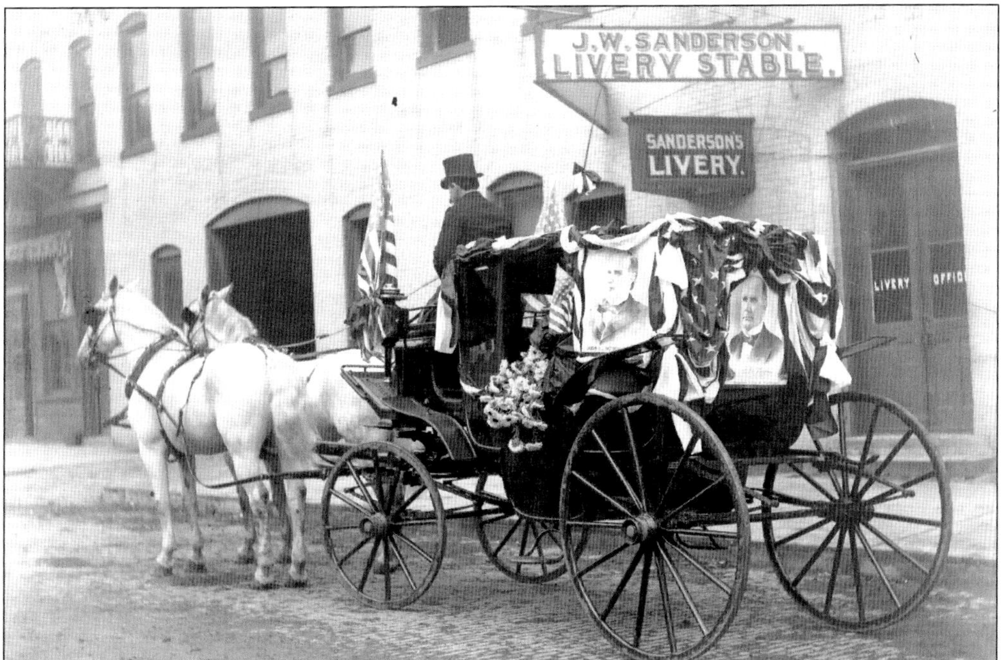

MOURNING A PRESIDENT. In 1901, Freeport mourned the assassination of Pres. William McKinley. This carriage joined a procession down a brick street in Freeport in front of the J. W. Sanderson Livery Stable.

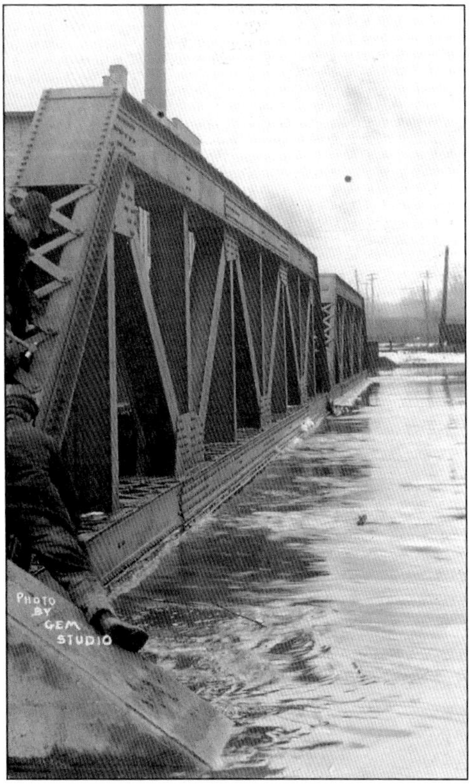

RAILROADS COPED WITH FLOODING. After a flood in February 1911, the Chicago, Milwaukee, and St. Paul Railway had the Pecatonica River licking hungrily at its right-of-way. Below, a crew of inspectors walks the precarious rails. The scene looks southwest near the Henderson Street, crossing north of the Stover plant of that day.

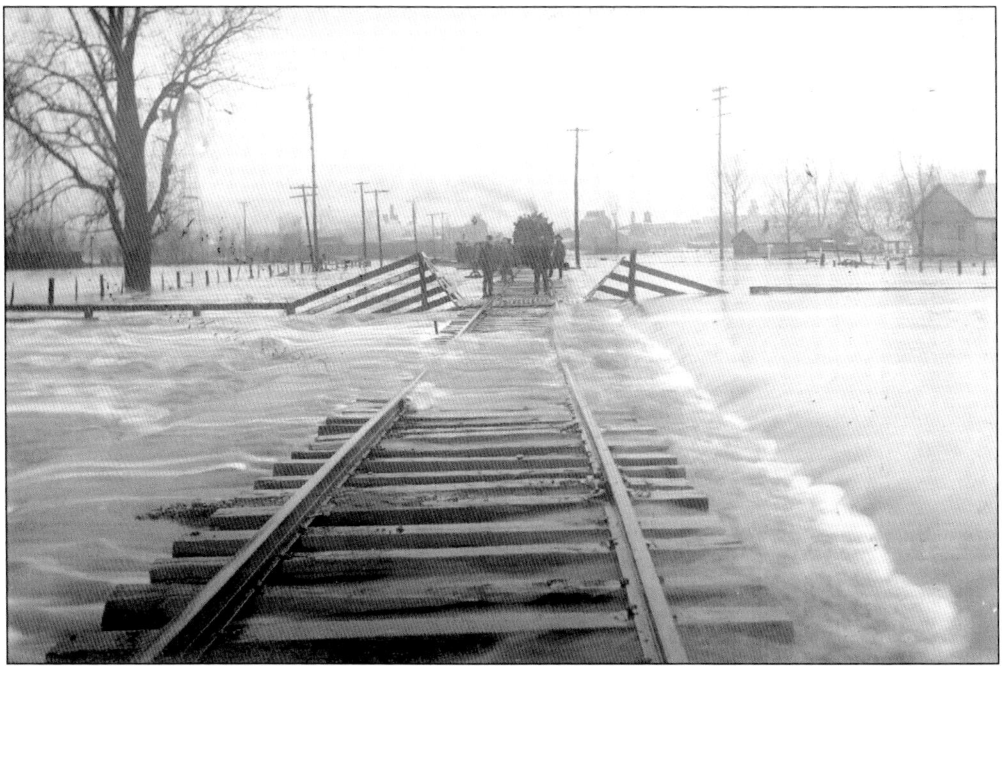

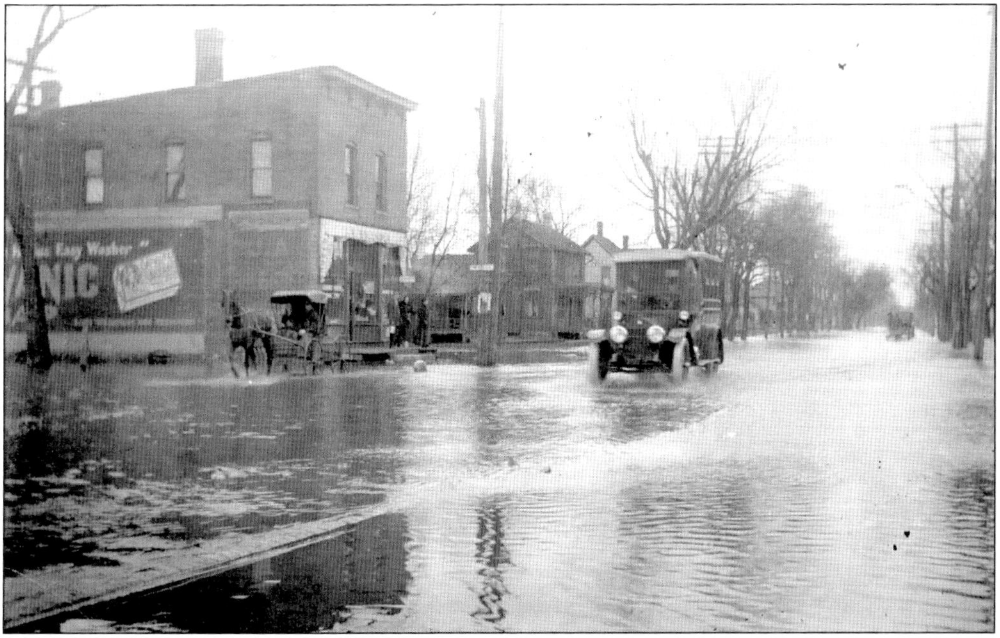

WATER EVERYWHERE. Freeport is a city of springs and creeks, and the Pecatonica River runs through it. Consequently, it has always been faced with flooding, especially east of the river during spring thaws and rainy seasons. Spectacular floods hit the town in 1911, 1916, and 1969, to name a few.

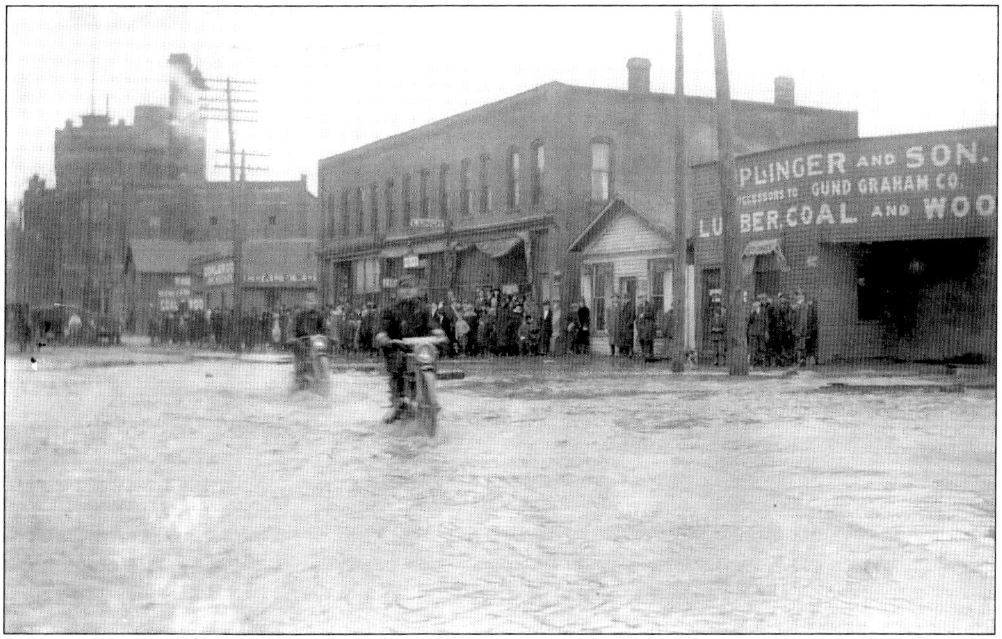

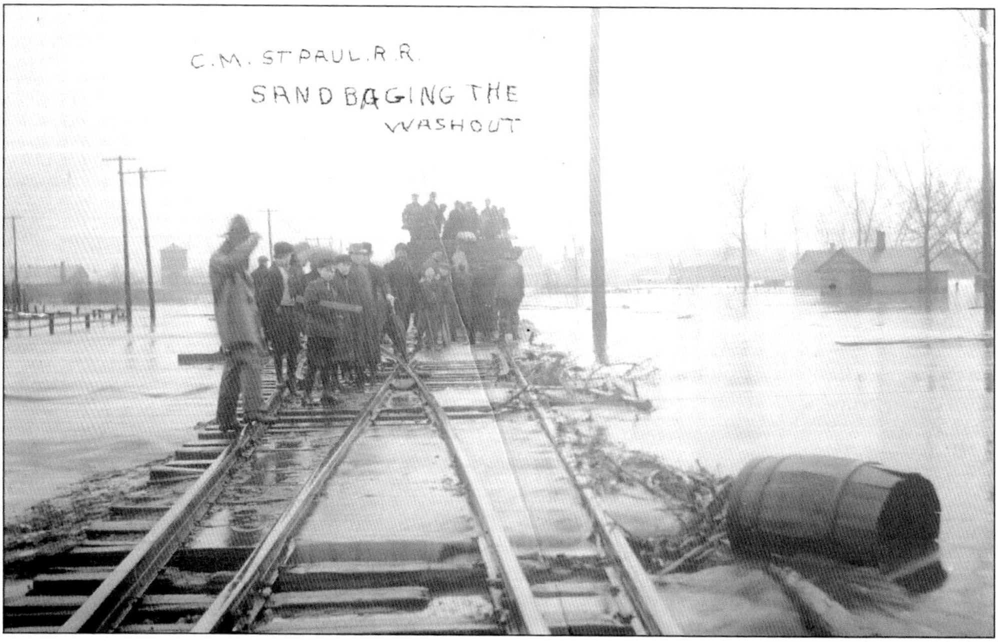

RAILROADS FOUGHT FLOODS. The Chicago, Milwaukee and St. Paul Railroad had to sandbag its tracks through Freeport when countless floods plagued the city throughout its history. Engineers changed the course of the Pecatonica River and the route of Illinois Route 26 in attempts to conquer the flooding.

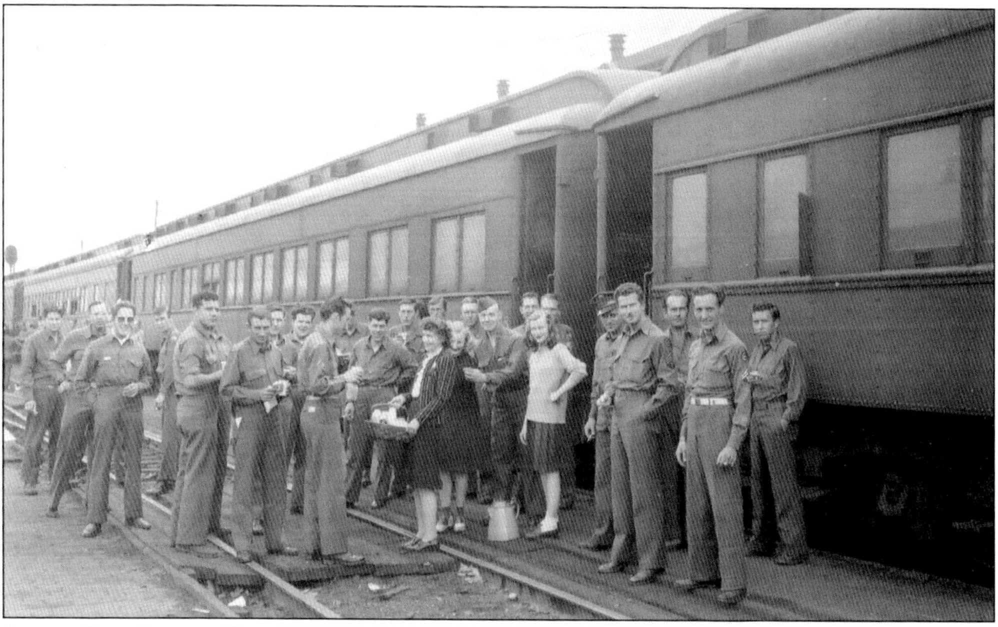

SNACK BAR SERVED TROOPS. Dozens of Freeport women helped serve sandwiches and cookies to troops passing through the city by train from November 1944 throughout 1945. The local snack bar at the Illinois Central Railroad depot served an average of two troop trains daily. Mrs. Karl Snyder was founder of the project, assisted by Margaret Hirtle and Mrs. Howard Hill. The total of servicemen and women served was approximately 239,000.

Two

RECREATION AND SPORTS

The Pecatonica River was a natural resource that provided much entertainment for the local population in its early days. Fishing was a chance for relaxation for many local businessmen. Social life involved much picnicking and boating along the riverbanks. Boating clubs provided opportunities for dining and dancing.

The public and parochial schools have kept the collective appetites for competitive sports on the edge.

Softball had its heyday during the early 20th century, bringing out crowds of fans to city parks for interleague play. Swimming, league play in baseball for all ages, and basketball, football, and soccer have filled many seasons for the youth.

For decades during cold winters when Yellow Creek turned solid, it has drawn blades to Krape Park where a warming house, piped outdoor music, and refreshment stand served those who loved to ice-skate. A pond in Taylor Park also drew skaters when winter reached the proper frigid levels.

Tennis courts and golf courses were magnets to those so inclined to frequent parks and clubs. Both the YMCA and YWCA provided open invitations for water lovers to develop their strokes. The Read Park swimming pool, at first a huge sand-bottomed, spring-filled facility, saw various improvements on its way to its present, modern state.

There has never been a lack of things to see and do in Freeport. It is a town of many tastes and feasts, but sports of every ilk have always drawn high billing.

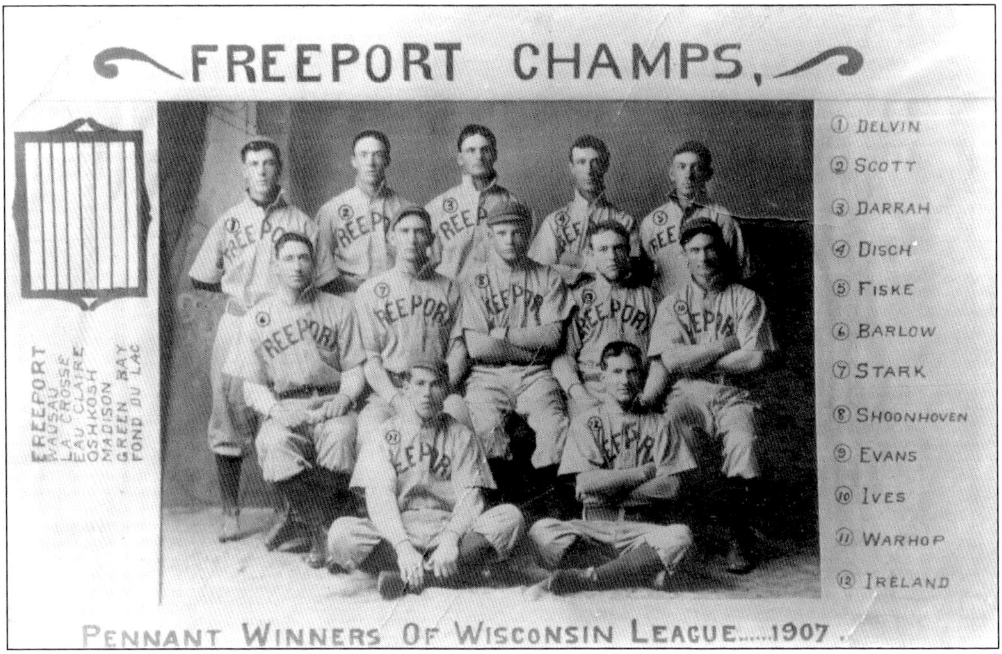

BASEBALL, A FAVORED SPORT. One name in this lineup of champions commands special attention. Jack Warhop went on to pitch for the New York Yankees. Warhop is the man seated on the floor on the right. As the label states, the Freeport team won the pennant for the 1907 season of the Wisconsin League.

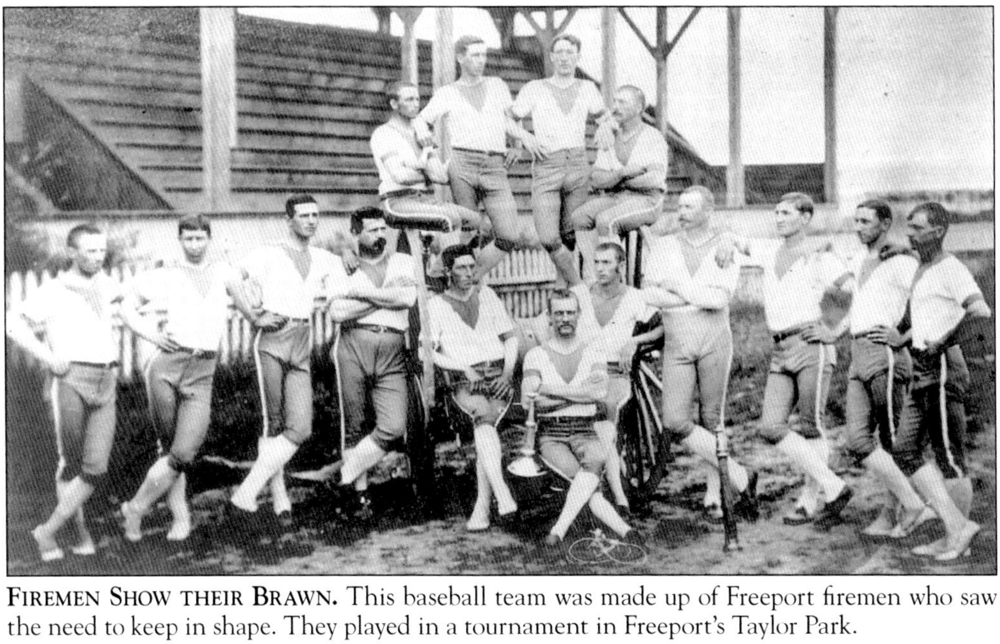

FIREMEN SHOW THEIR BRAWN. This baseball team was made up of Freeport firemen who saw the need to keep in shape. They played in a tournament in Freeport's Taylor Park.

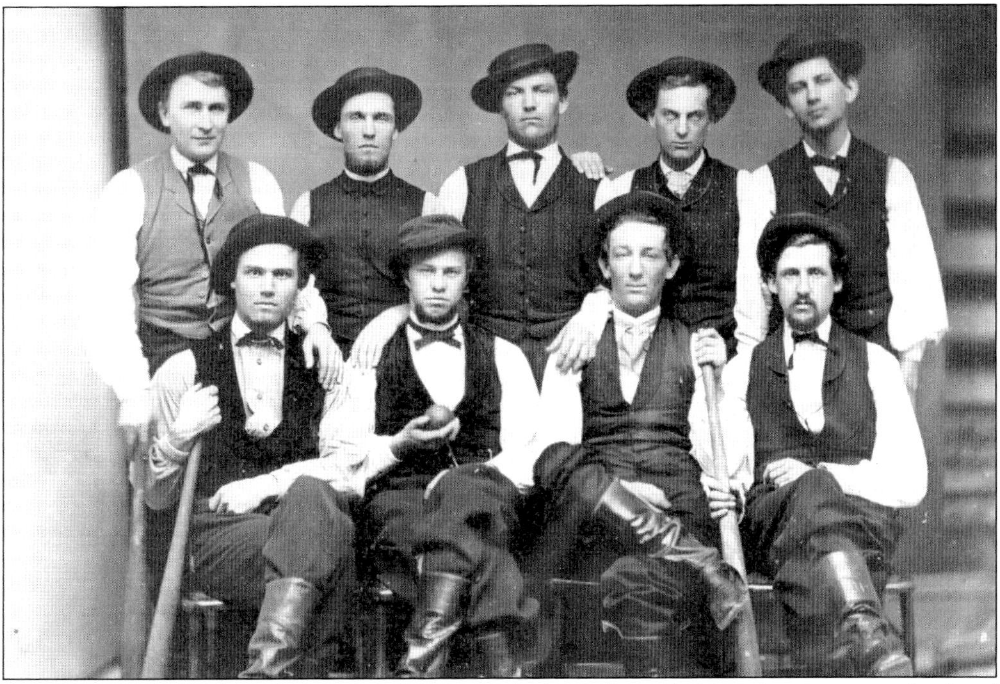

AN ATYPICAL BASEBALL TEAM. These tough looking, boot-clad hombres composed a local baseball team in 1897. Note the length of the bats. Perhaps the one with ball in hand is the pitcher.

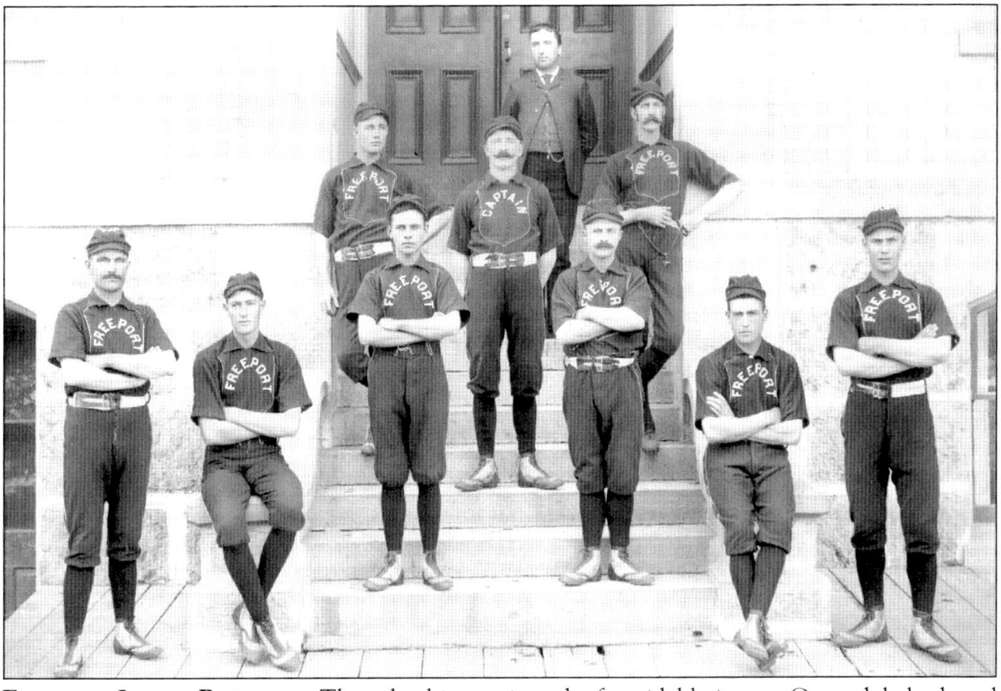

FREEPORT LOVED BASEBALL. These huskies projected a formidable image. Capped, belted, and cleated, they were ready to go to the park for play. Judging from the boardwalk and the handlebar mustaches, this might have been taken around the dawn of the 20th century.

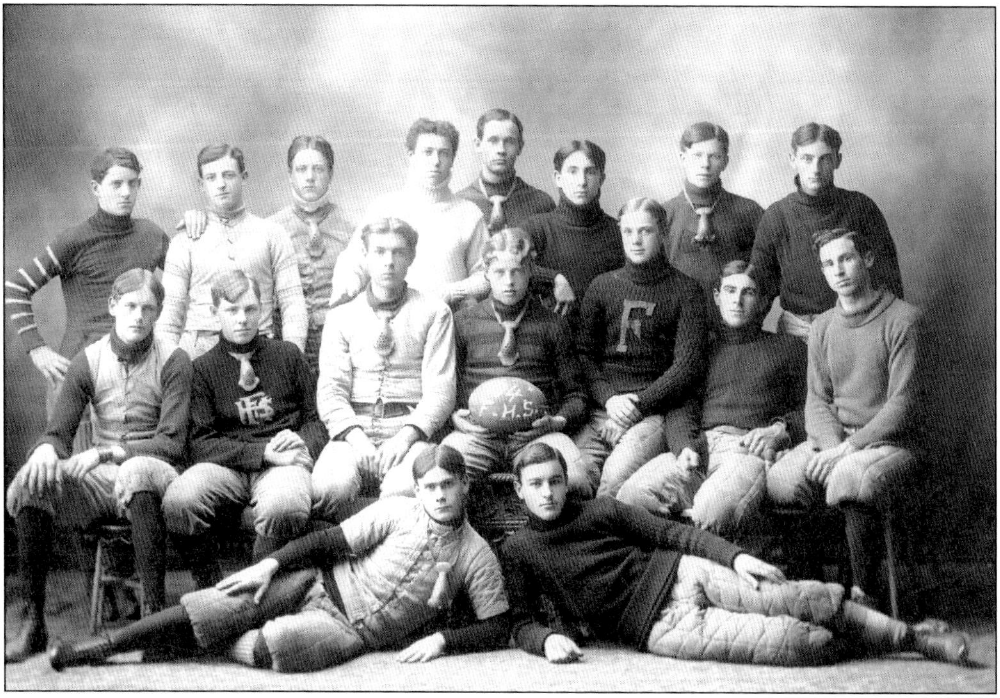

The 1904 Freeport High Heroes. These fellows composed the 1904 Freeport High School football squad.

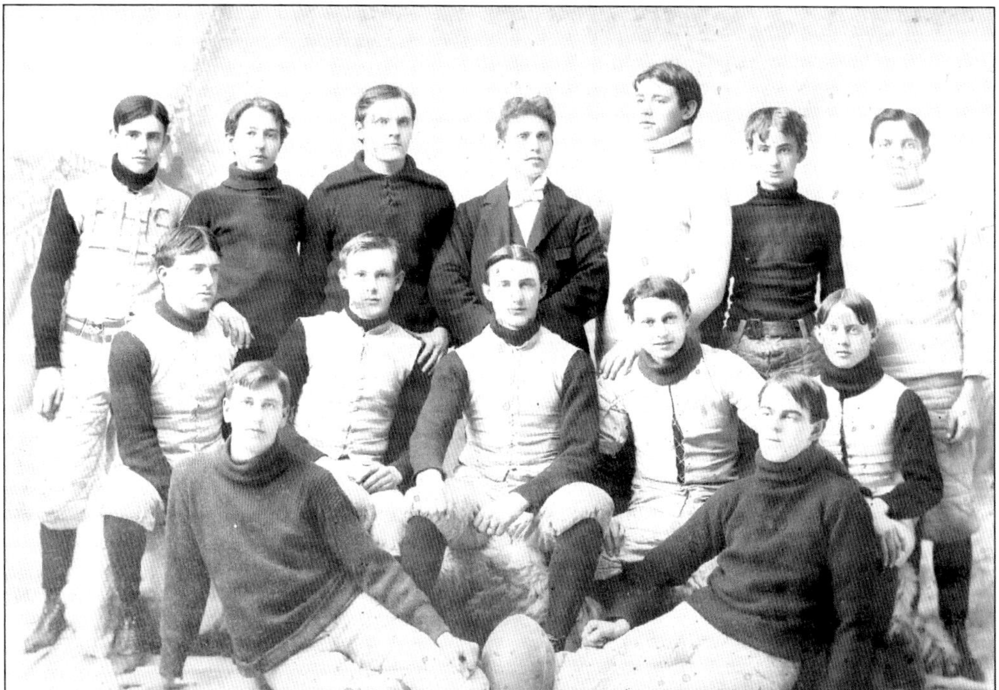

The Football Team. In 1896, these fellows carried the ball for Freeport High School.

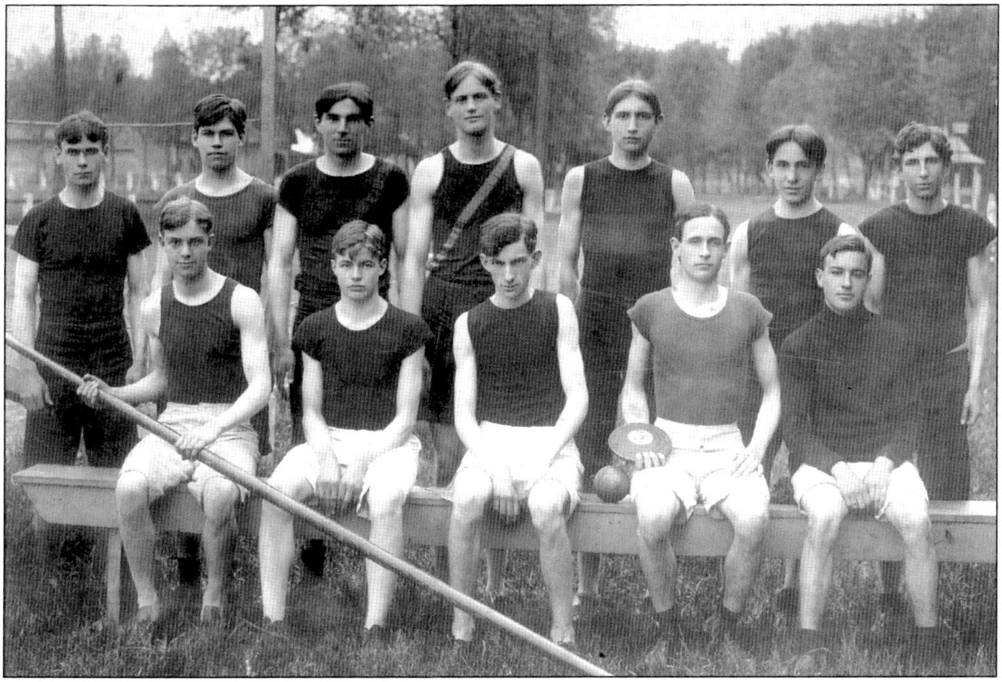

MUSCLES SHOWING. Freeport High School's track team in 1905 or 1906 was made up of a resolute bunch. Runners, pole-vaulters, and discus throwers alike were toughened for a field day.

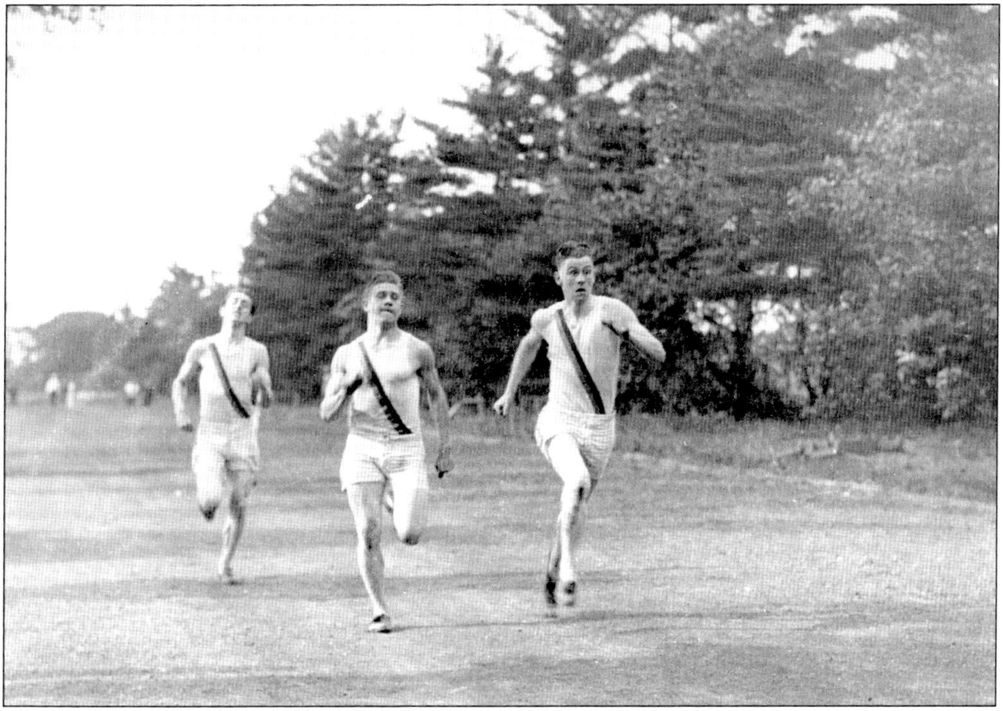

AT THE STARTING LINE. Members of the Freeport High School track team vie with those from the high school in Beloit, Wisconsin, in 1916.

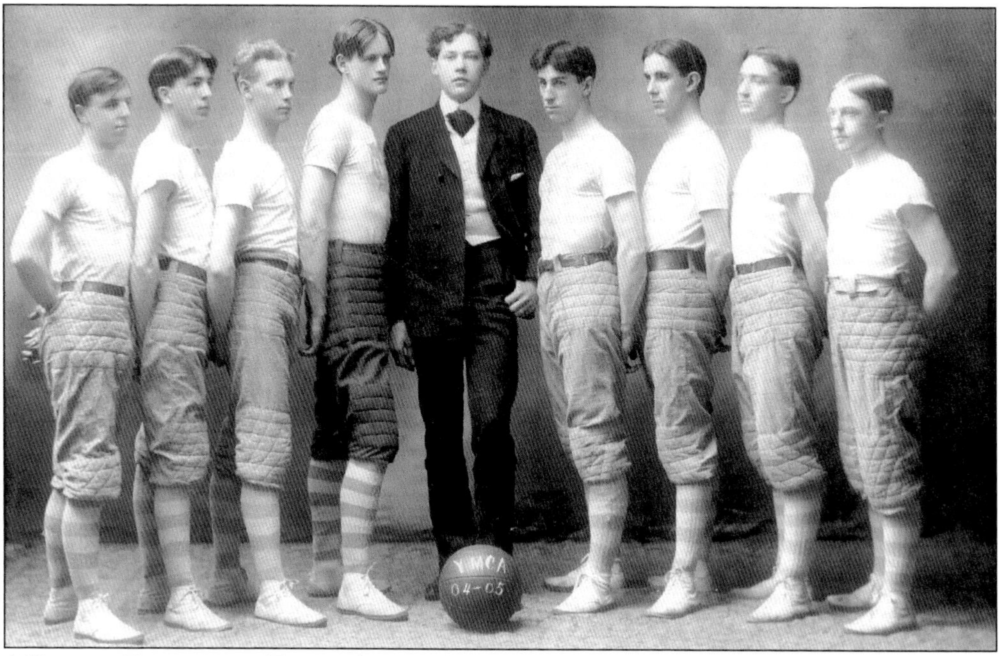

A Pioneer Basketball Team. This was the 1904 team of YMCA basketball players. According to local historian Leslie Fargher, basketball originated as a sport in the Springfield, Massachusetts, YMCA training school. Fargher said it was some years before the sport was adopted by schools or colleges.

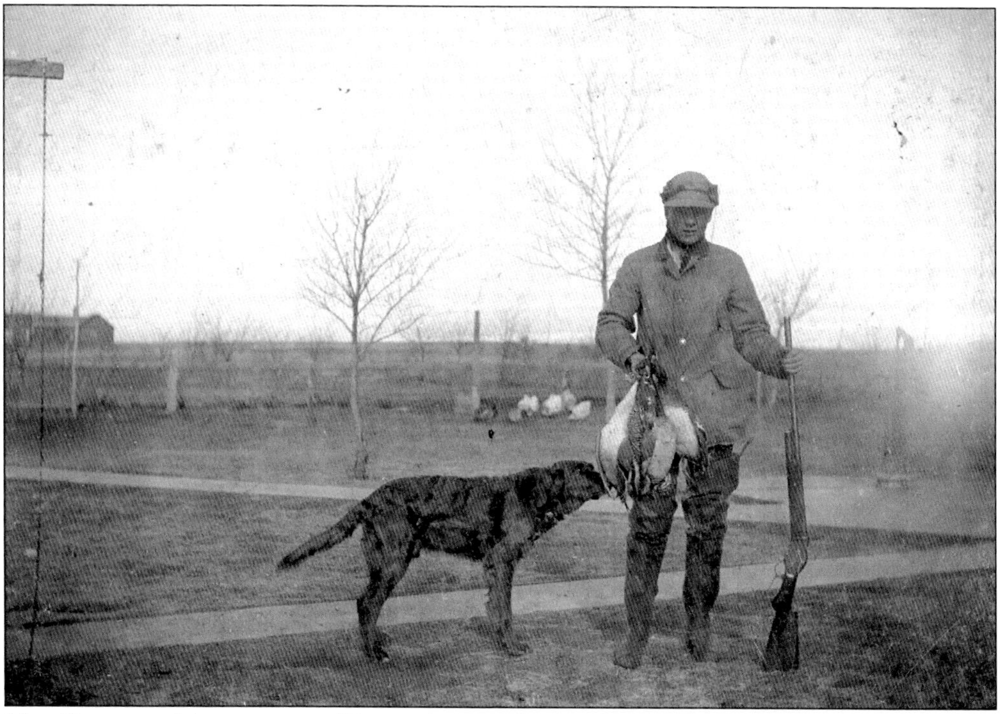

Men Provided Meat for the Table. A young hunter shows off the wild game he shot in this 1890s photograph. While hunting was a sporting skill for men, it also had a practical side.

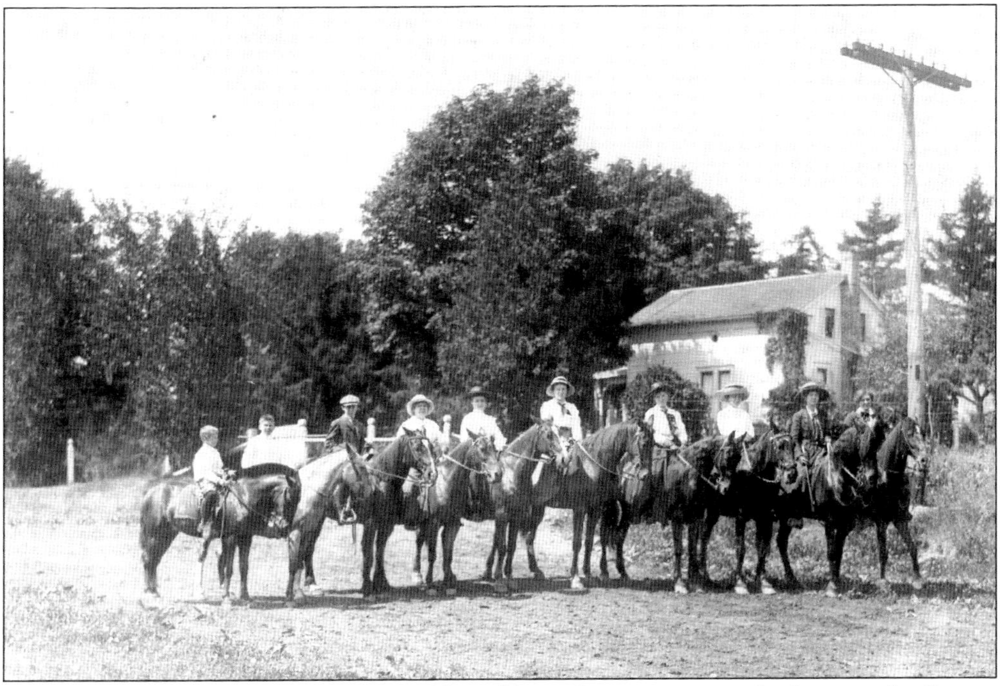

HORSES BIG IN FREEPORT. The Saxby stable and horse farm was just north of present-day Empire Street on Saxby Avenue. This 1916 photograph is of the Freeport Saddle Club. Alda Saxby's daughter Elizabeth is the sixth person from left on her horse Charlie.

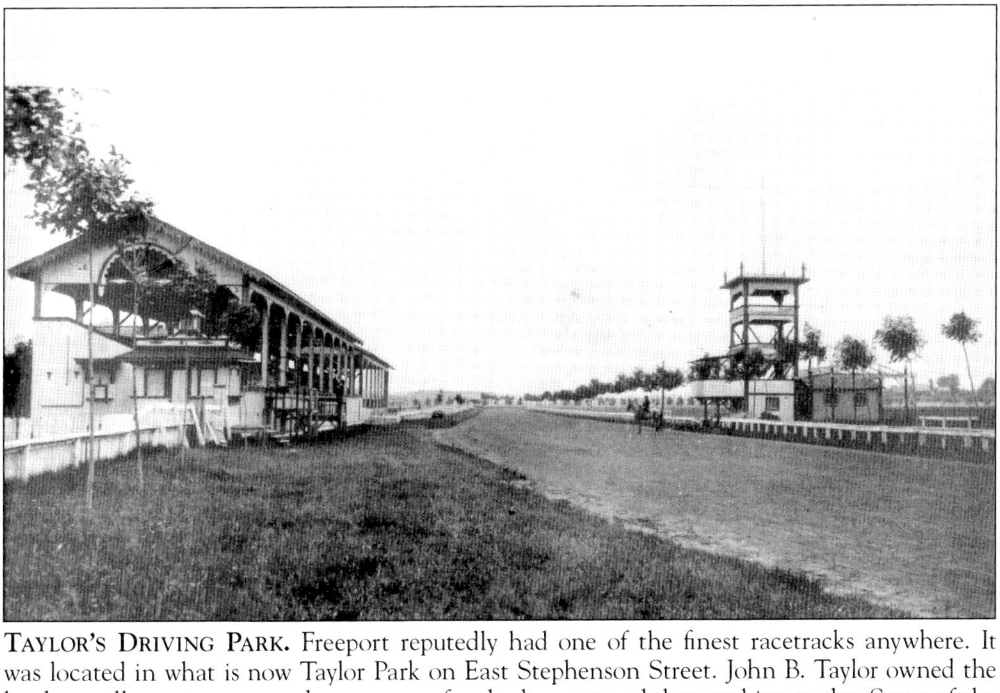

TAYLOR'S DRIVING PARK. Freeport reputedly had one of the finest racetracks anywhere. It was located in what is now Taylor Park on East Stephenson Street. John B. Taylor owned the land as well as a tannery and a processor for the harness and shoe-making trades. Some of the most prominent trackmen in America patronized the track. Stephenson County Fairs also were held there.

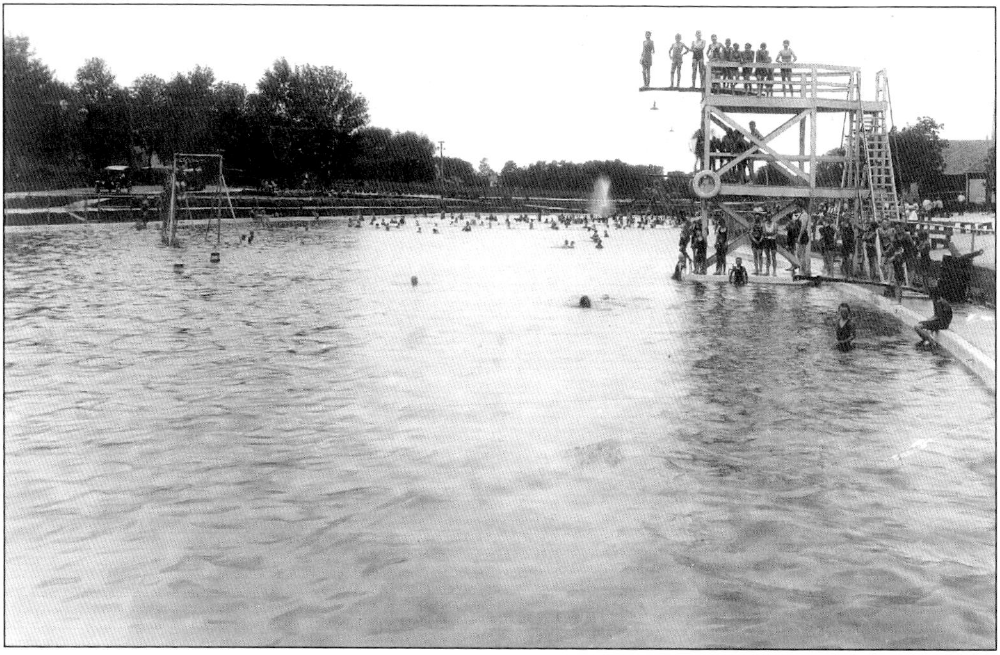

SUMMER FUN. Read Park first opened in 1923 with the land given to Freeport Park District by F. A. Read, a local merchant. A large spring-fed swimming pool and a lagoon for fishing, shown below under construction, were added. Both of the new ponds were popular among local seekers of recreation. Construction of the pool shown was completed in 1929 at a cost of $20,000. The park ultimately included ball diamonds and courts for shuffleboard, tennis, and other sports. (Courtesy of the Kokie Griffin collection.)

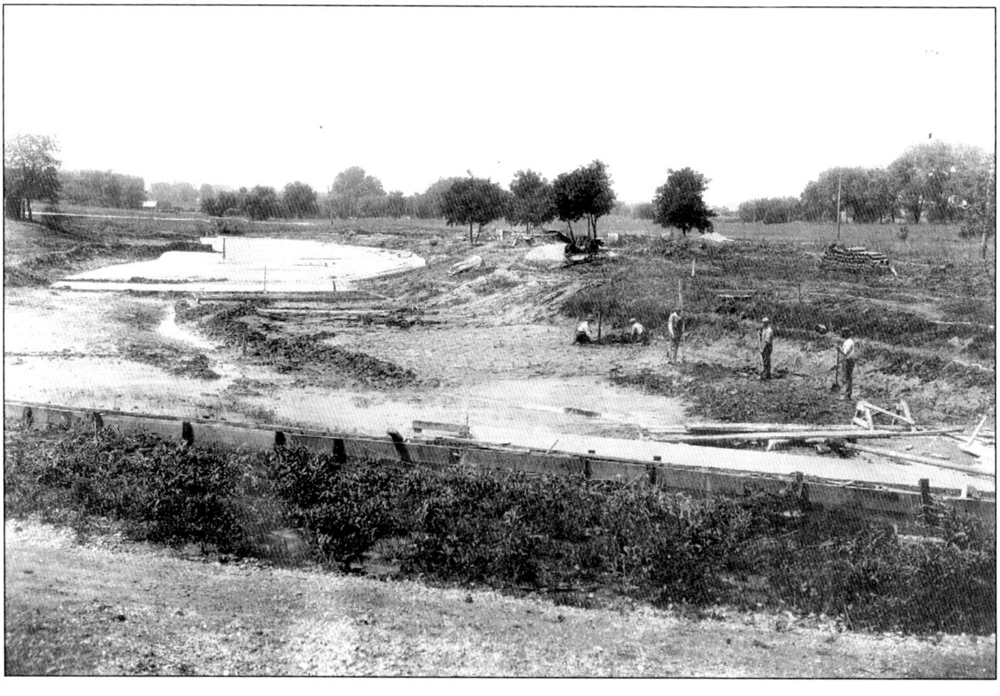

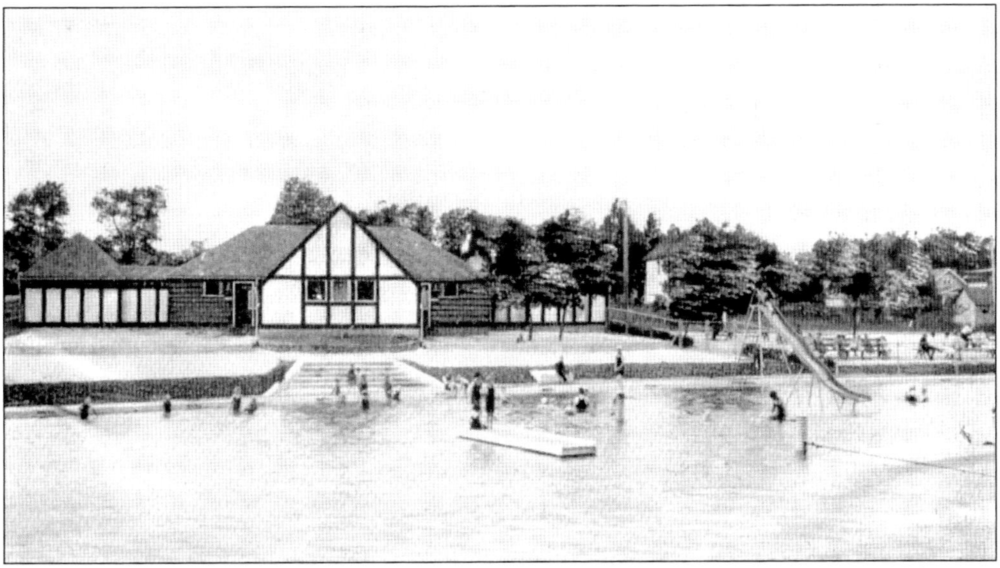

NEW, IMPROVED READ PARK POOL. In 1946, the original Read Park pool was closed because of a polio epidemic and because it did not meet modern state requirements. A new, smaller pool was completed in 1949. The bathhouse was remodeled at that time, as shown above. (Courtesy of the Freeport Public Library.)

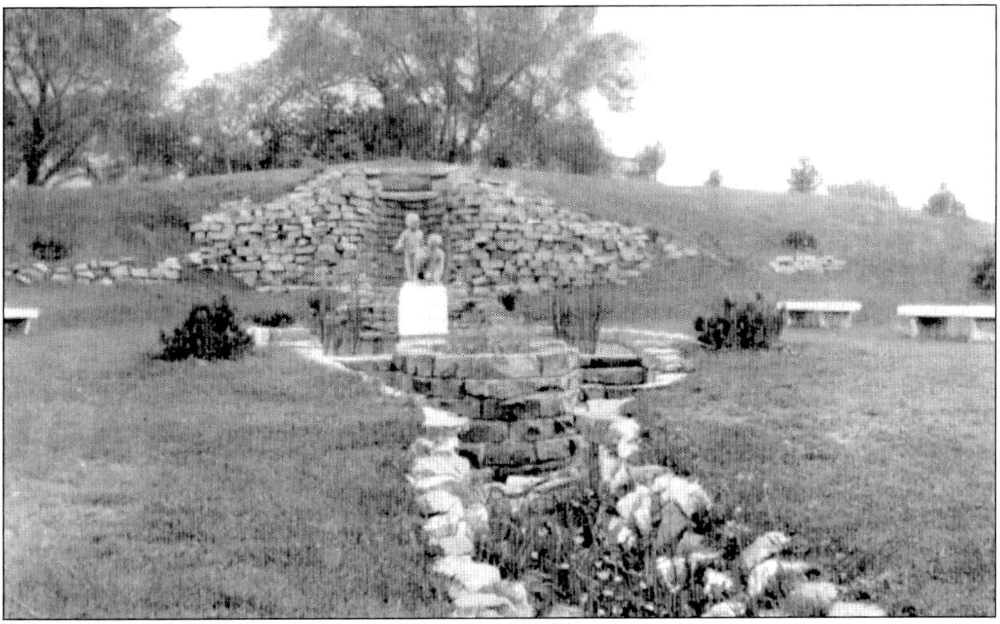

READ PARK MEMORIAL. This bronze statue of two children playing in front of a waterfall was erected in Read Park as a memorial to Mrs. Edward Morgan, given by her husband, Edward Morgan, and daughters Mrs. B. C. Trueblood and Mrs. Edward Winslow. Later, the entire area west of the swimming pool including the memorial was renovated and landscaped through the planning and assistance of the Civic Garden Club. (Courtesy of the Freeport Public Library.)

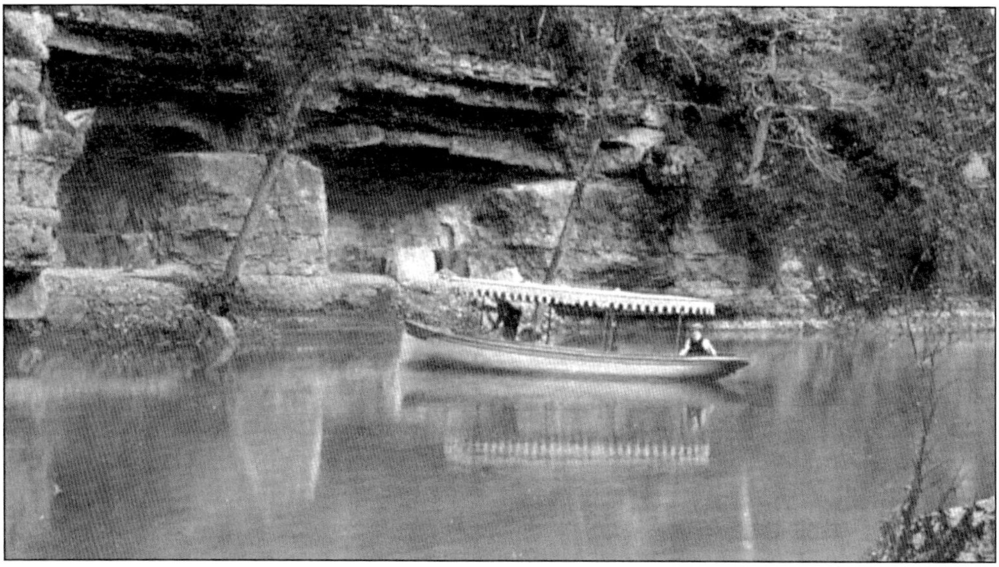

CAVES AND CLIFFS ARE LANDMARKS. Cliffs along Yellow Creek provided adventure for picnics and boating in Globe Park. This later became Krape Park, which continues to draw people from miles around. Twin Caves draw interest among boaters along the creek. (Courtesy of the Freeport Public Library.)

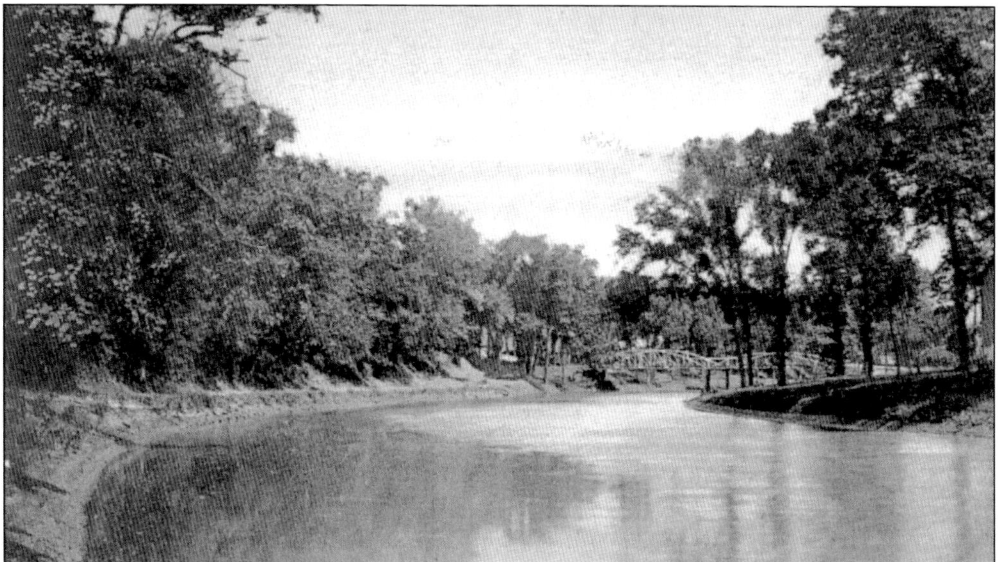

GLOBE PARK FAVORED RECREATION AREA. Globe Park, situated along the Yellow Creek valley, was a favorite scenic, hiking, and picnic area for the early settlers. It first was known as Beebe's Woods and then was named Globe Park by its owner Dr. W. W. Krape. Freeport Park District purchased the land in 1913 and named it Krape Park after its previous owner. (Courtesy of the Freeport Public Library.)

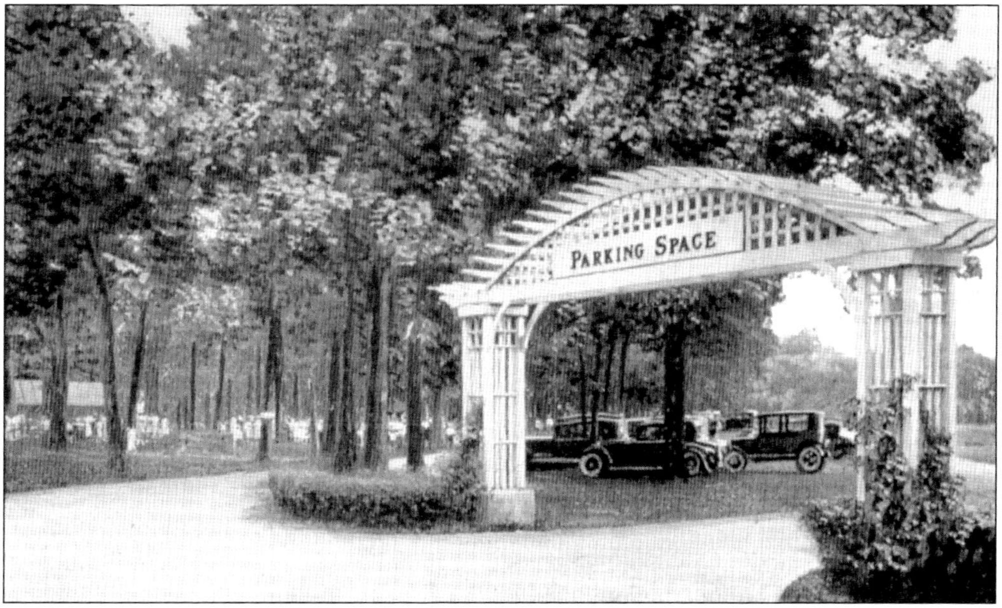

KRAPE PARK WAS LIVELY PLACE. Krape Park had a different look back in the second decade of the 20th century. Something big was going on the day this photograph was taken. The park already had been landscaped by the young Freeport Park District formed in 1911. Extensive road construction and development of buildings later took place during the Great Depression through the public works programs of Pres. Franklin D. Roosevelt. (Courtesy of the Freeport Public Library.)

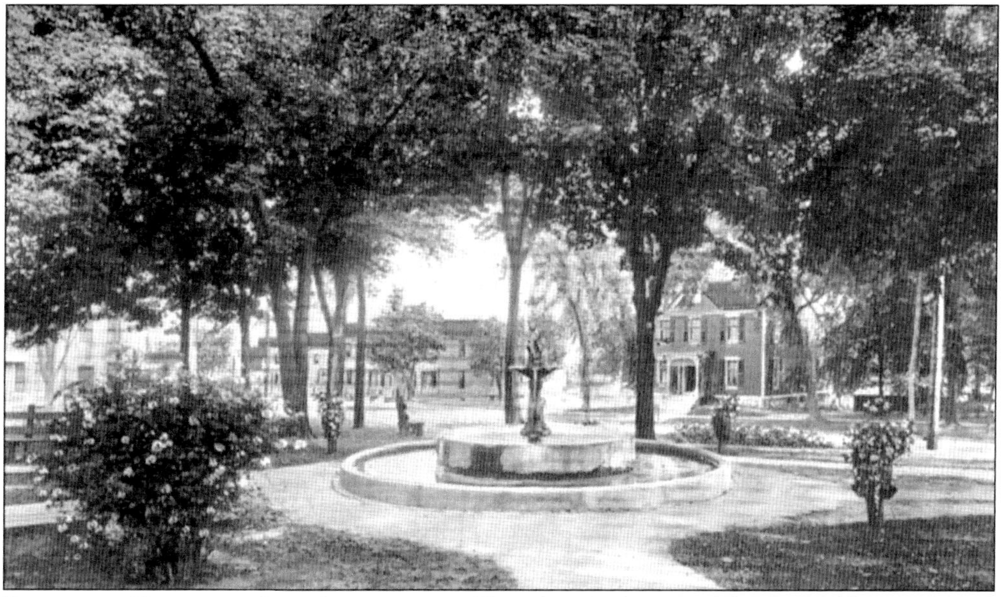

KNOWLTON PARK WAS CITY CENTERPIECE. Knowlton Park, one of the city's oldest, was a gift of Dexter Knowlton, a pioneer merchant and landowner. It is bounded by West Pleasant and Broadway Streets and Locust and Blackhawk Avenues. Supposedly Knowlton gave the land for the park, located on the main road into Freeport from the east, to draw traffic past his store. (Courtesy of the Freeport Public Library.)

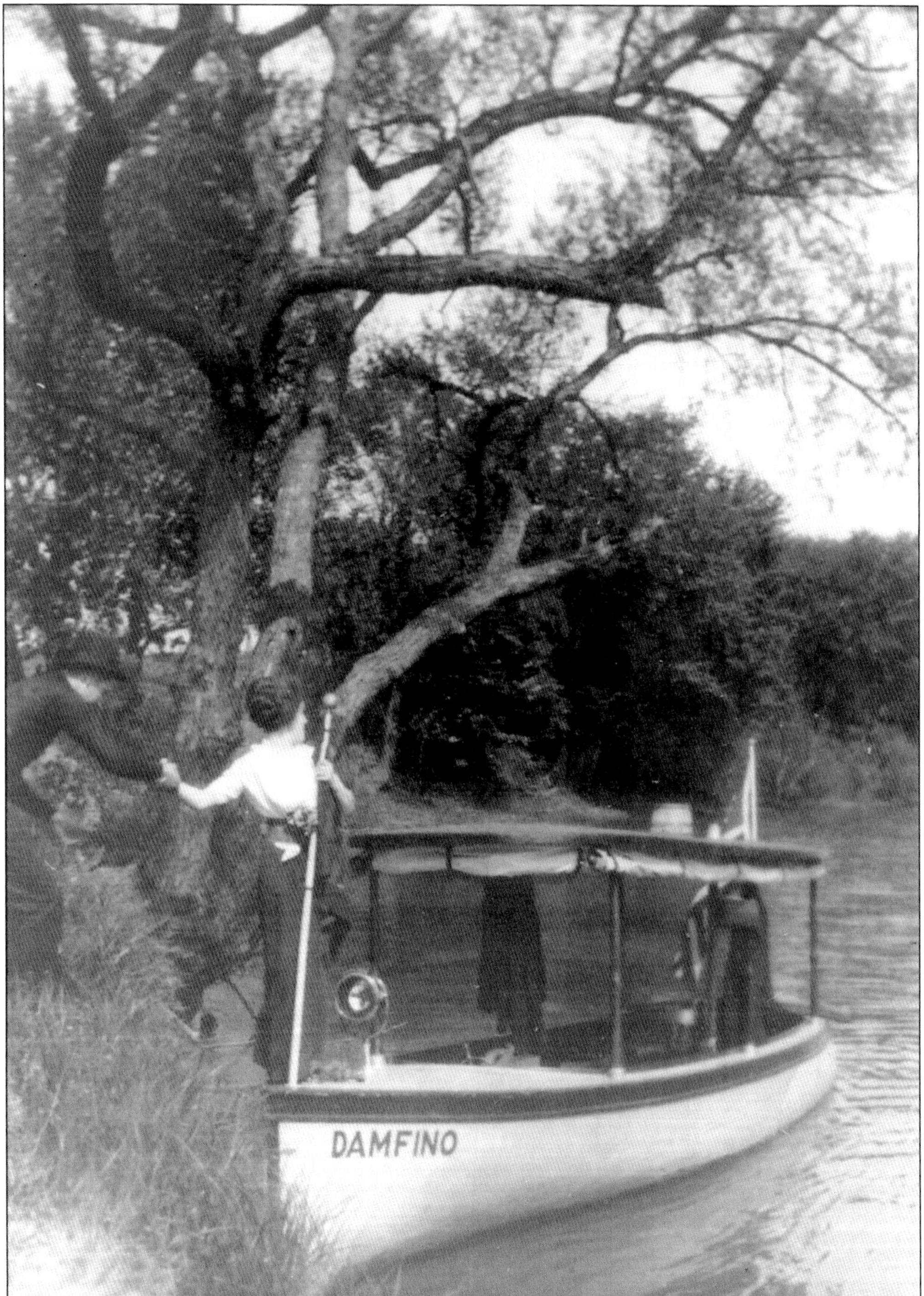

FLOATING DOWN THE RIVER. The Pecatonica River was widely used for recreation in the early 20th century. Boating was popular for a romantic Sunday afternoon's entertainment. The scenery was pleasant and the river clear. The owner of the boat may have named it *Damfino* with tongue in cheek. (Courtesy of the Freeport Public Library.)

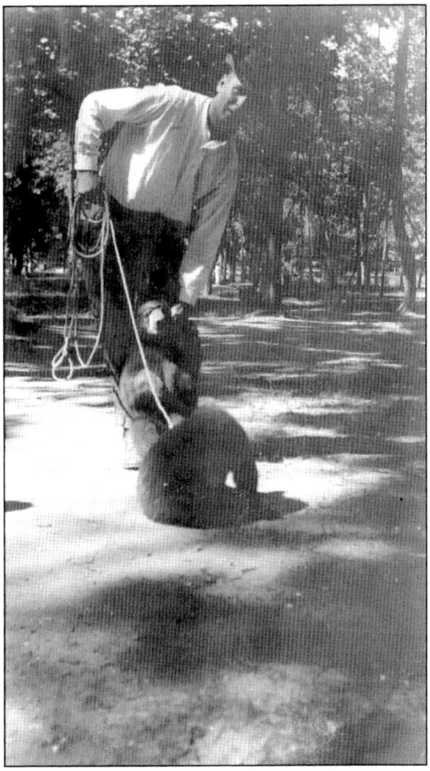

FREEPORT ZOO WAS LOCAL ATTRACTION. In 1918, a county zoological society established a zoo in Krape Park. Animals were donated by Dr. J. A. Poling and W. T. Rawleigh. In 1920, the Freeport Park District board purchased the entire Rockford Zoo. With donations from local businessmen, by the end of 1918, 40 species of animals resided in the zoo. Before it closed in 1928 due to cost of feeding the animals and complaints of the odor, zoo inhabitants included lions, tigers, bears, kangaroos, alligators, wolves, elk, deer, birds, and many species of native wildlife.

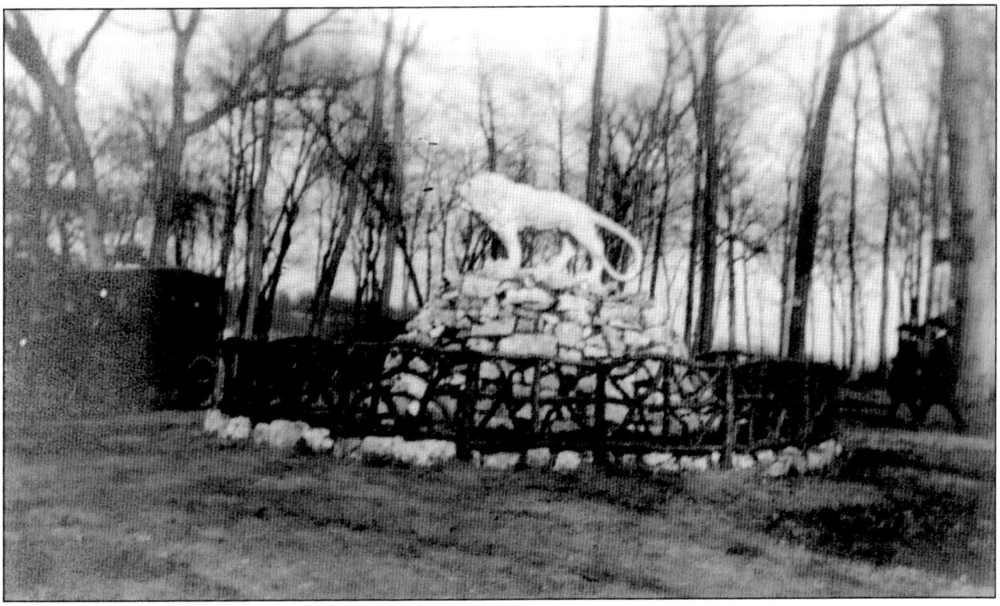

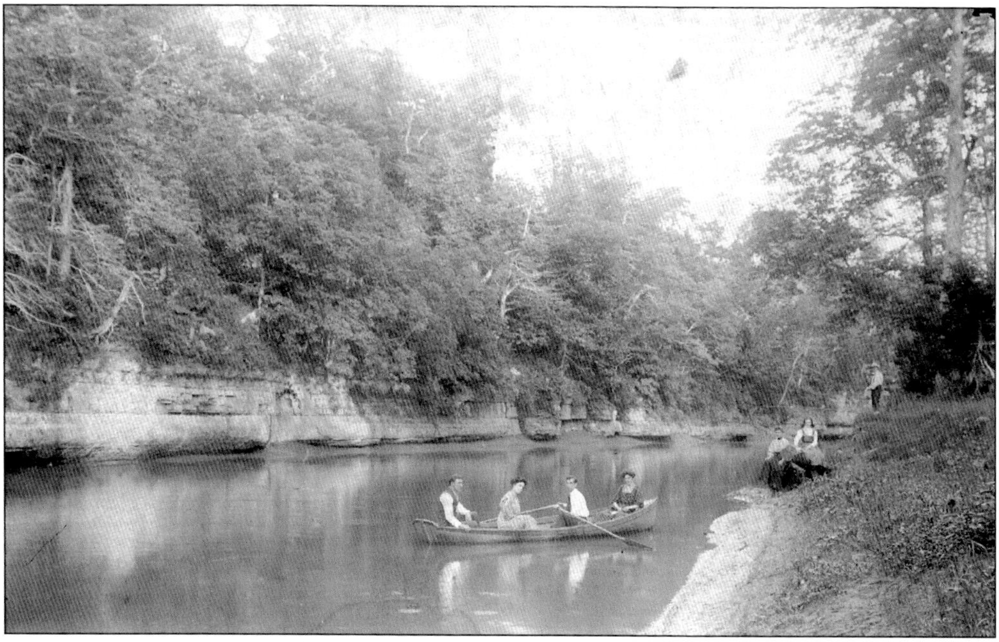

YELLOW CREEK PROVIDED RECREATION. Even in those late-Victorian days, it was proper for young couples to go rowing down the river on a warm summer's day. This scene was on Yellow Creek in Krape Park.

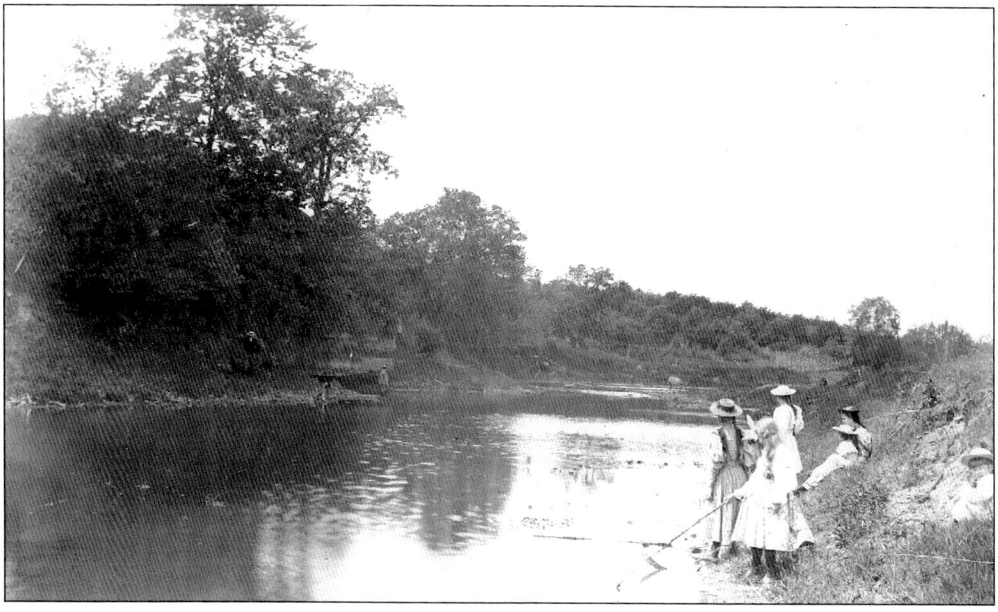

DABBLING IN THE CREEK. These young ladies of the late-Victorian era forgot their good dresses and bonnets when lured to the banks of Yellow Creek. The photograph was taken about 1895. It looks west from the Illinois 26 bridge. (Courtesy of the Freeport Public Library.)

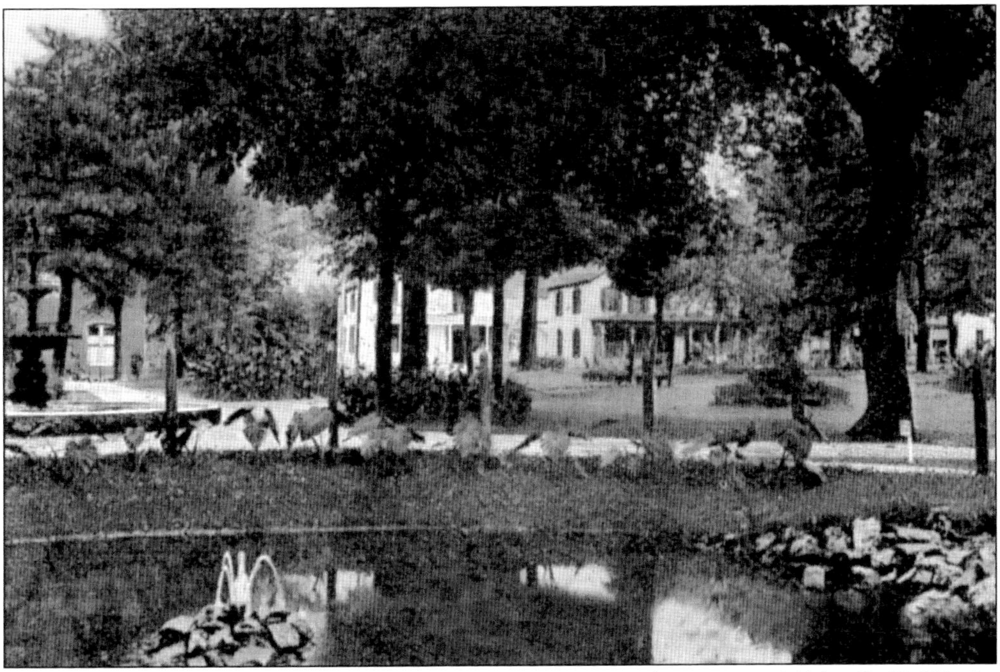

FREEPORT'S OLDEST PARK. This square block was given to the city in 1849 by O. H. Wright and Judge George Purinton and thus given the name Wright-Purinton Park. It became more commonly known as Third Ward Park and was, for years, a well-kept area landscaped with a bandstand, a fountain, and flora. It then became a playground for Henney Elementary School and later for Martin Luther King Community Center. (Courtesy of the Freeport Public Library.)

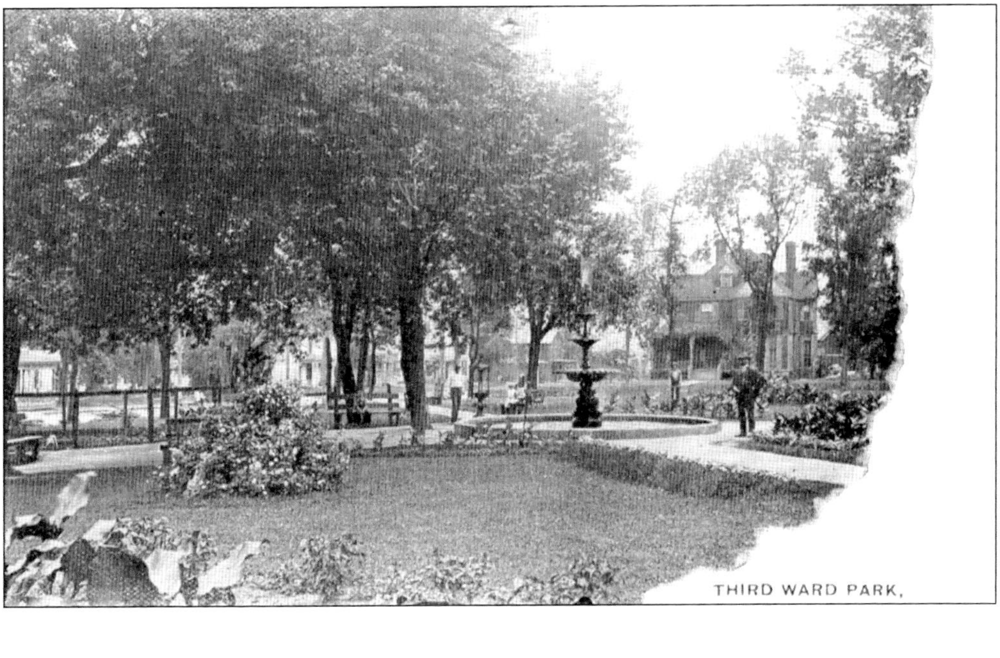

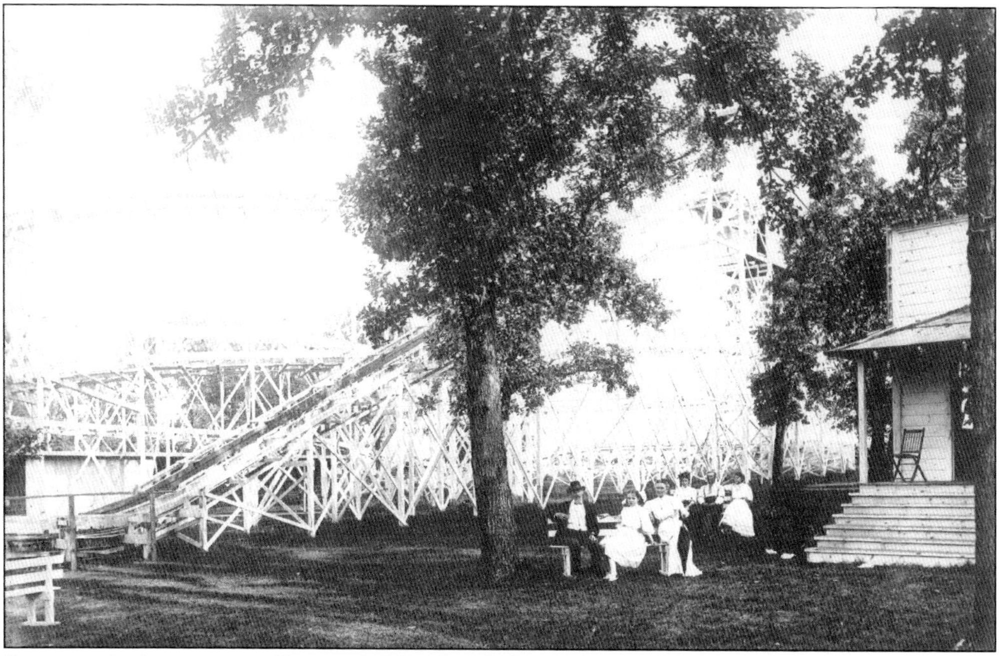

FREEPORT'S AMUSEMENT PARK. Highland Park, located south of West Stephenson Street along Park Boulevard around 1910, had a roller coaster and a merry-go-round. Families packed picnic dinners and headed to the park on streetcars to spend the day. As Krape Park developed, the amusement park lost its attraction and was closed prior to 1918.

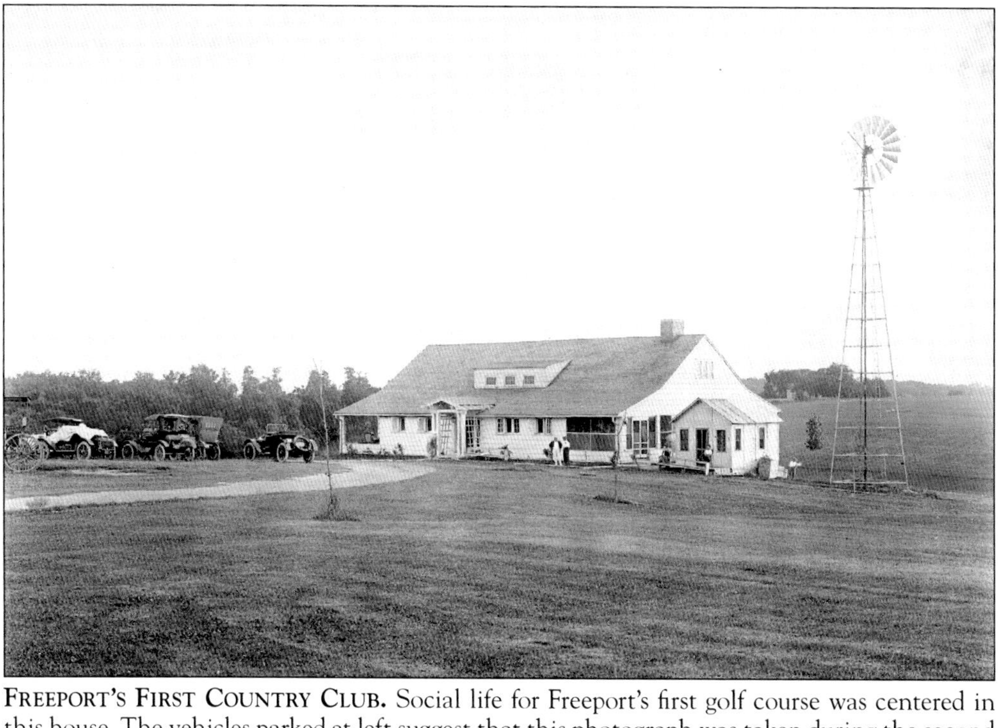

FREEPORT'S FIRST COUNTRY CLUB. Social life for Freeport's first golf course was centered in this house. The vehicles parked at left suggest that this photograph was taken during the second decade of the 20th century.

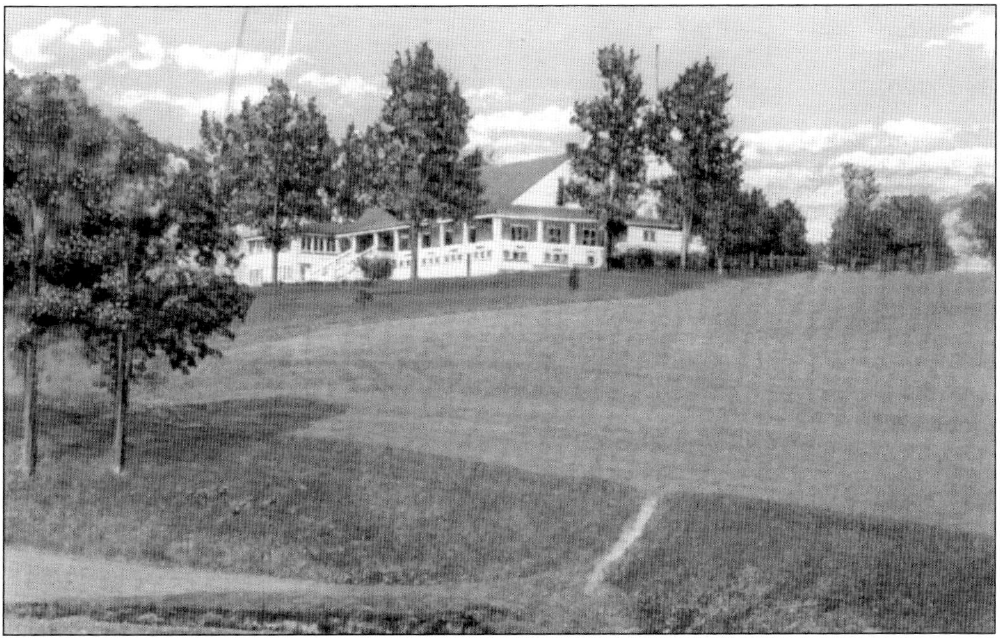

A GOLFER'S HAVEN. This white-frame clubhouse at Freeport Country Club was built in 1912 or 1913 to give avid golfers a place to socialize. It overlooked the golf course that adjoined present-day Krape Park. (Courtesy of the Freeport Public Library.)

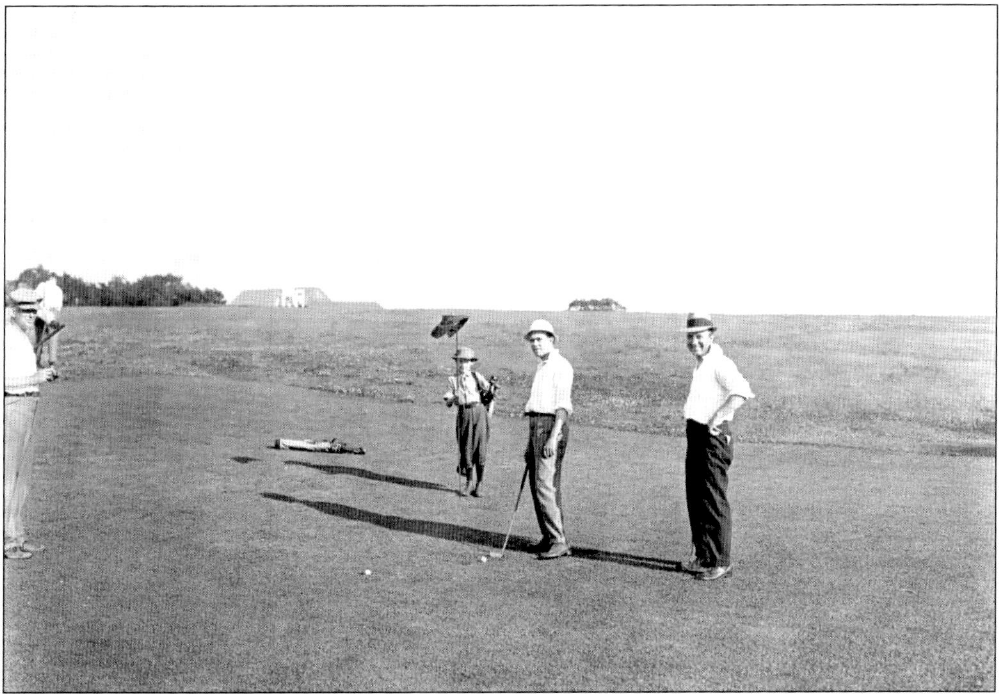

GOLFING ALREADY IN THEIR BLOOD. These men have already caught the golfing bug. The Freeport Country Club course was located southwest of the city at the edge of farmland. Roy Farwell is the man at the far left. The caddy is identified as Bob Edwards, and the golfers are Dr. E. L. Griffith and Dr. Paul Breyer.

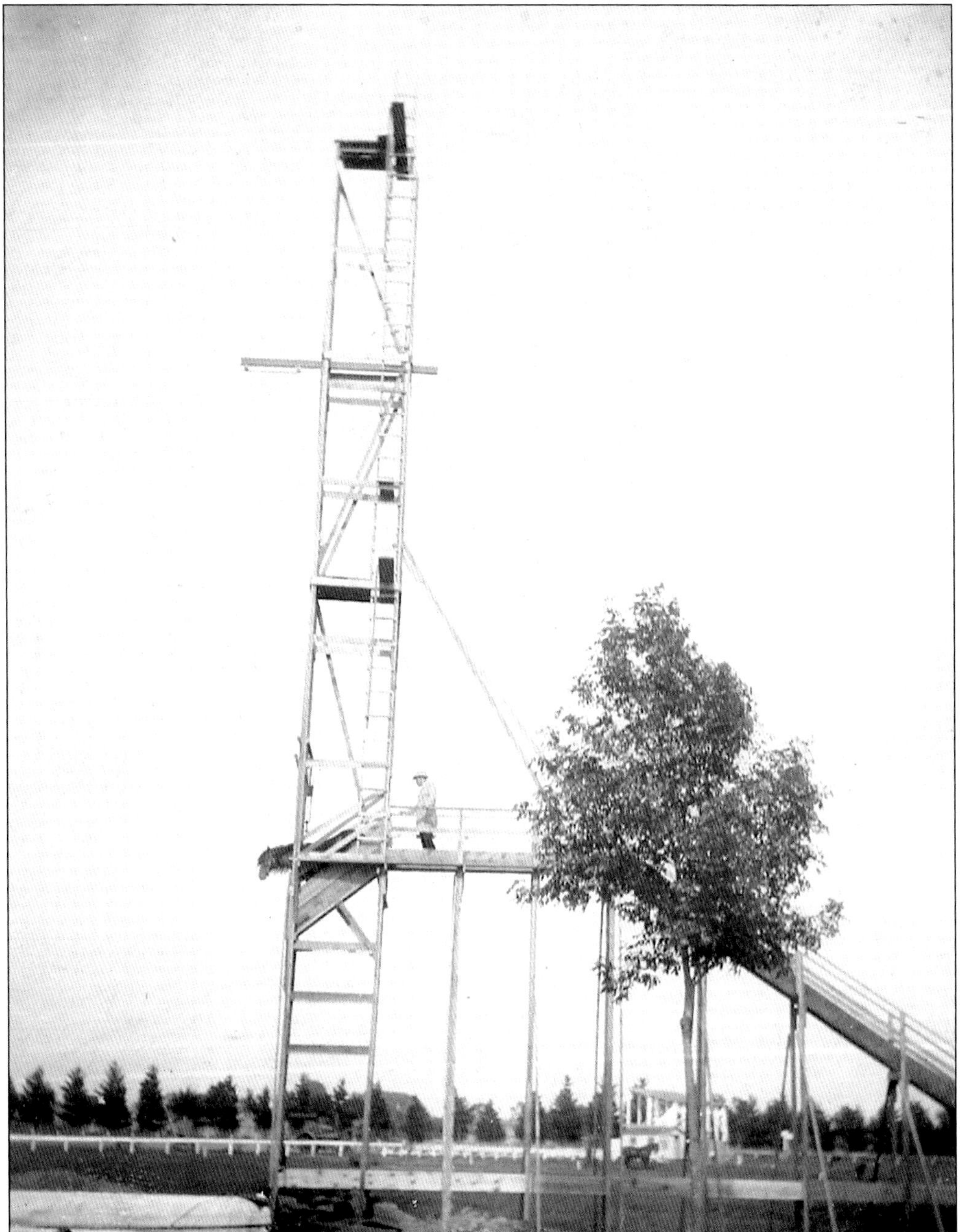

A Wild West Show. Dr. William Carver, a nationally famous daredevil in Wild West shows, performed stunts for audiences in Taylor Park. His horses and elk jumped from the tower into a pond to impress the crowd. His trained bull dogs performed, and Carver rode in the park's sulky races. His show was ranked in popularity with those of Buffalo Bill. (Courtesy of the Freeport Public Library.)

Three

PEOPLE AND INSTITUTIONS

Freeport is made up of a broad, ethnic diversity. A majority of its ancestry comes from a German background, but in the 1830s, the lush hills of Stephenson County beckoned also to immigrants from other European countries.

Following the Civil War and the expansion of the railroads, workers from the South were also attracted to the region in search of work and more desirable living conditions.

Agriculture was at first the main means of livelihood, but after the necessities of sustenance and shelter were satisfied, the need for assuaging the hungers of mind and soul arose. Schools, churches, and other aesthetic institutions sprung up to satisfy both.

This chapter offers a meaningful glimpse into what made Freeport what it is today.

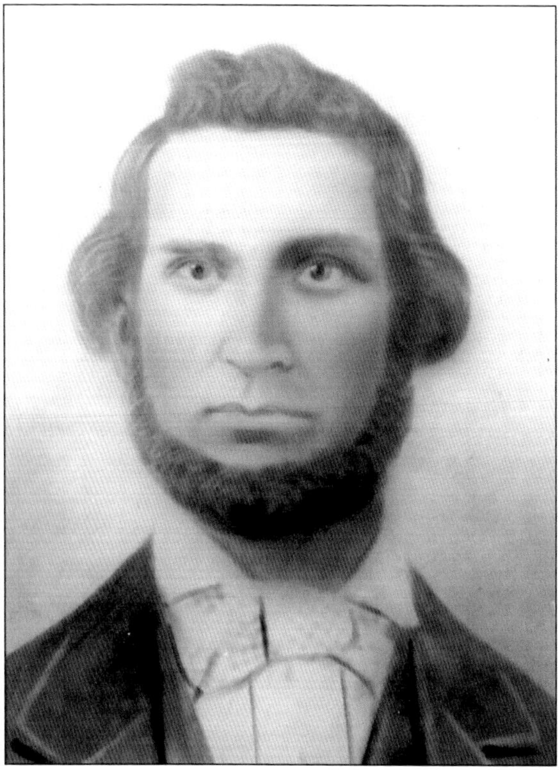

Freeport's Sly, Shrewd, and Eccentric Founder. According to legend, William "Tutty" Baker, Freeport's founder, received his nickname from the Native Americans who occupied this land when he arrived because he stuttered. Freeport got its name from his wife, Phoebe, who thought him to be too generous in hospitality. He assisted arriving settlers in getting their wagons across the Pecatonica River on his raft then reputedly offered them free board at his home.

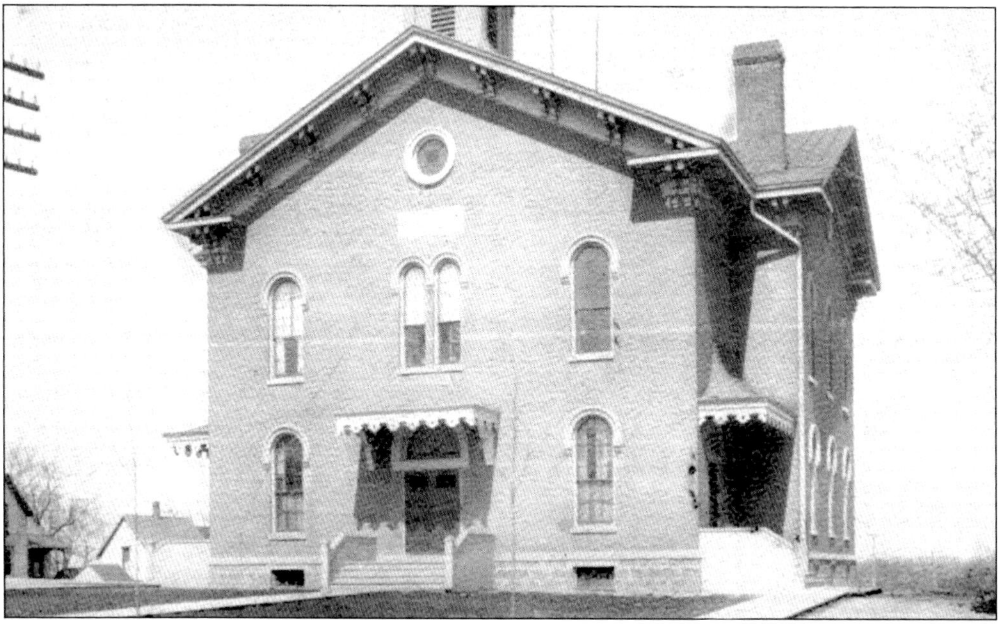

Freeport Gets a School. After the free school law became effective in 1855, the city experienced a growth spurt because of the arrival of the railroad. A school was built not far from the Pecatonica River and was appropriately named the River School. An election saw the approval of funds for the purchase of a site and construction of a school on North Van Buren Avenue at Ringold Street.

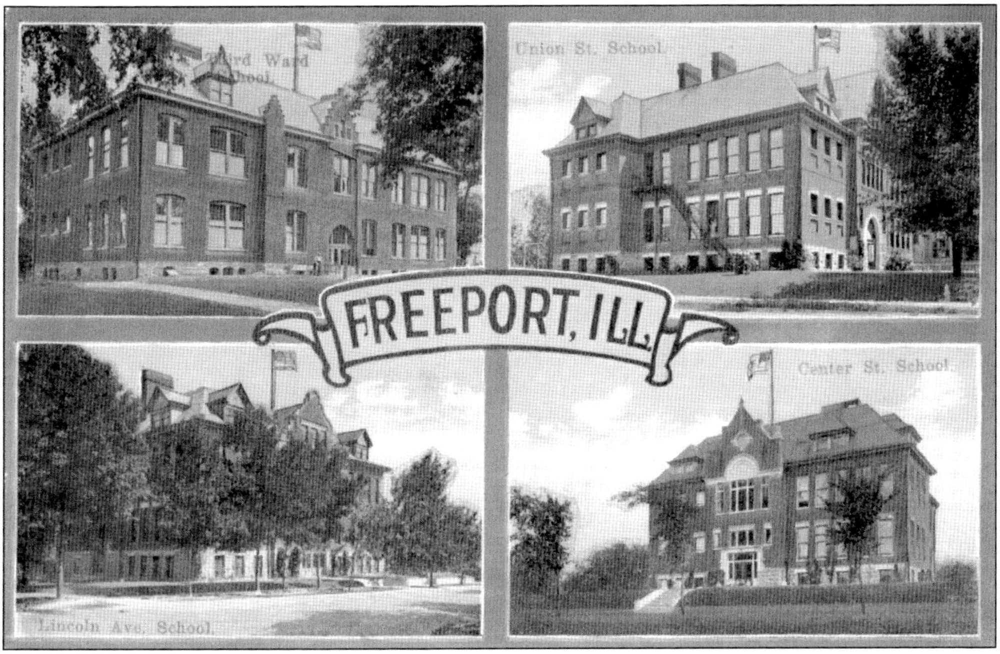

ECHOES OF FORMER DAYS. These former school buildings are not in use today by the Freeport School District. Clockwise from top left, Third Ward School, built in 1866, is now the site of the King Community Campus. Union Street School sits idle on South Chicago Avenue. It opened in 1897 and served until 1960 when new elementary schools were constructed and it became the district's administration building. Lincoln School now houses businesses at Lincoln Boulevard and West Avenue. It was first occupied in 1899 and was the second building on that site. Center Street School opened in 1906 but was replaced with the present school in September 1968. Freeport High School held class in the building below for about 20 years beginning in 1906.

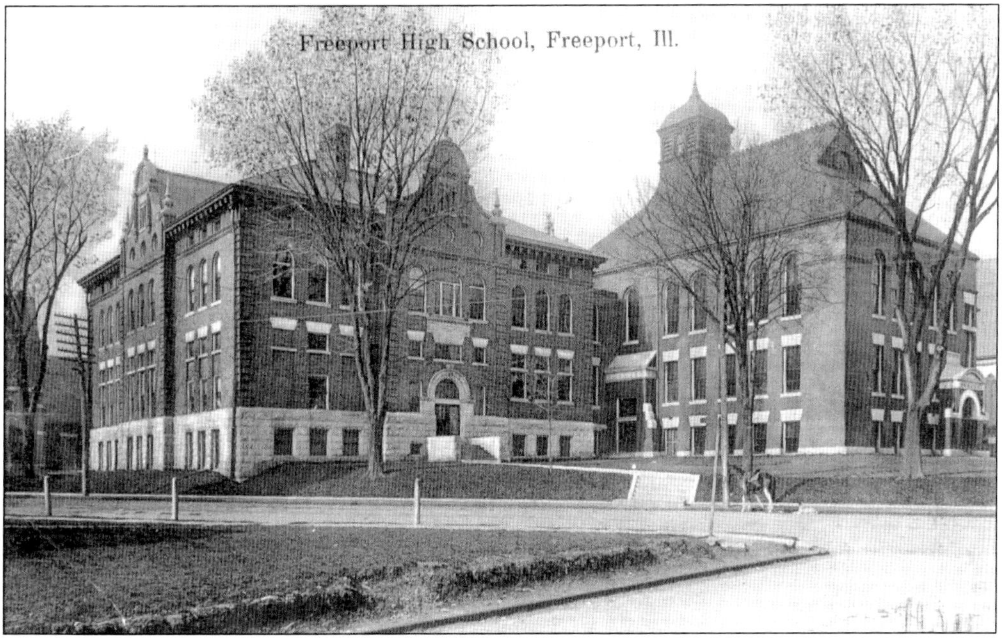

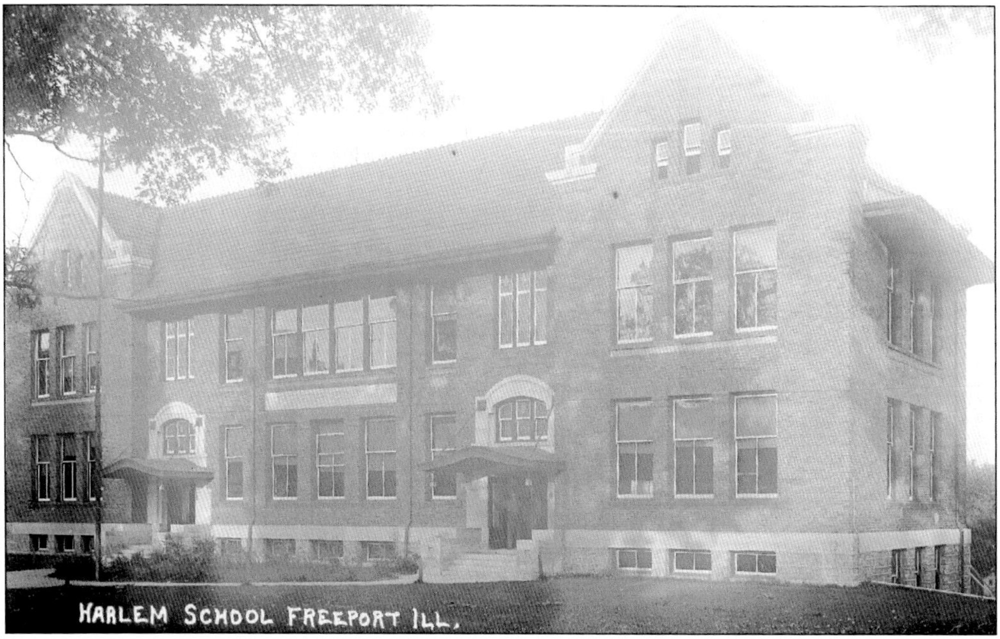

HARLEM SCHOOL NOW A MUSEUM. This was Harlem Elementary School, built in 1911 and 1912 at 121 North Harlem Avenue. It was eventually closed and sold by the Freeport School District and now houses both Stephenson County Senior Center and Freeport Arts Museum.

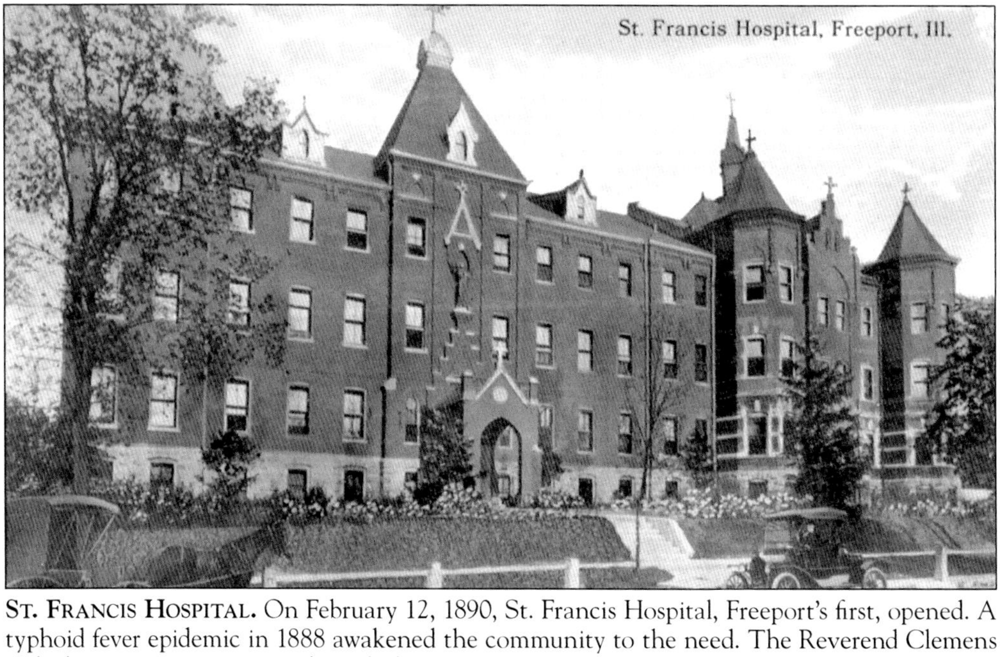

ST. FRANCIS HOSPITAL. On February 12, 1890, St. Francis Hospital, Freeport's first, opened. A typhoid fever epidemic in 1888 awakened the community to the need. The Reverend Clemens Kalvelage, a priest at St. Joseph Catholic Church, was a force in acquiring the institution, which served the community until mid-July 1965. Kalvelage raised public donations for financing the project. Large extensions were added in 1902, 1925, and 1926.

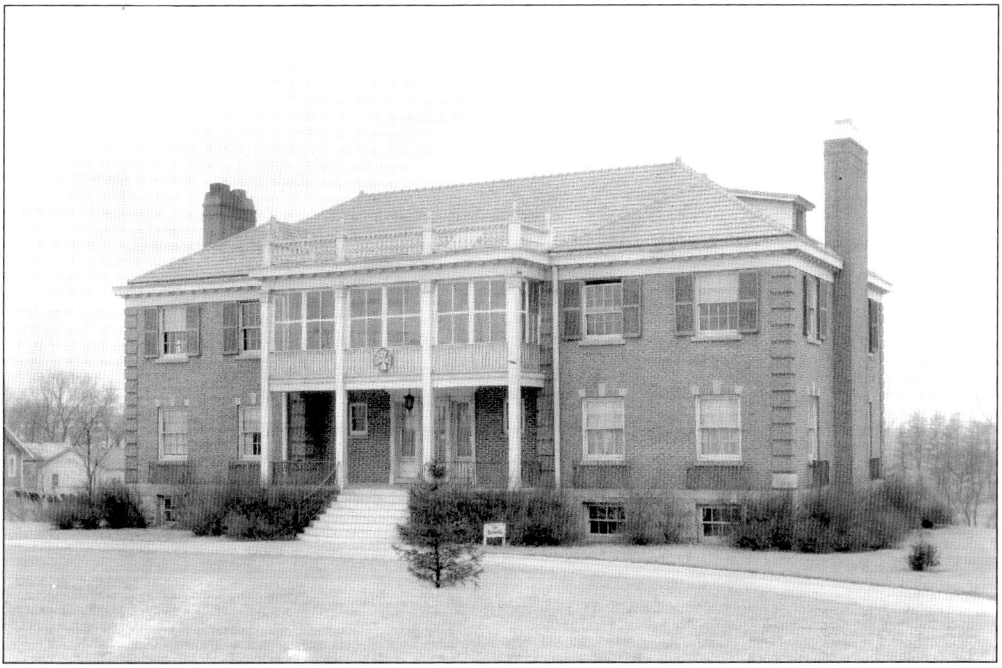

AN ORPHANAGE IN TOWN. King's Daughters' Children's Home was located near the north end of Harlem Avenue. It was instituted in 1926 as an orphanage by the King's Daughters Society. Many children were raised there and given good care and good education.

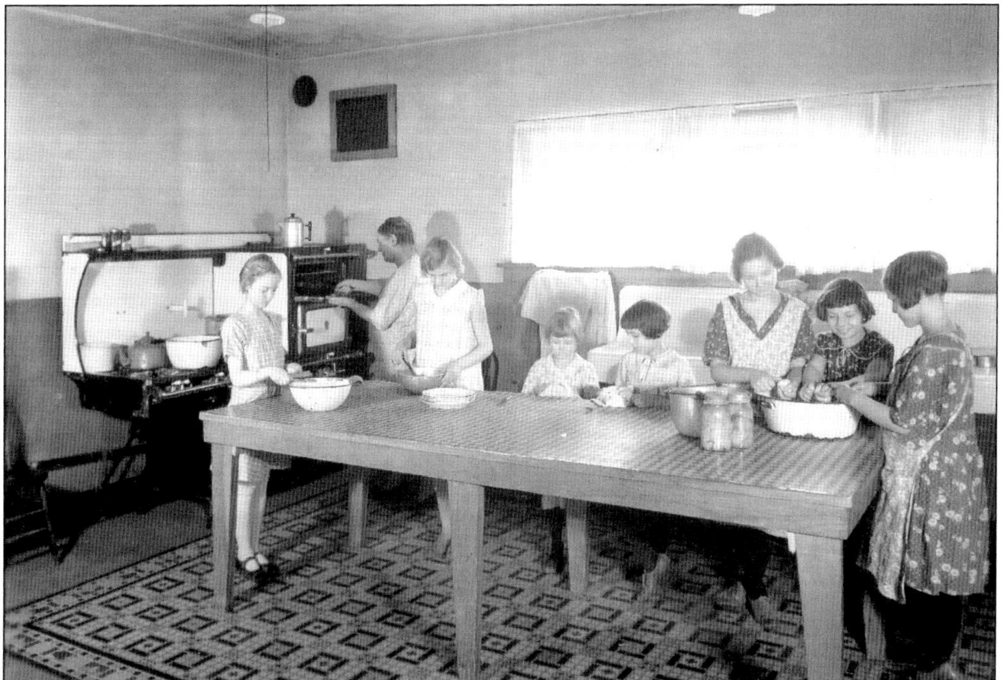

LEARNING TO COOK. Female residents of King's Daughters' Children's Home spent time in the kitchen learning how to cook and help prepare meals.

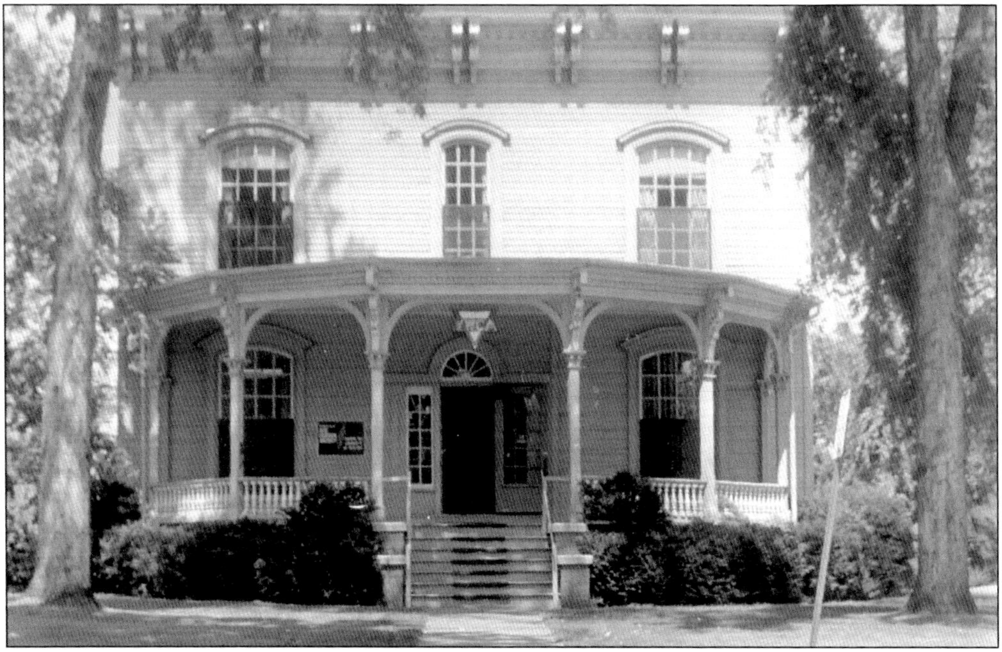

A Stately Home for YWCA. In the fall of 1917, a house at 514 West Stephenson Street in Freeport became the home of the brand new YWCA. The dwelling that had served as a private clubhouse for young men remained the YWCA center for a good half century before the association built a new facility at 641 West Stephenson Street.

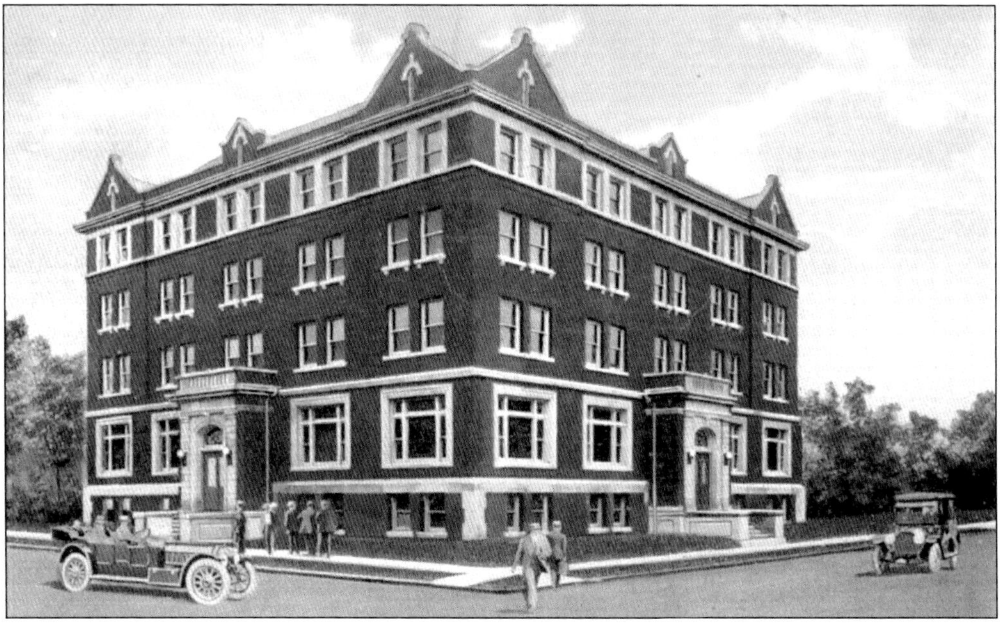

YMCA. The Freeport YMCA was organized in 1868 at the promotion of evangelist Dwight L. Moody, who had spoken here. After occupying rented rooms and several locations in downtown, the building shown was dedicated in January 1916. That building was sold and is now made up of offices and apartments. The YMCA now has a sports complex on the Highland Community College campus.

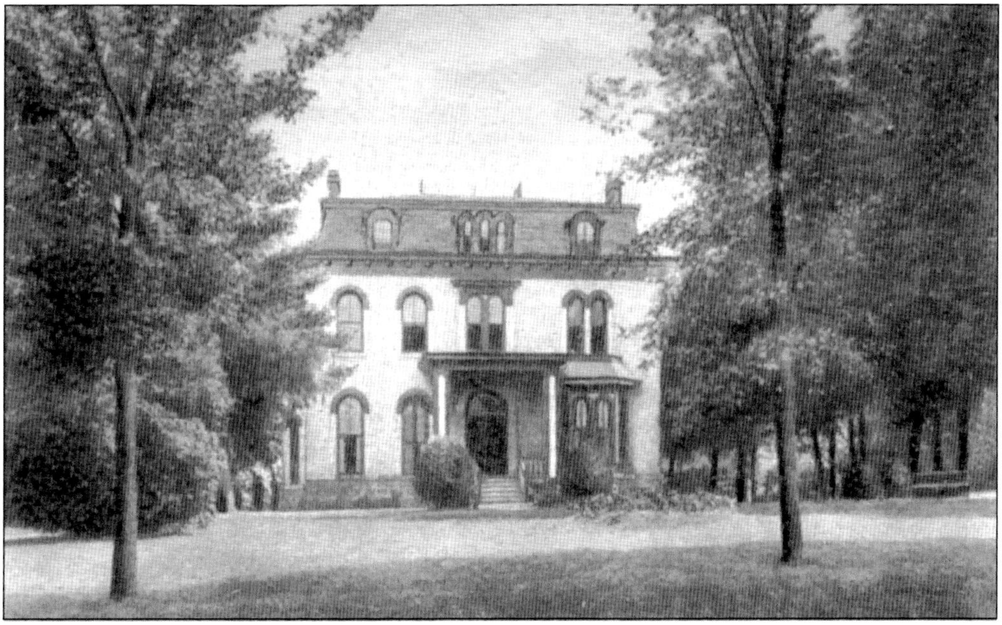

A HOUSE BECOMES A HOSPITAL. This Victorian house, built in 1866, became Globe Hospital, Freeport's first nondenominational hospital. It opened in 1902 as a 40-bed institution and was opened in a house then owned by Dr. William W. Krape, a dentist who founded the Knights of the Globe, an insurance-related society. In January 1924, the hospital was taken over by the Deaconess Society of the Evangelical Church, and its name changed to the Evangelical Deaconess Hospital and Training School for Nurses. In 1960, the institution became Freeport Memorial Hospital and later FHN Memorial Hospital. (Below, courtesy of the Freeport Public Library.)

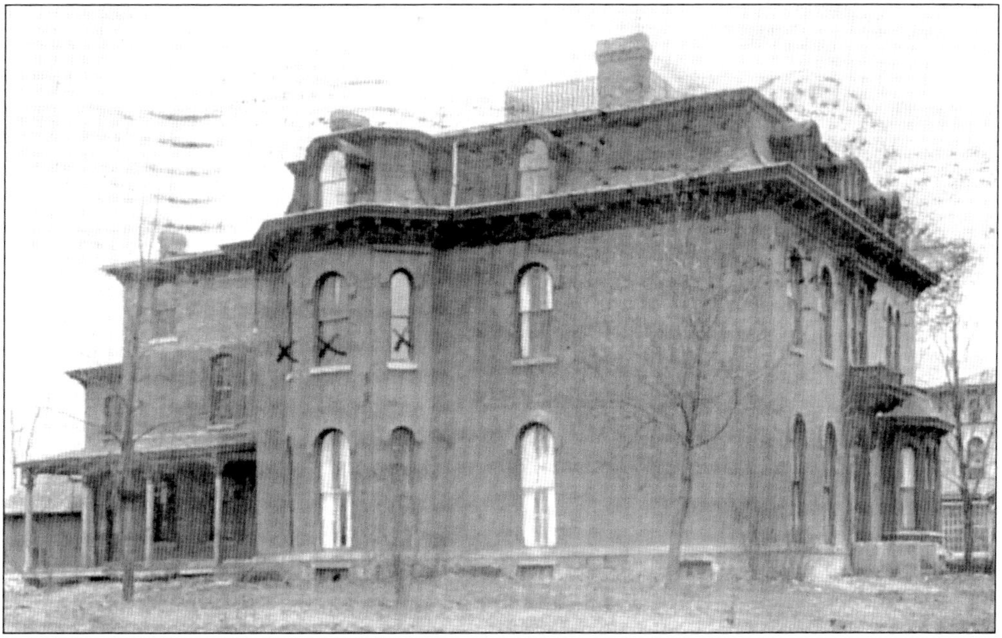

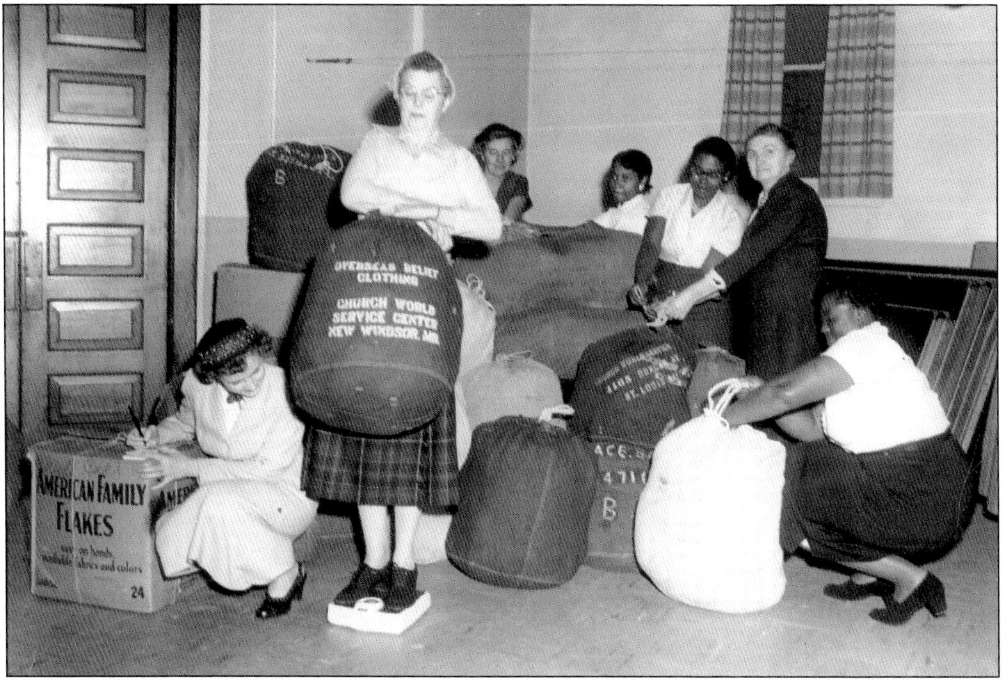

CLOTHING FOR WORLD RELIEF. Women gathered on November 4, 1955, at Trinity United Methodist Church to mail donated clothing for World Community Day. Women in the foreground packing and weighing the contributions are identified, from left to right, as Mrs. Munich, Mary Barrett, Mrs. Hauger, Mrs. Fehr, and Mrs. Salter.

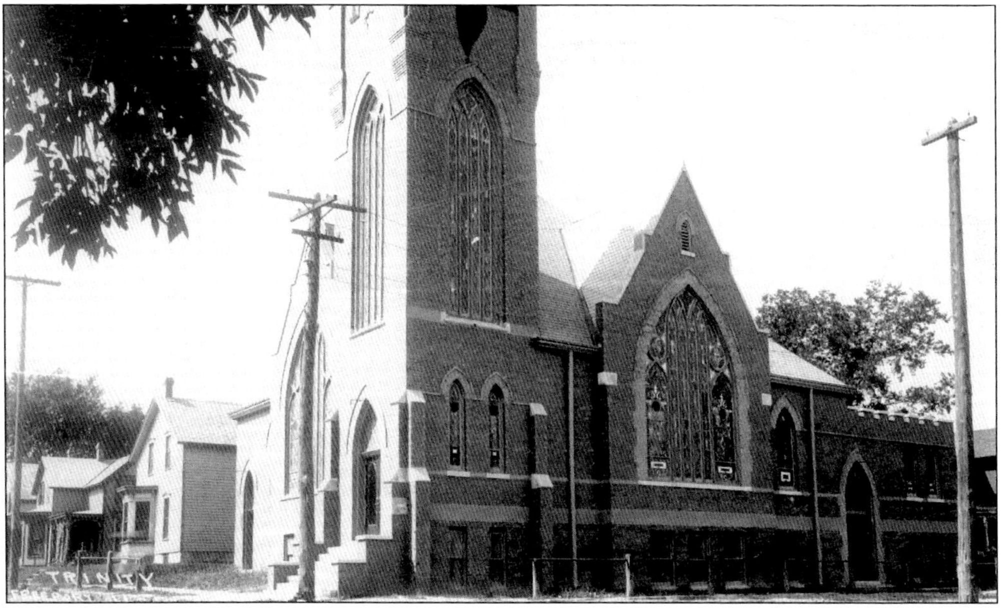

CHURCH ON CHICAGO AVENUE. Trinity Evangelical United Brethren Church occupied this corner spot at 602 South Chicago Avenue. The edifice was dedicated on March 15, 1908. It cost $15,000 to build. The church building is currently occupied by Mount Carmel Missionary Baptist Church.

A FREEPORT LANDMARK. The tower of St. Joseph Catholic Church at West Washington Place stands 175 feet in the air and is said to be the highest point in Freeport. This Gothic structure, erected in 1871, was built to serve a German-speaking group that had formed its own parish from a combined German-Irish congregation. The lofty steeple is visible far and wide and is one of Freeport's most prominent landmarks.

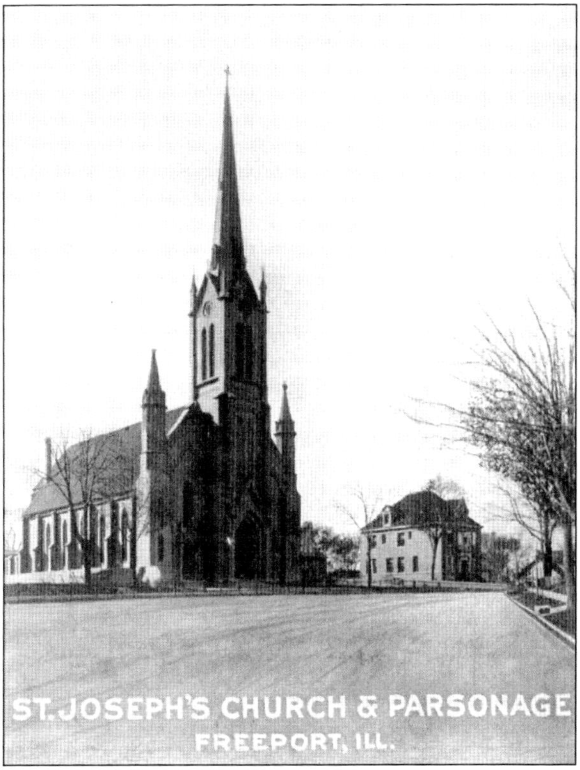

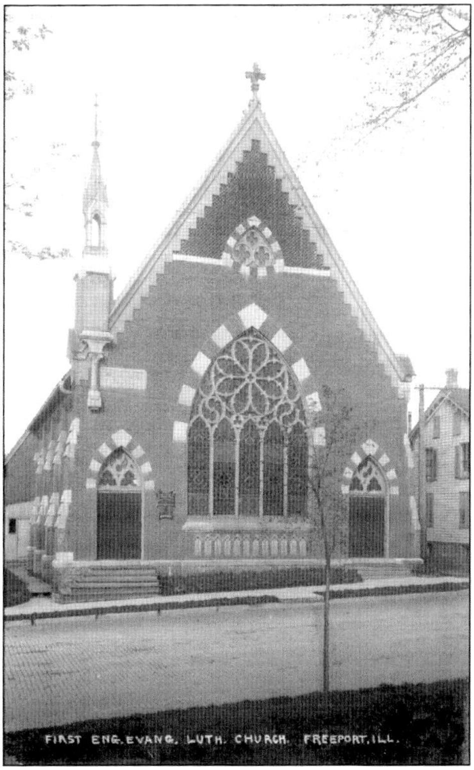

AN ORNATE LITTLE CHURCH. First English Evangelical Lutheran Church at 303 South Galena Avenue was organized in 1881. This small, ornate edifice was completed within the next few years. Throughout its more than 125 years, the congregation has added an educational unit and acquired most of the city block where it sits.

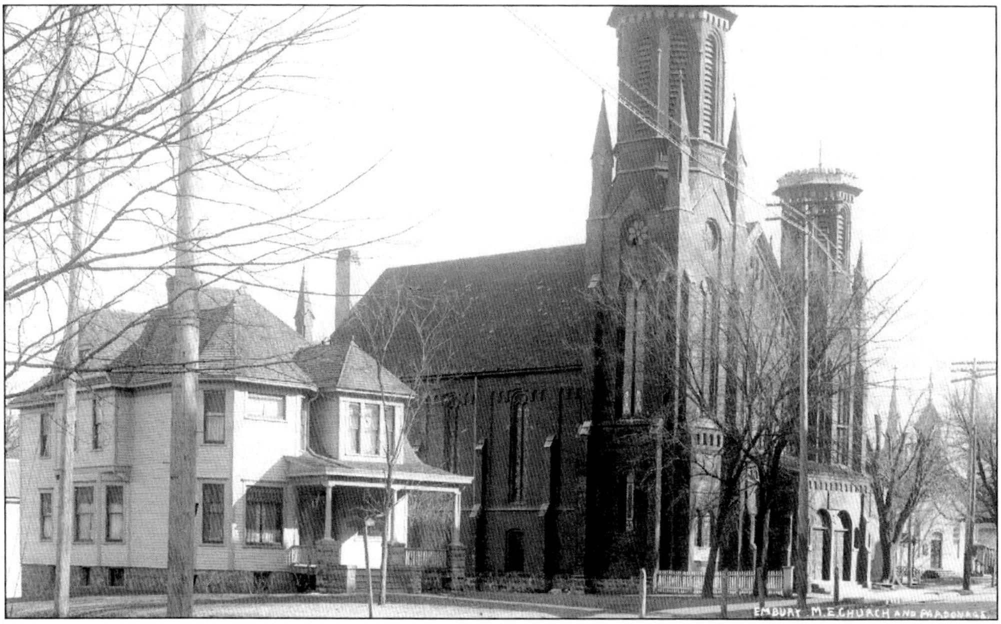

METHODISTS SAT UP HIGH. Embury United Methodist Church was organized in 1865. Its house of worship was built in 1867 at 515 South Galena Avenue. The massive structure that houses the congregation today was built in 1909. The scene below shows its sanctuary.

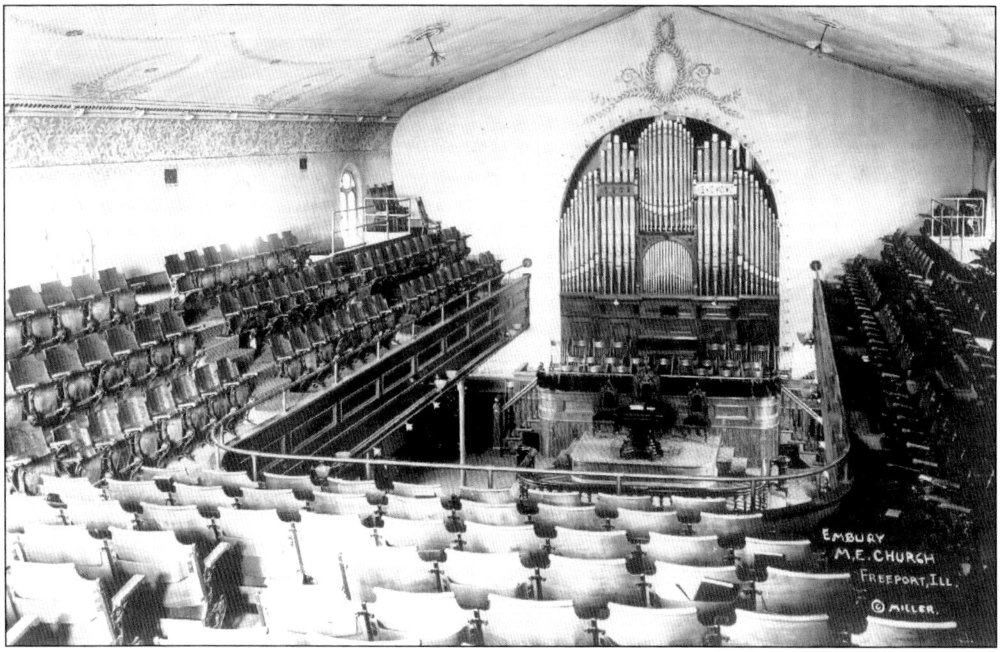

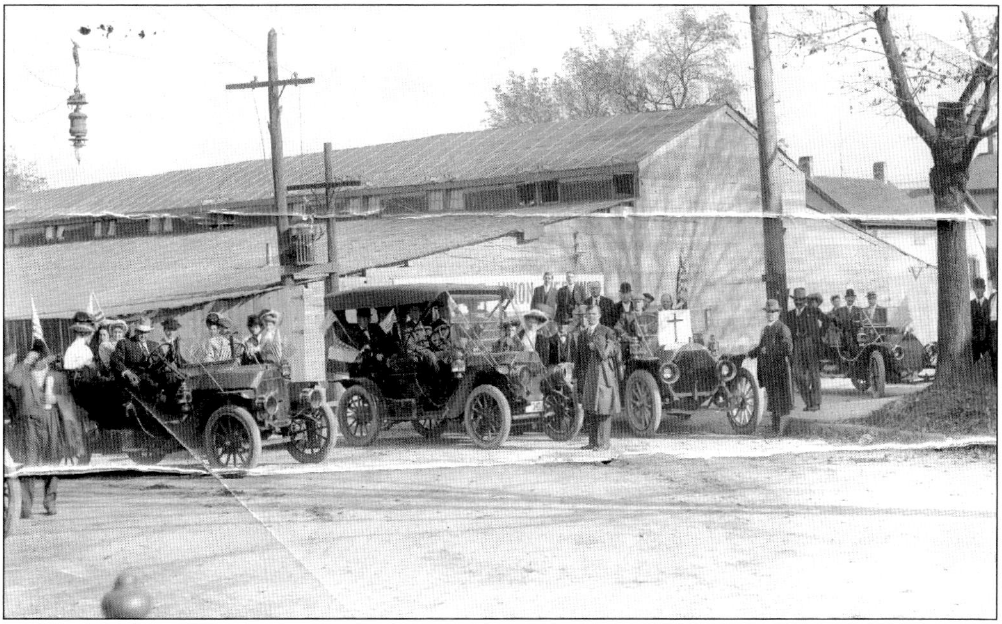

FAMOUS EVANGELIST VISITS. Nationally known evangelist Billy Sunday visited Freeport in 1906. Sunday conducted weeks of rousing revivals at the Tabernacle in Oakdale Park and in other locations. Sunday's preachings raised the ire of city fathers because of his criticism of church apathy, tolerance of gambling and booze, and society women's frivolities.

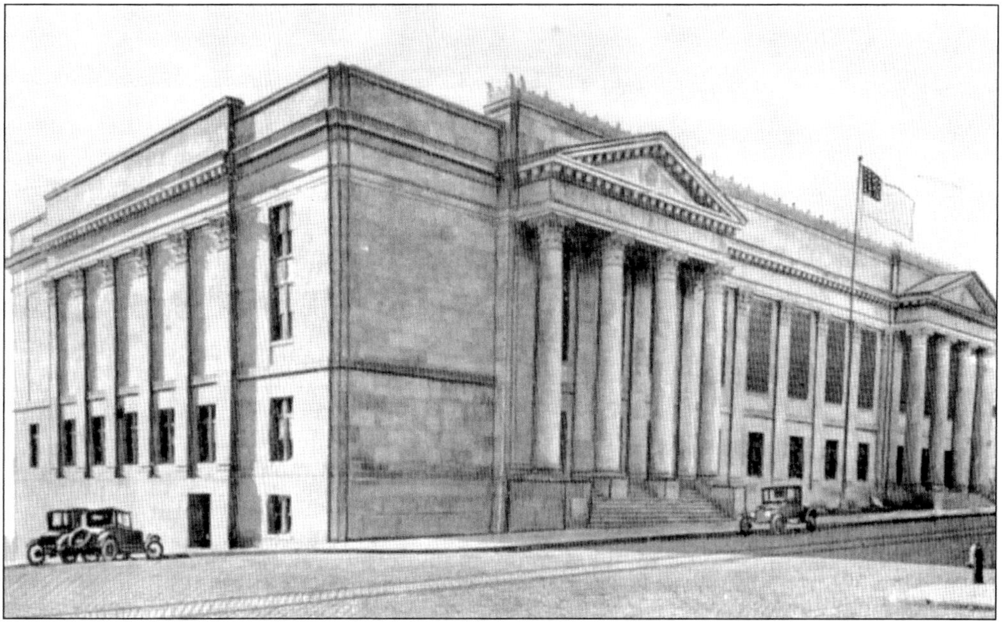

FREEPORT'S PRIDE. The Masonic temple at 305 West Stephenson Street has gallantly served the artistic appetites of Freeport and environs since 1928. It furnishes an ideal theater for all types of stage productions and has a ballroom/dining room utilized during its 80-year history for large banquets, dances, receptions, expositions, and for lodge, club, business, and community activities.

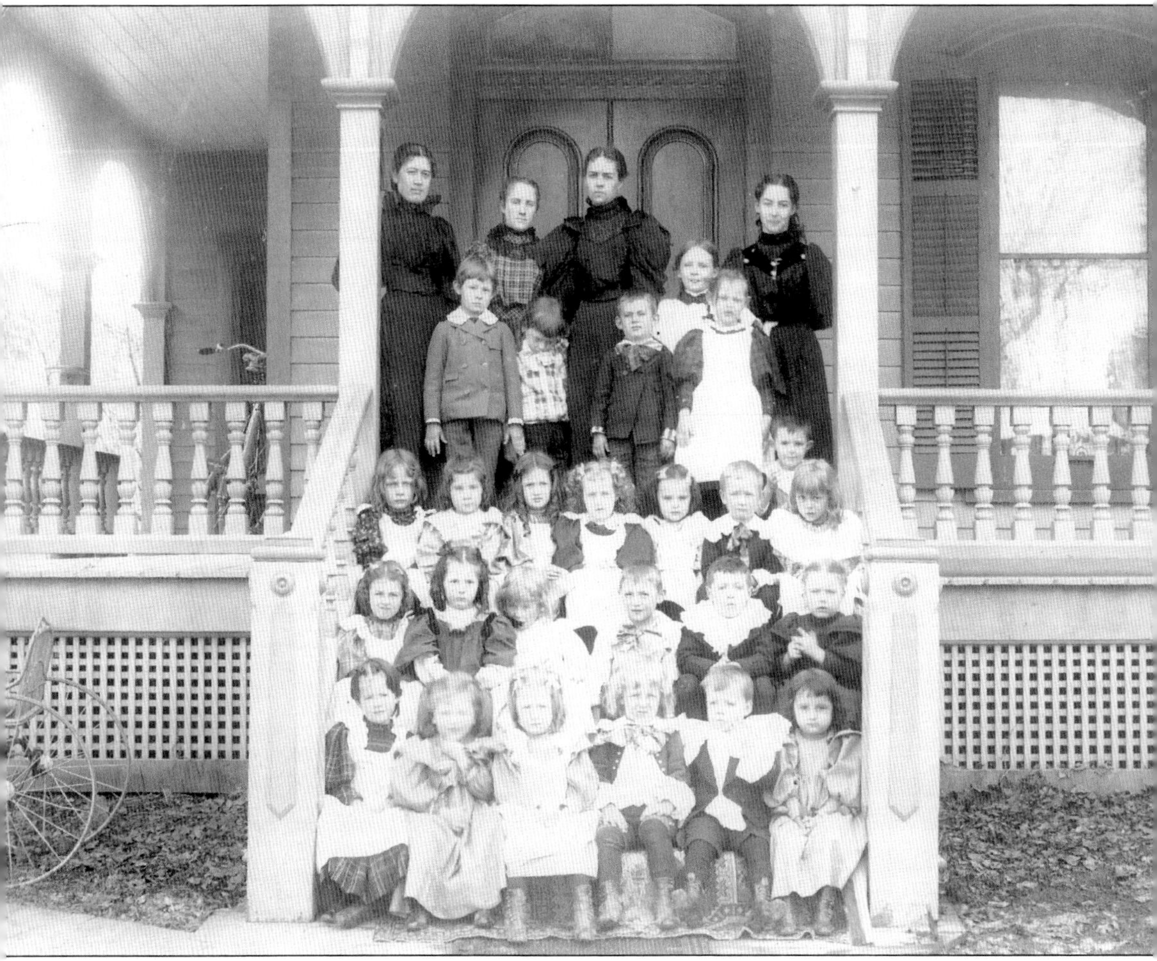

A New Concept in Education. Anna Snyder held a private kindergarten in her home at 861 West Stephenson Street. This 1896 photograph shows 25 children, and among them is Donald Breed, the later owner, publisher, and editor of the *Freeport Journal-Standard*. Breed is the small boy who is second from left at the top. Other familiar surnames from Freeport history are Gund and Knowlton. Teachers standing in the rear, from left to right, are Jessie Blanchard, Pansy Runner, and Anna and Helen Snyder.

Four

MUNICIPALITY

The City of Freeport was incorporated in 1855, then groaned and grew. Its swelling population demanded many things. The people wanted wells and cisterns, streets and sidewalks, fire and police protection, and a government responsive to their wants and complaints.

A mayor, Thomas J. Turner, and six aldermen were elected, and the city was on its way. One by one, as the years went by, the citizens' needs were met. Fine, large homes were built, and the city's industrious citizens found employment in local, growing industries.

The cornerstone of the city hall was laid on May 30, 1899. That building remains the city hall today, 110 years later. Bids for a post office building were taken in 1902. That building, having doubled in size, also continues to serve.

Freeport proceeded to meet all the challenges of a maturing city, not without its conflicts, but always rising to the occasion and filling admired diligently to ensure Freeport's citizens are safe at home and at work.

The following chapter offers glimpses of some of the grunt and grind it has taken Freeport to be the city it is, endeared to its faithful dwellers for more than 150 years.

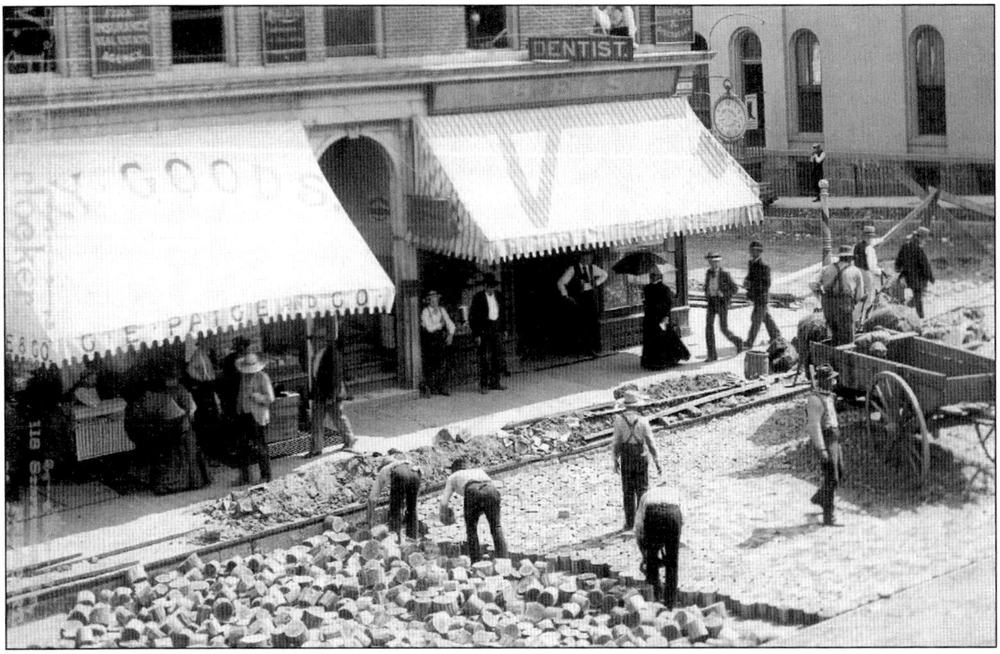

STEPHENSON STREET GETS PAVED. In 1890, the Freeport City Council approved paving downtown Stephenson Street with brick, but an outcry from citizens arose because of the cost. Thus, the council voted to use the cheaper cedar wood blocks. Later years saw the street paved, first with bricks and later with asphalt. (Courtesy of the Freeport Public Library.)

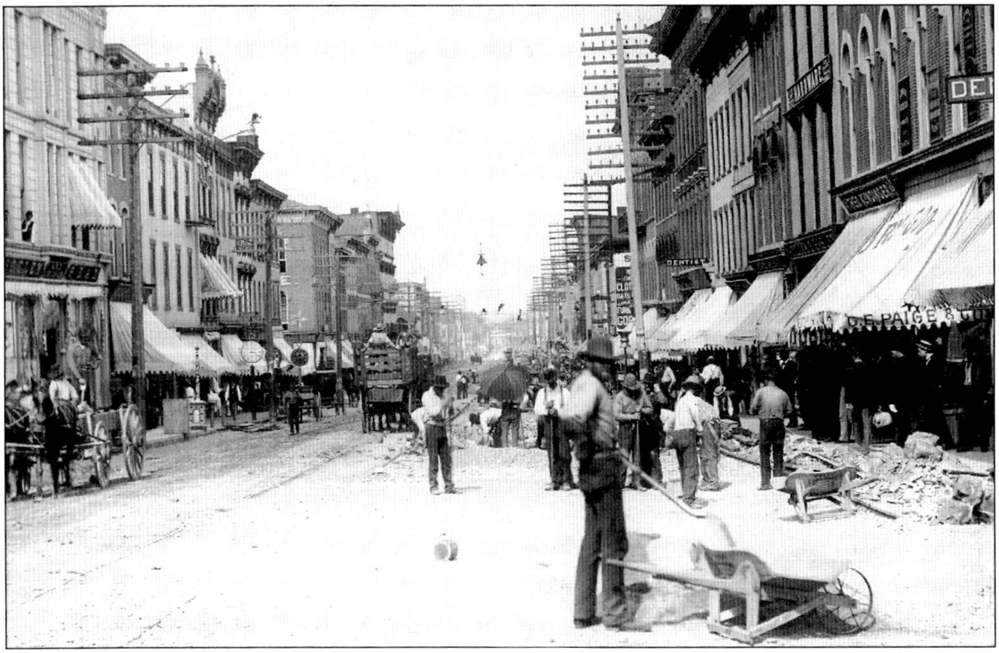

A MAJOR STREET IMPROVEMENT. Laying pavement in 1890 was a back-breaking job, especially because of the cedar wood blocks. This scene was of Stephenson Street looking east from Van Buren Avenue. The F. A. Read Department Store is the building at the left edge. (Courtesy of the Freeport Public Library.)

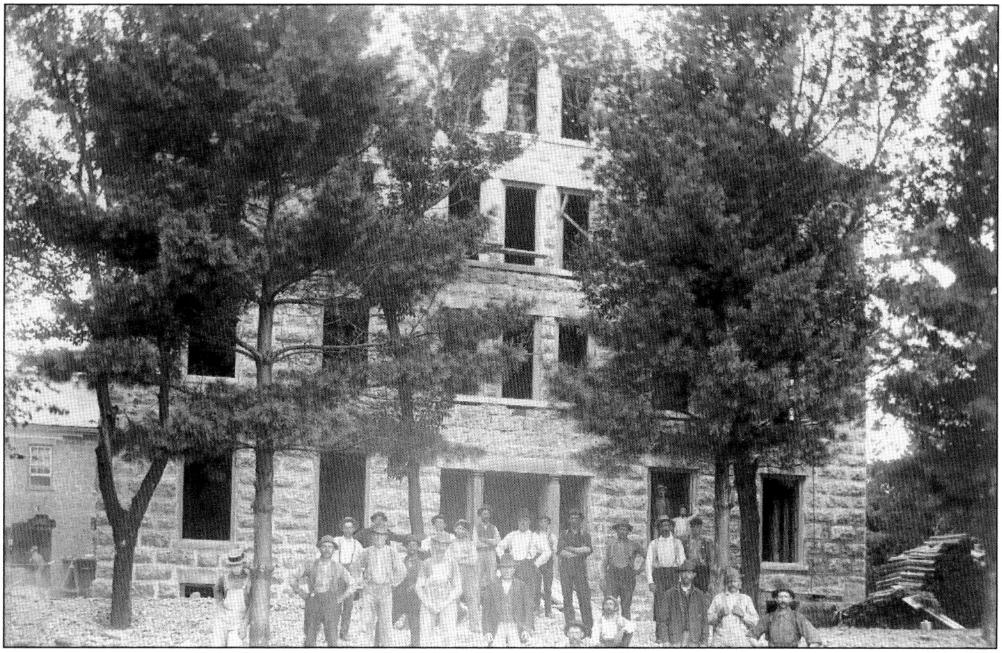

Earning their Keep. These residents of the Stephenson County Home, commonly called the poor farm, actually earned their living. Each resident contributed to the running and upkeep of the farm, which supplied meat, vegetables, and dairy products for the residents' diets. This building burned in 1927, with only some of the stone outer walls salvageable. (Courtesy of the Freeport Public Library.)

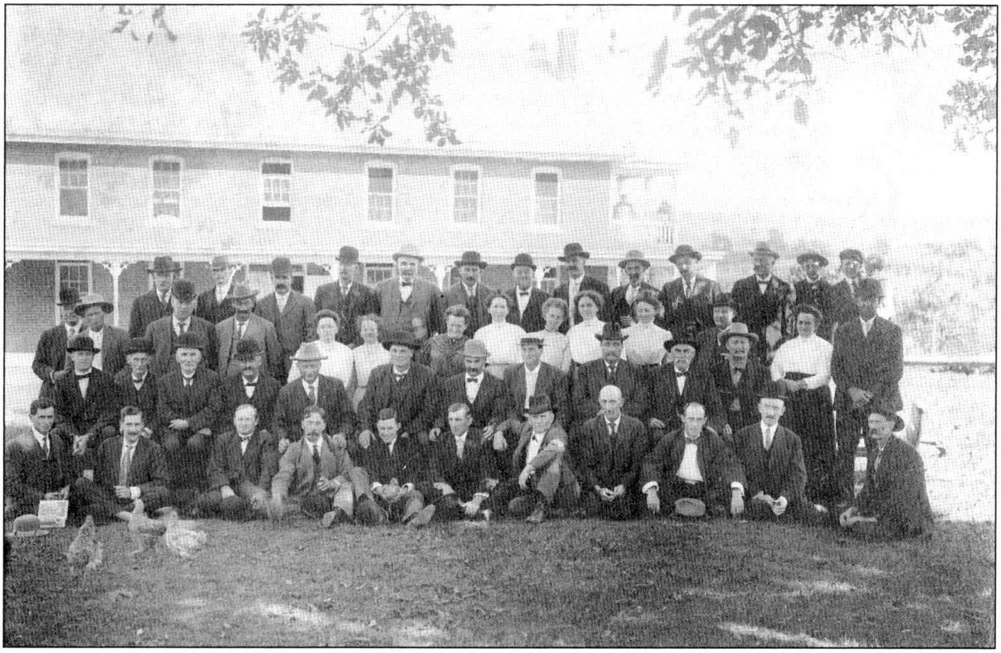

Poor Farm Supervisors. This photograph is labeled "Supervisors at the Poor Farm in about 1915." Hats were the order of the day for the gentlemen. A few unconcerned chickens wandered into the picture.

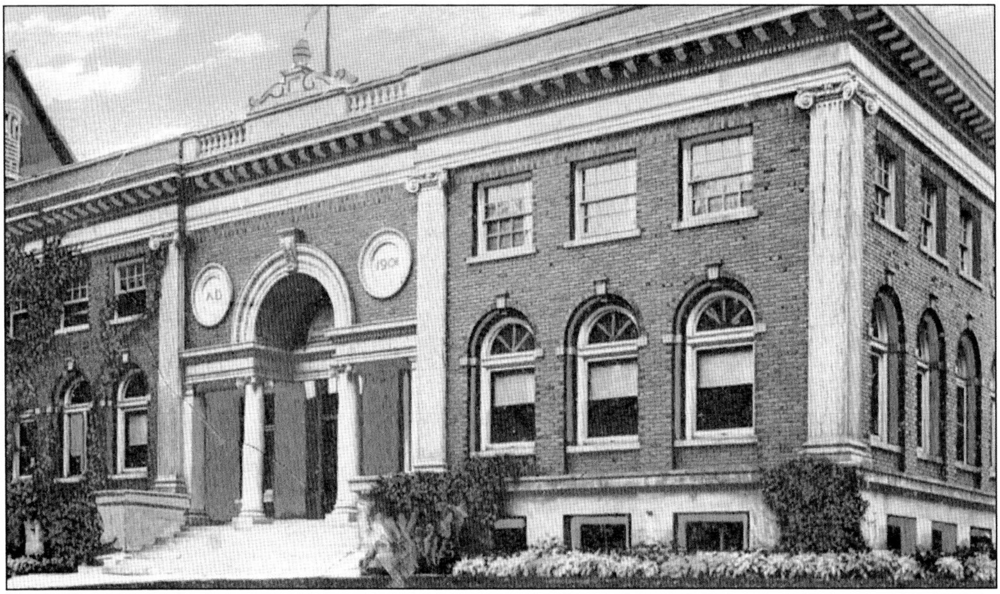

A SILENT SERVANT. Freeport's Andrew Carnegie Library stands empty today, having surrendered to the eminence of a new and modern library opened in December 2003. This old library impartially served generations of citizens from all walks of life. Winifred Taylor, daughter of pioneer notables Oscar and Malvina Taylor, is credited as the founder. This building, opened in 1902, materialized through a $30,000 gift from financier Carnegie and citizens' contributions of about $10,000. (Courtesy of the Freeport Public Library.)

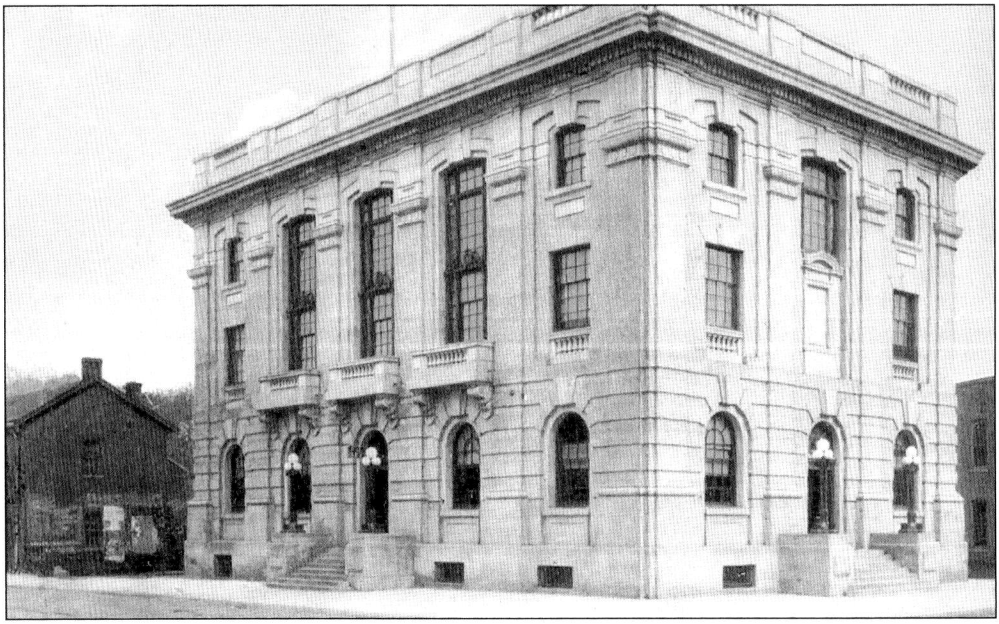

NEW POST OFFICE IN 1903. Freeport's first post office was established in about 1837 in a small storeroom on what is now Main Street. The entry of the railroad removed the need for the stagecoach lines. Various downtown buildings served as the post office temporarily until the building went up. This building was remodeled and nearly doubled in size in 1931 and 1932, also housing the federal court. (Courtesy of the Freeport Public Library.)

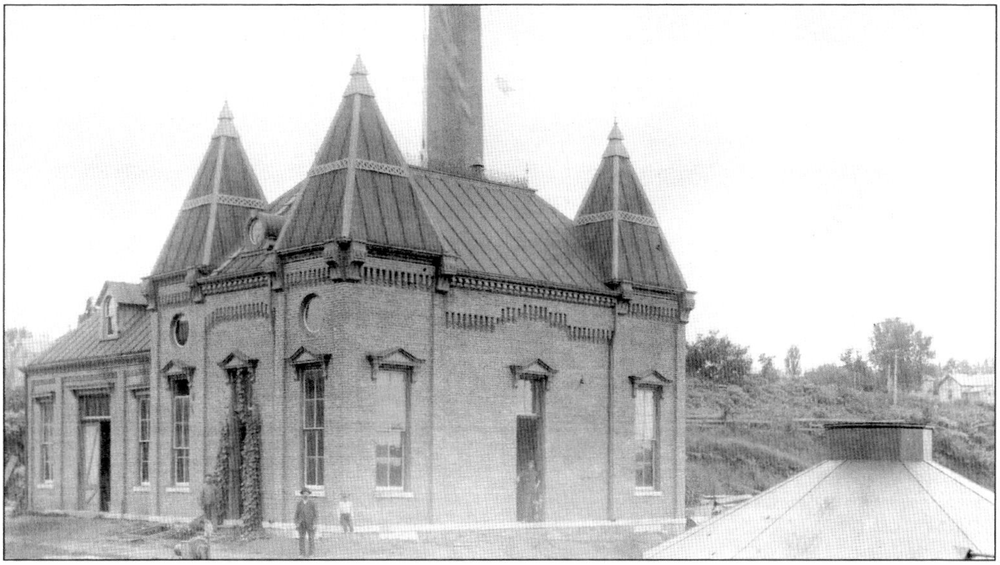

FREEPORT WATER WORKS. This building at 706 North Brick Avenue was Freeport Water Works in 1885. According to *History of Stephenson County, 1970*, Freeport newspapers began pleading the case for a water system in 1880. A private company first came to the fore, and the laying of the first cast-iron pipe began on July 31, 1882. The next month, work began on a pumping station engine house. Water was first let into the mains on November 20, 1882, and on December 18, 1882, the Freeport City Council approved the system. (Courtesy of the Freeport Public Library.)

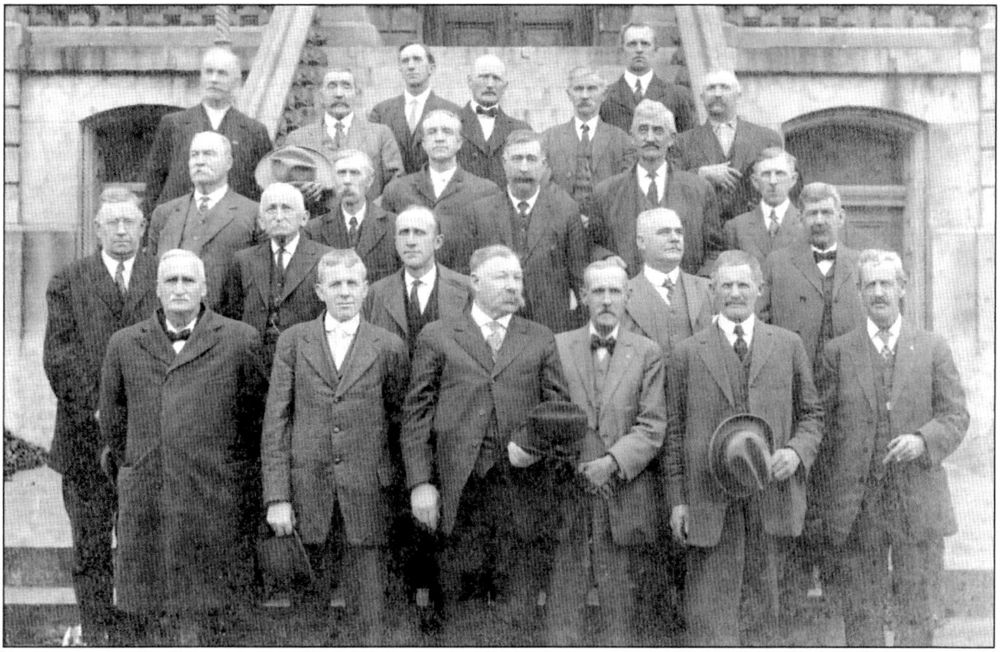

IN CHARGE. Standing second from right in the first row, David I. Felts is pictured on November 10, 1916, among the Stephenson County supervisors. Having served from 1902 to 1933, Felts set a record in Rock Grove Township for the longest term on record since 1890, a whopping 31 years.

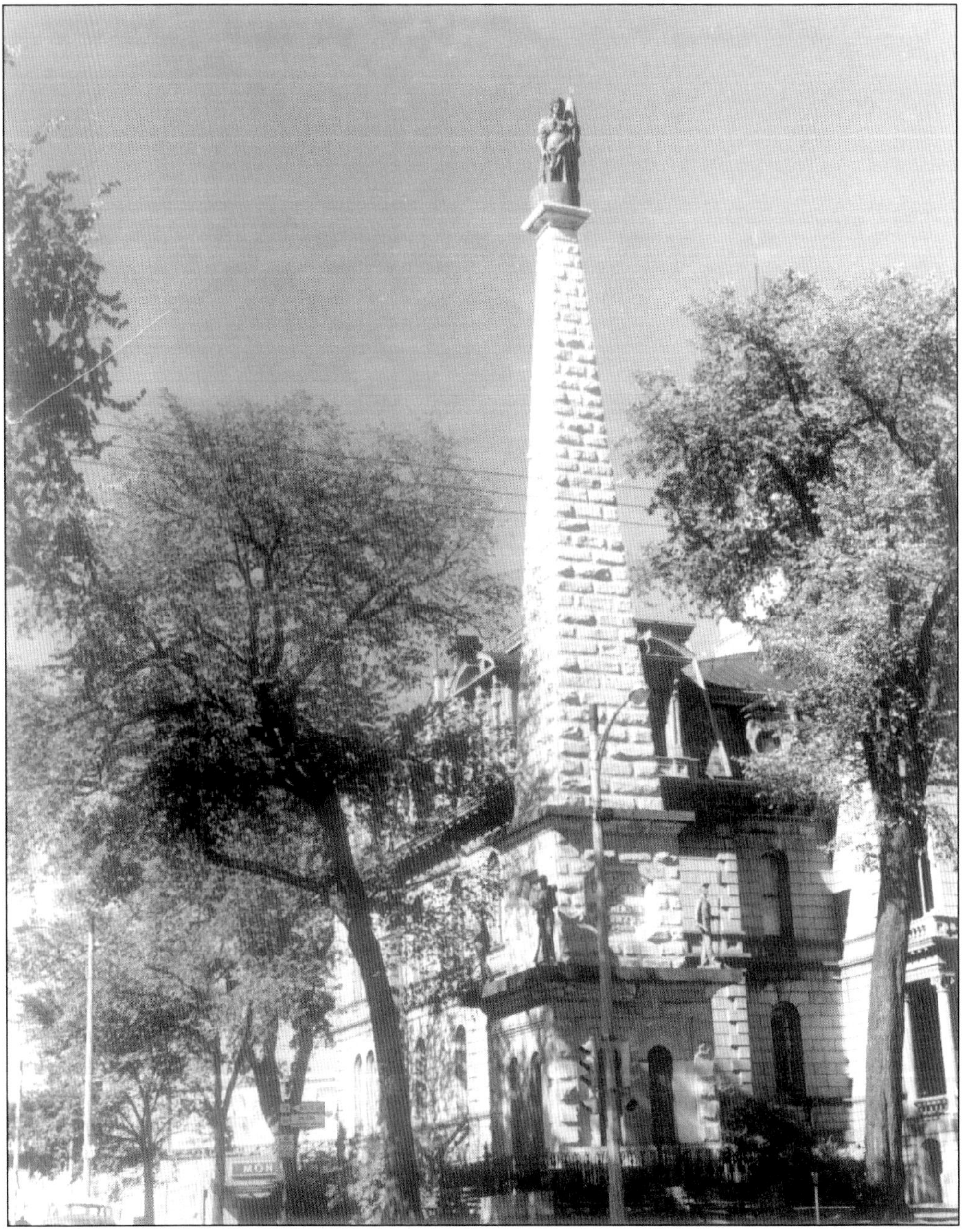

STEPHENSON COUNTY'S CIVIL WAR MONUMENT. The Stephenson County Soldiers' Monument Association was formed in 1868 to design and construct a monument to honor the county's citizens who had given their lives for their country. A contest was held to determine the design, with the winning one being submitted by Gen. S. D. Atkins, a community leader and veteran of the Civil War. The cornerstone was laid October 19, 1869. The monument of Joliet marble had a 12-foot-square base and was 83 feet high. The statue at the top, named Victory, was the work of celebrated artist Giovanni Meli. On October 1, 1960, Victory was destroyed by lightning. The four figures at the corners of the base, also done by Meli, represent each of the arms of the service: infantry, cavalry, artillery, and navy.

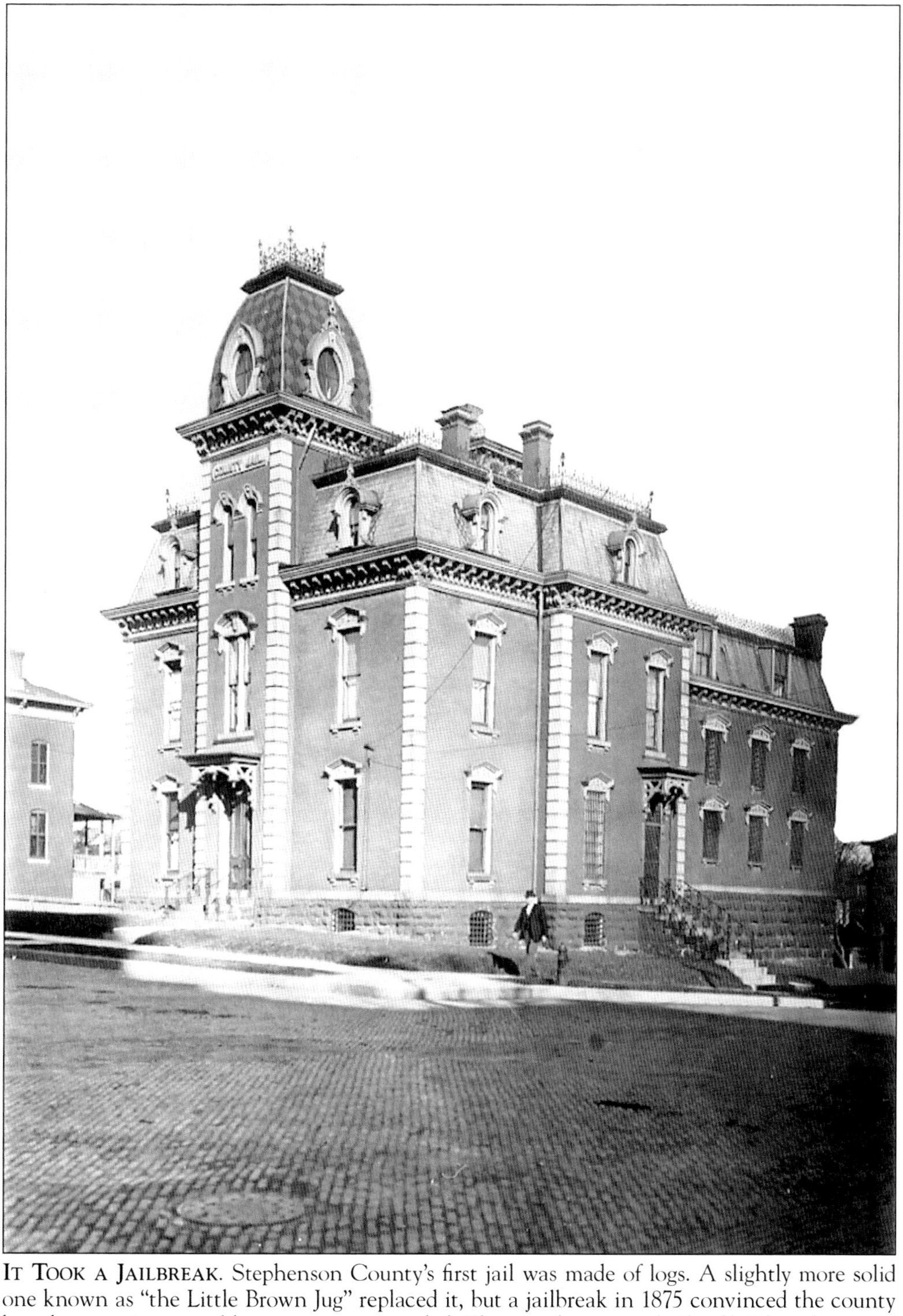

IT TOOK A JAILBREAK. Stephenson County's first jail was made of logs. A slightly more solid one known as "the Little Brown Jug" replaced it, but a jailbreak in 1875 convinced the county board a more impregnable structure was needed. The one shown was built of brick and stone at Exchange and Galena Streets in the late 1870s and also contained a residence for the sheriff. This jail was destroyed by fire in 1962. The new, modern jail is at the southeast edge of town.

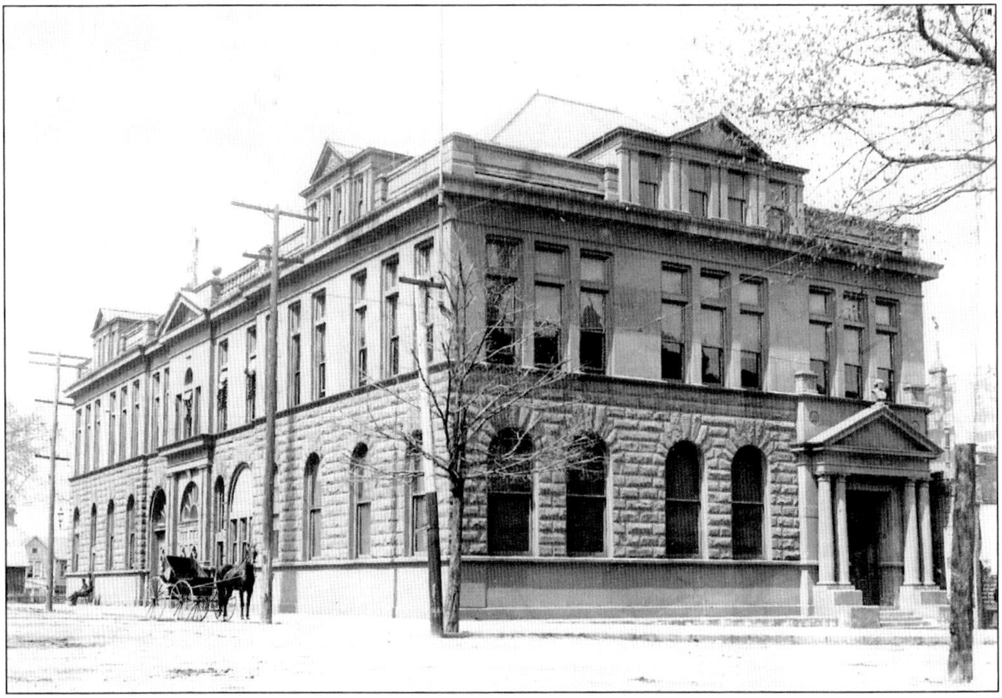

CITY HALL. The cornerstone of Freeport's city hall was laid on Memorial Day in 1899. Albert Baumgarten was mayor. Architect D. S. Shureman tricked city fathers when they refused to allow his name to be etched on the building. He had the names of famous literary people added in such an order that the sequence of first letters spelled his name. The building first housed the water, police, and fire departments.

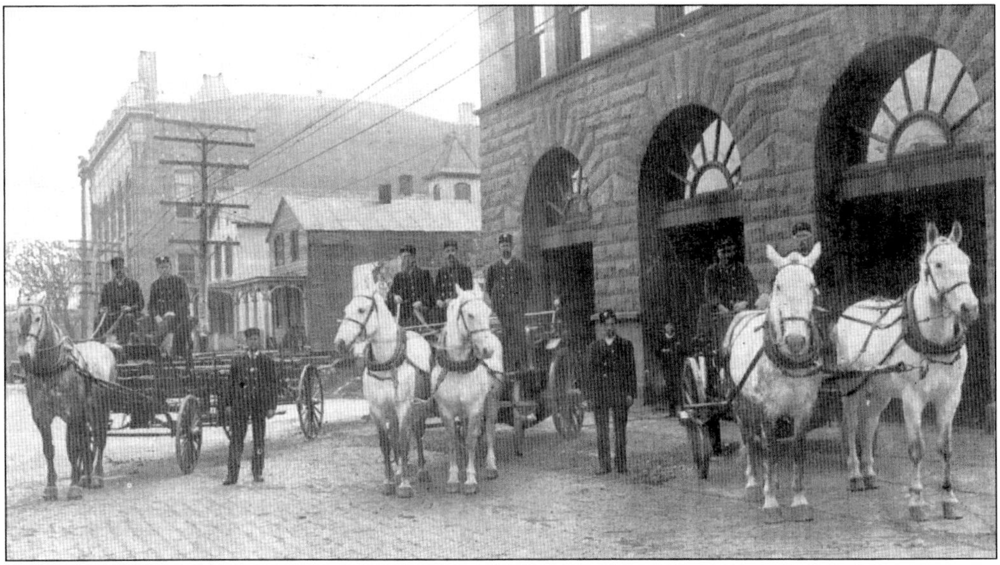

WHITE STEEDS PULLED FIRE WAGONS. Before automobiles, firemen not only had to shine the wagons, but they also had to feed, groom, and clean up after the horses that clip-clopped over the brick streets to the site of the alarm. This station was at the rear of city hall along Exchange Street. (Courtesy of the Freeport Public Library.)

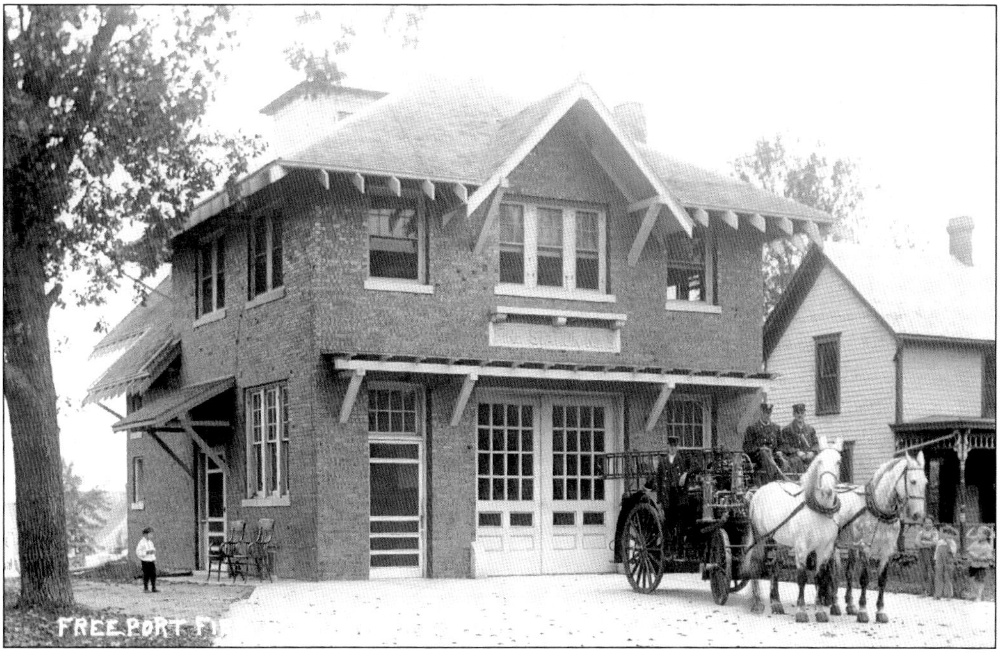

FREEPORT FIRE STATION. When the residents of West Freeport wished to become a part of the city of Freeport in 1911, Freeport Fire Station No. 3 was erected. The provision of this station was one of their conditions for annexation. The station now serves as the Freeport Rural Station.

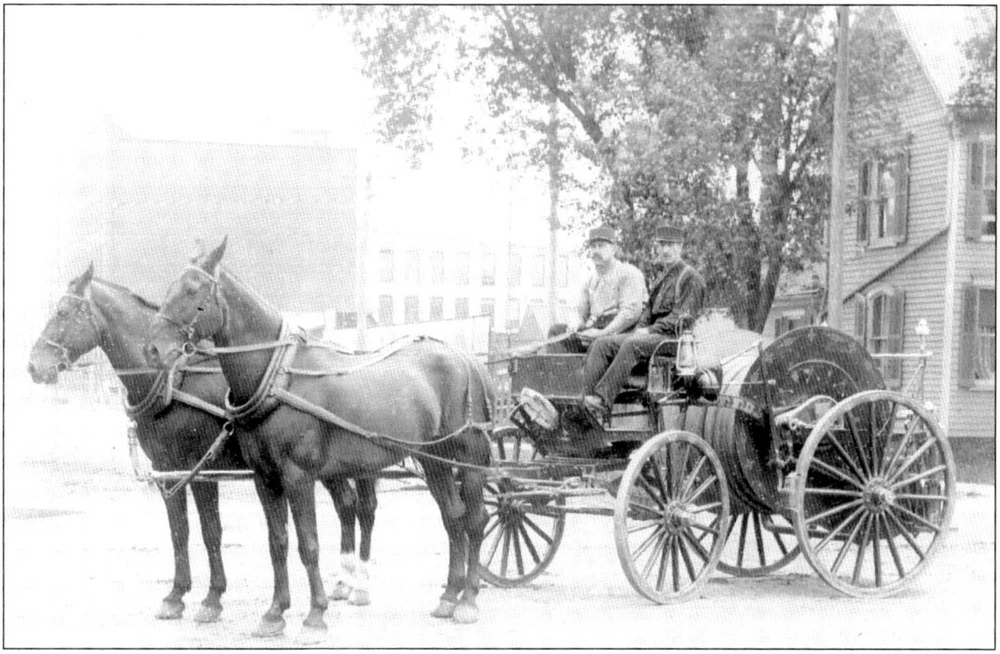

FIRE DEPARTMENT LIVESTOCK. Two legendary members of the Freeport Fire Department in 1904 were this team of horses, Dick and Dewey. Firemen Charles Borsdorf, the driver, and Potter Faubell must have had to crack the whip to get their faithful friends to the scenes of fires. The picture was taken at the corner of Galena Avenue and Spring Street.

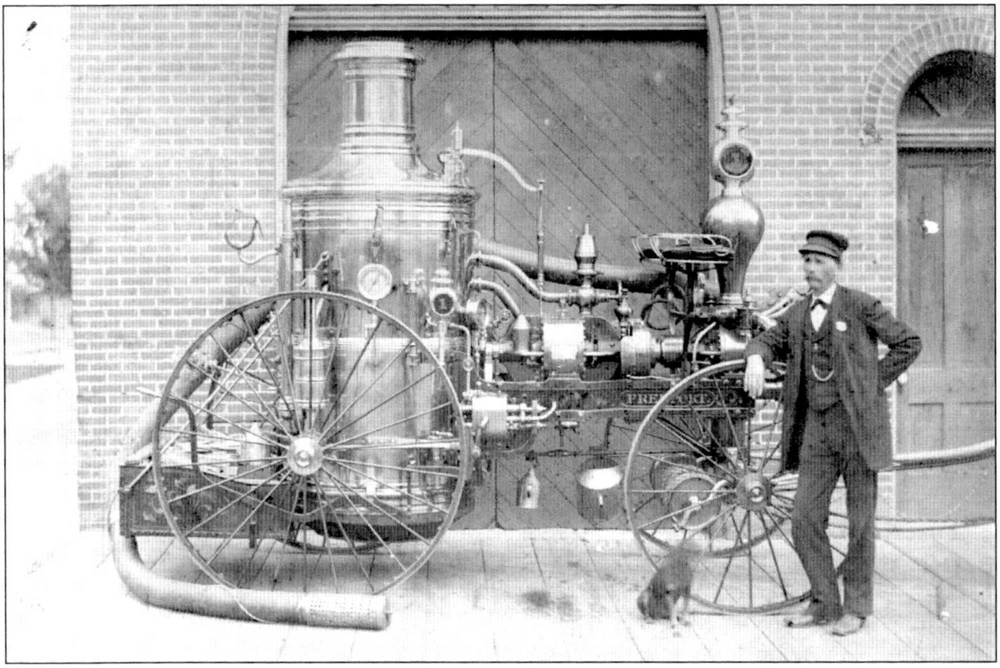

Firefighters Had a System. When firefighting depended on small steam engines like the one above, tunnels were dredged underground to store storm water. Many of the tunnels still exist under downtown streets. In the early days, the only fire alarm was the cry of "fire!"

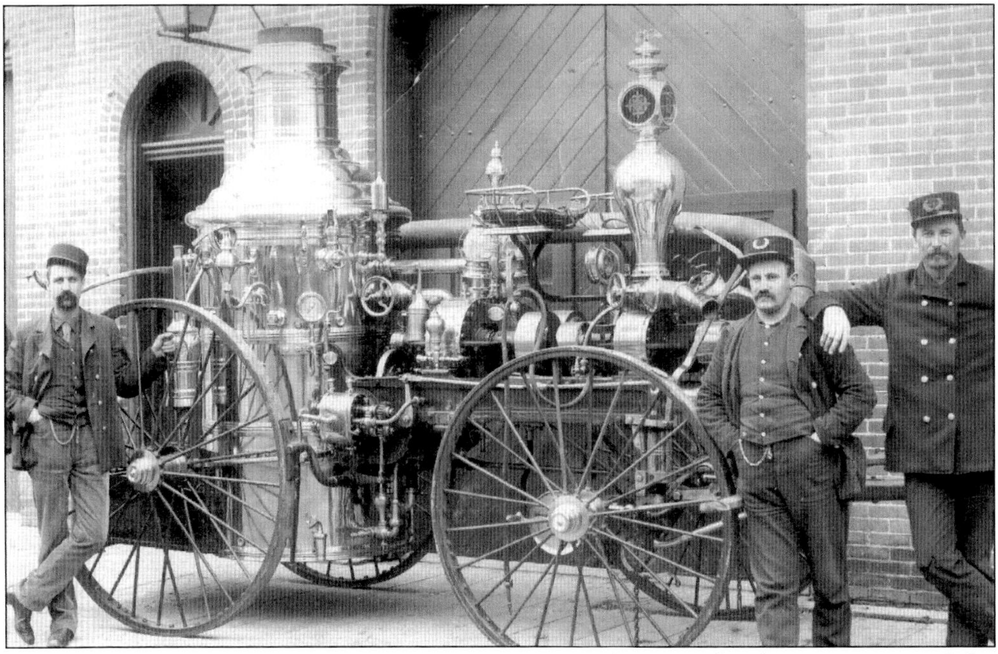

A Streamlined Steam Engine. Freeport was protected in 1885 by this steam-powered fire engine. The building in the background is the city hall and engine house. Longtime fire chief John Bodemeier stands at right. These jaunty, mustached men are in dress uniform and sport pocket watches complete with chain.

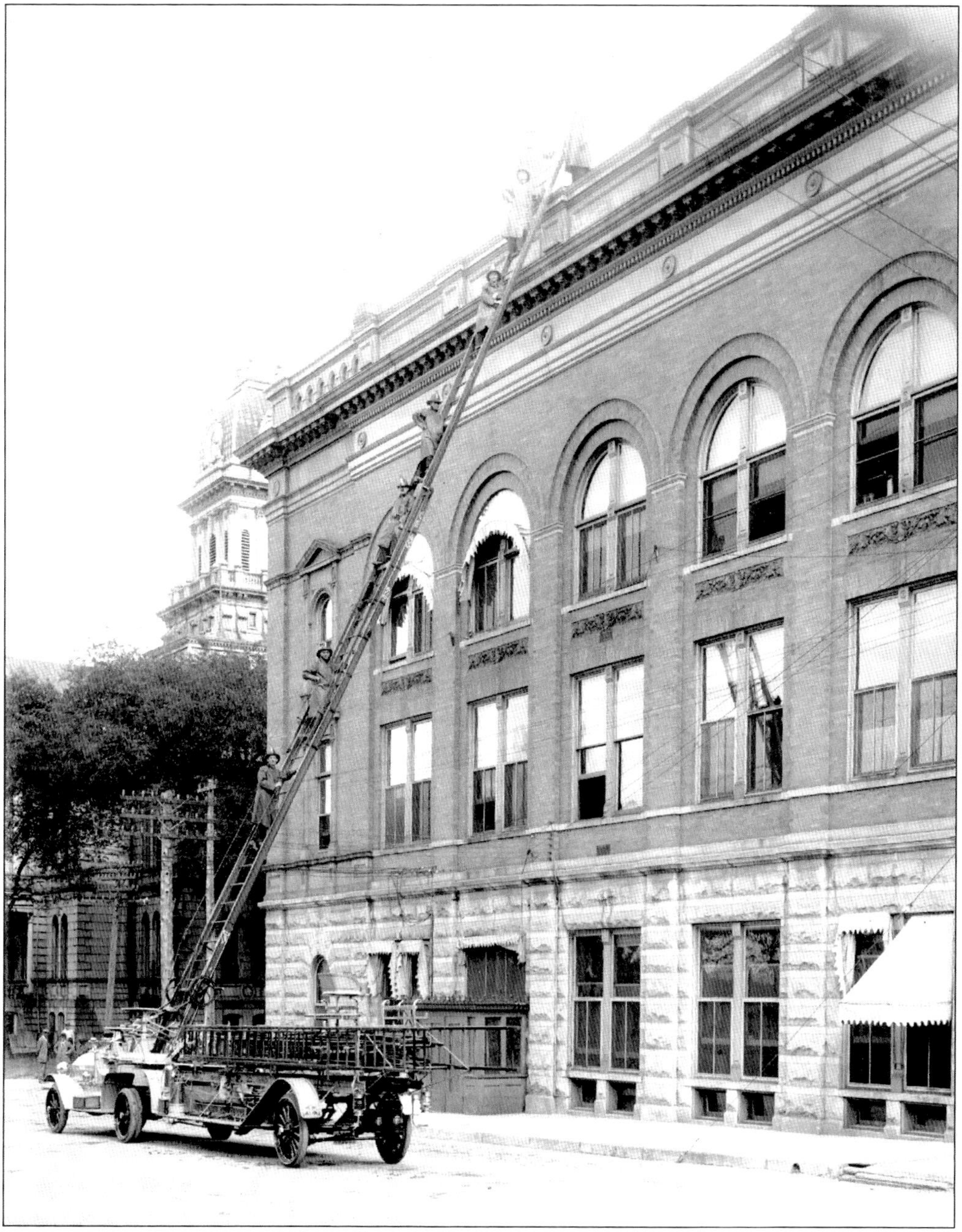

MODERN EQUIPMENT. Firefighters from Freeport's station No. 1 were apparently checking out the roof of the massive building that faces Galena Avenue across the street from what was the Stephenson County Courthouse at the time. The view is from the Exchange Street side of the building that was once the home of the German Insurance Company. In 2009, the building is home to various professional offices. The *Freeport Journal-Standard* was located there for many years prior to moving to its present location at 27 South State Avenue. Firefighters from bottom to top are Earl Kahley, Dutch Dreier, Frank Botdorf, Harry White, Herman Seitz, Rudolph Datt, assistant chief Charles Borsdorf, and John Ludke.

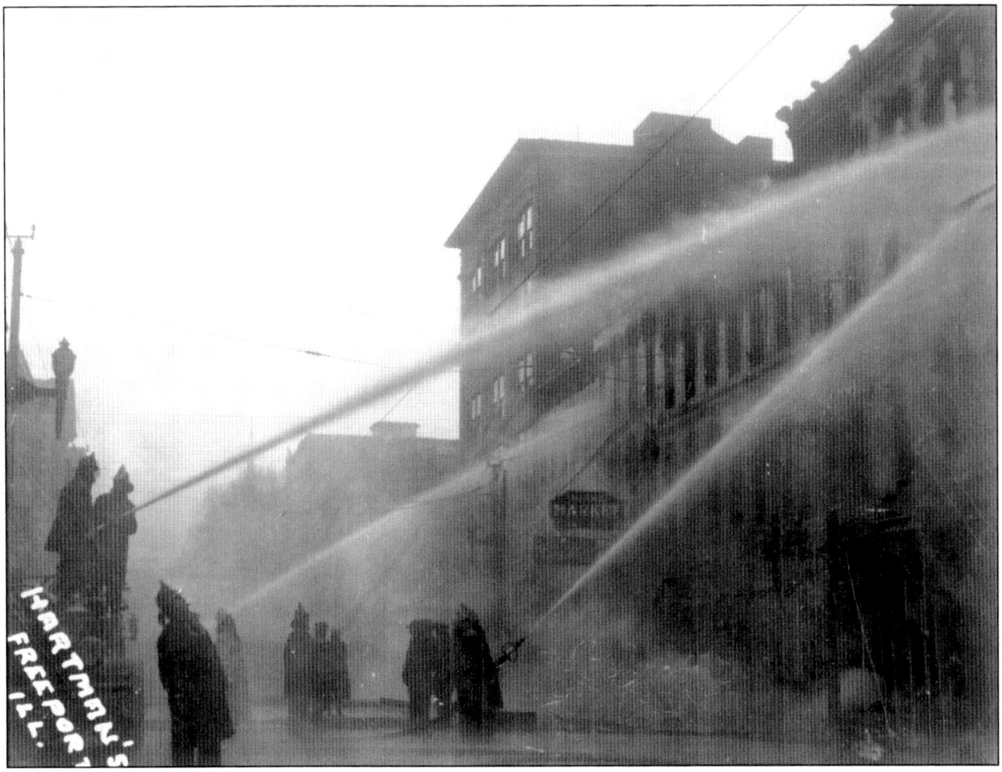

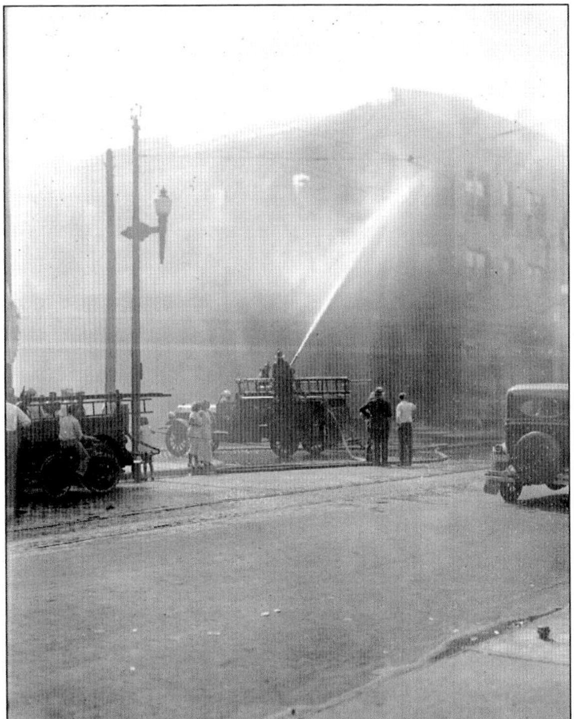

DOWNTOWN BLOCK GUTTED. The late Leslie Fargher, Freeport's legendary historian, called the blaze "the most disastrous fire in the history of Freeport." He thought it took place in March 1927. He said about 100 feet of downtown store buildings fronting on Stephenson Street and extending a block back through to Exchange Street were destroyed by the conflagration. Businesses burned out included the C. H. Little Company, the armory building, the Charles A. Pfeiffer clothing store, and the J. C. Penney Company store.

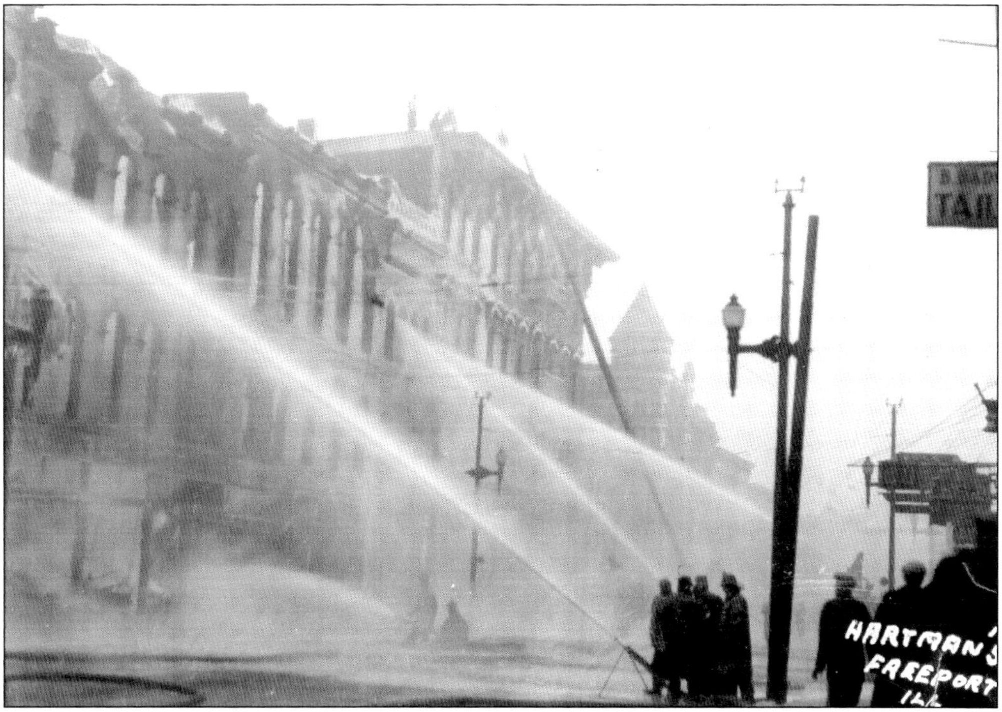

BLAZE RAVAGES FREEPORT. Firefighters work feverishly to extinguish a fire consuming buildings in downtown Freeport.

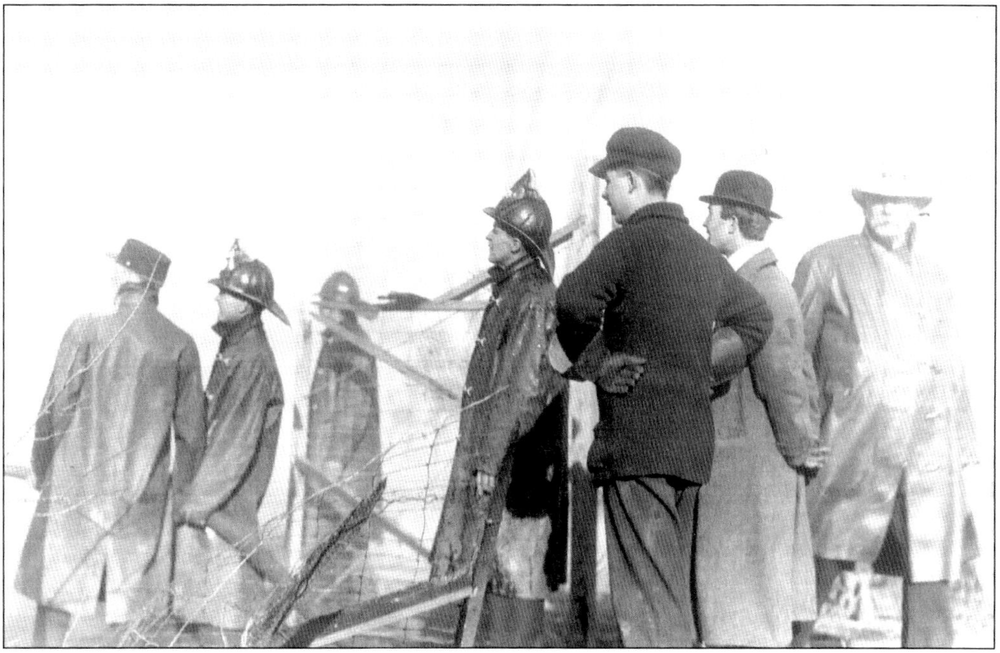

ROBUST HEROES. The Freeport Fire Department surveys its work at a fire in 1915 at the Goddard farm. A paid department was instituted during the administration of Mayor James McNamara between 1881 and 1885, with John F. Rodemeier (far right) becoming the city's first paid fire chief.

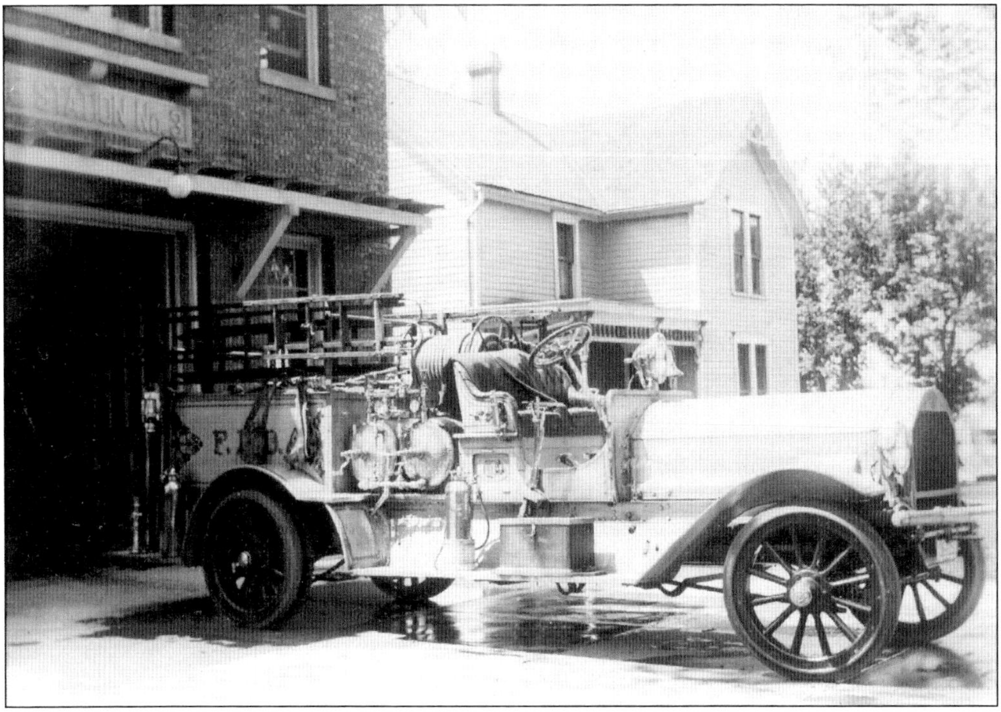

AT THE READY. Freeport's fire departments have a long tradition of keeping their equipment spotless and ready to roll.

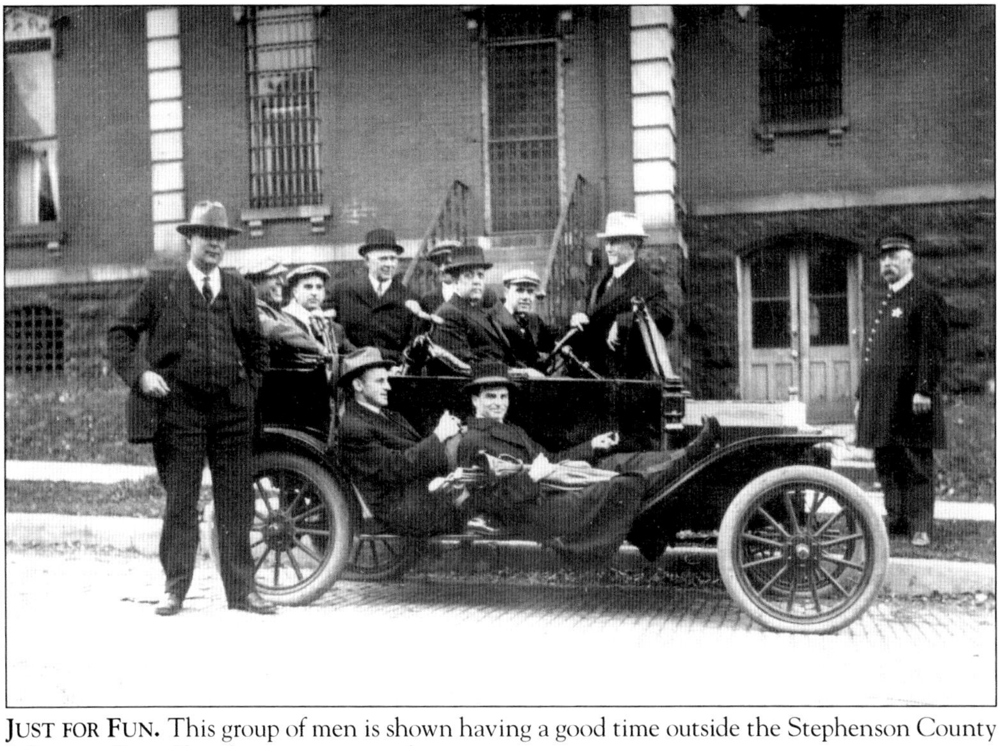

JUST FOR FUN. This group of men is shown having a good time outside the Stephenson County Jail as a police officer keeps an eye on them.

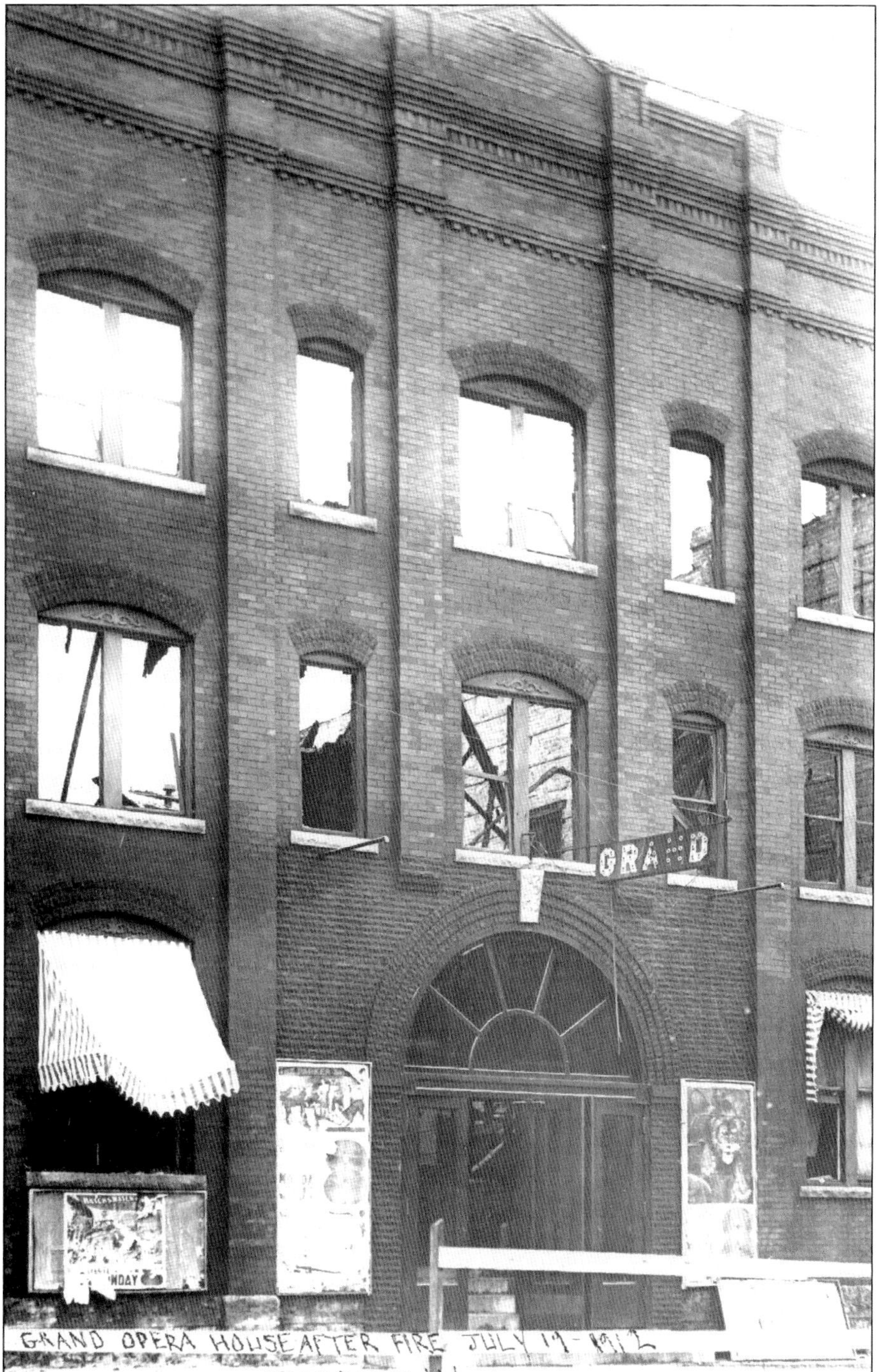

GRAND OPERA HOUSE. On July 14, 1912, the interior of Freeport's Grand Opera House at what is now 224 West Main Street was destroyed by fire. The structure of the building was saved and restored to house businesses on the street level and apartments upstairs.

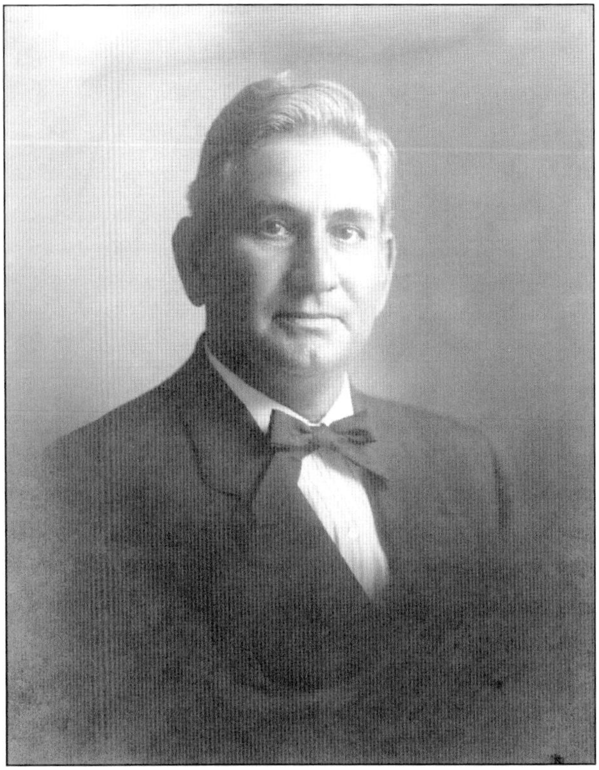

FREEPORT DIGNITARY. Democrat Charles Franz was elected mayor in 1913. He went on to serve as an Illinois state representative. (Courtesy of the Ted Luecke family.)

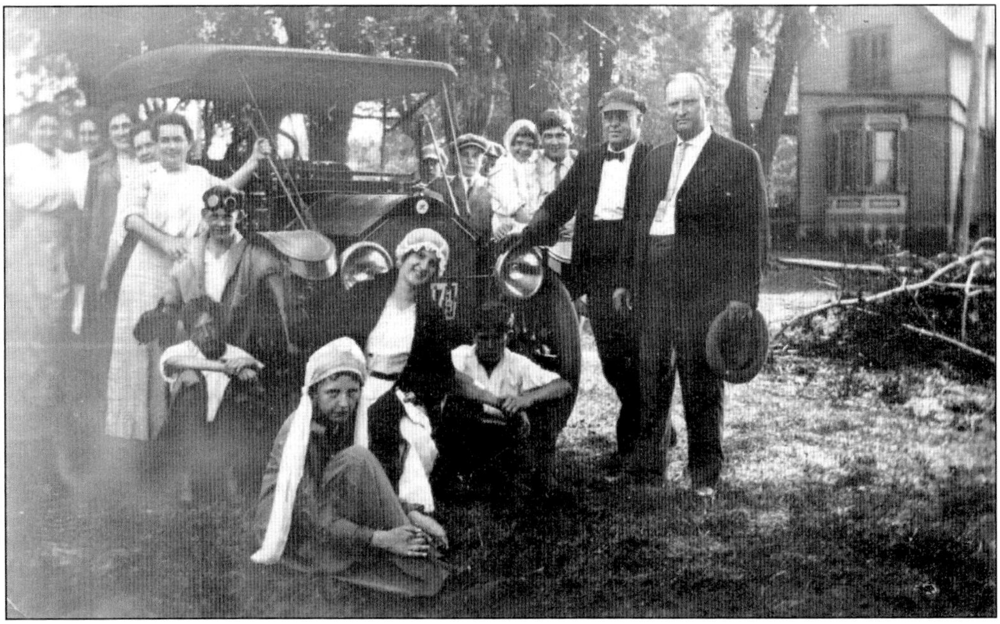

WHAT IS GOING ON HERE? Mayor Charles Franz is the man on the right. The activity in the photograph is not known, but it could have been some kind of political rally. Franz faced some revolutionary issues during his tenure as mayor, beginning in 1913. A referendum allowed movie houses and pool halls to be open on Sundays. Also a number of streets were renamed and renumbered to establish uniformity. (Courtesy of the Ted Luecke family.)

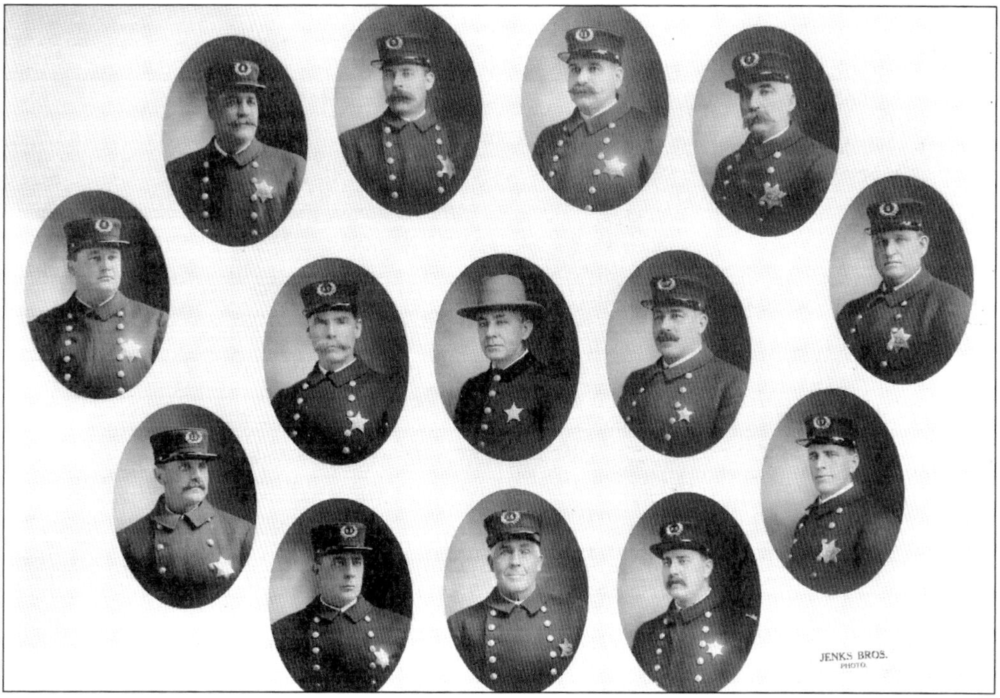

FOURTEEN MEN WORE STARS. These 14 smartly uniformed officers made up the Freeport Police Department. The city had grown enough to support this sizable force in the early 1900s. (Courtesy of the Freeport Police Department.)

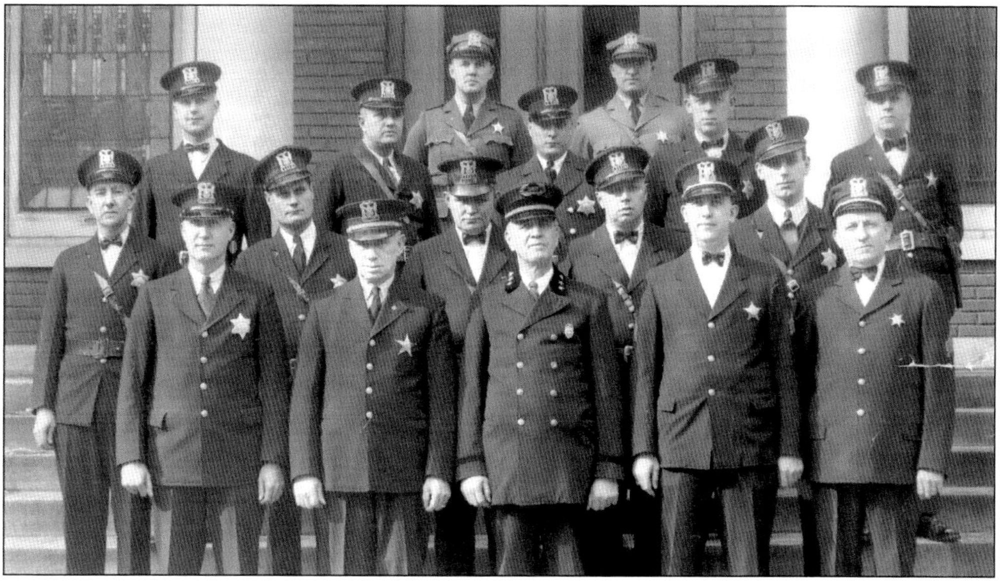

SERVE AND PROTECT. Pictured in 1935, Freeport Police Department officers from left to right (first row) are Fred Manthei, Bert Tavenner, Adam Wilkey (chief), William Jogerst (assistant chief), and Walt Pearse; (second row) Fred Held, Ed Brown, Joe Maltry, Lloyd Walton, and Charles Roberts; (third row) Ed Haller, Richard Cowan, Bob Kerlin, C. Robbins, and John Feld; (fourth row) Leo Mordick and Wendell Wolf. Three officers had motorcycle beats. (Courtesy of the Freeport Police Department.)

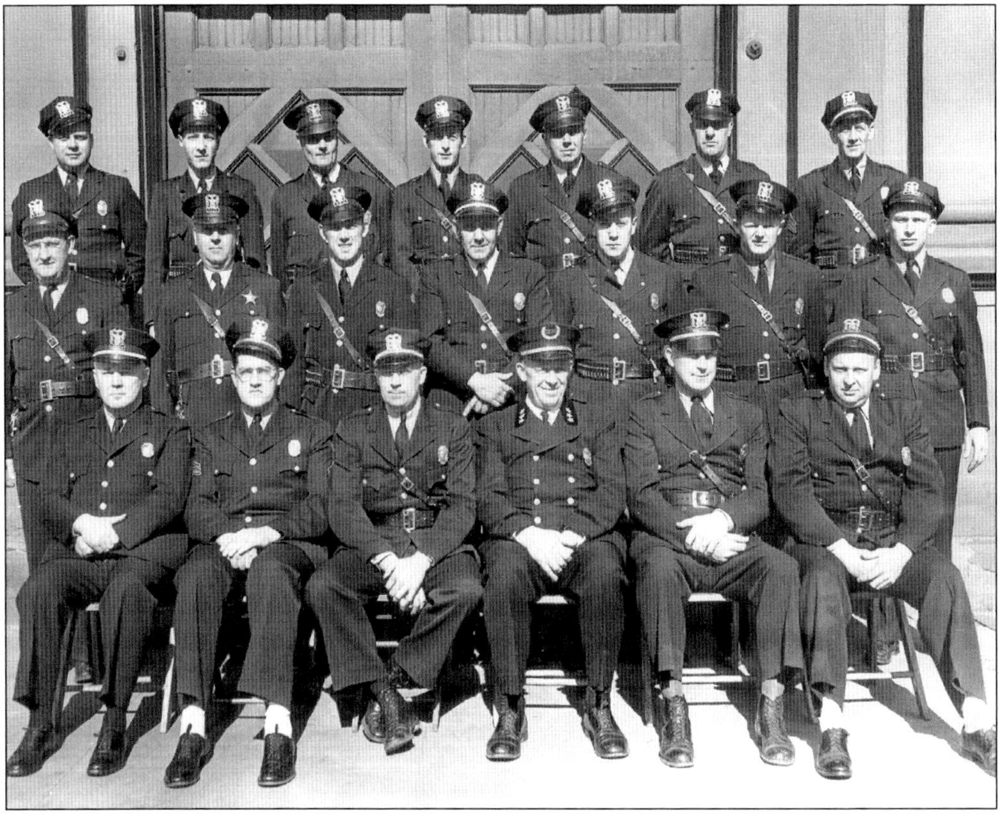

LOCAL HEROES. Freeport police officers have a long tradition of protecting and serving the local community. (Courtesy of the Freeport Police Department.)

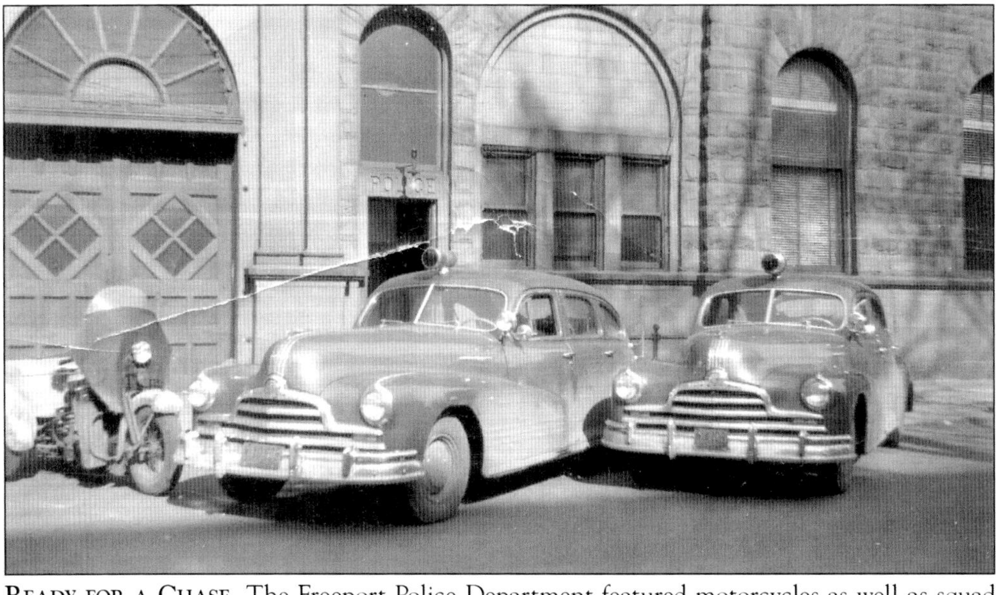

READY FOR A CHASE. The Freeport Police Department featured motorcycles as well as squad cars, even in its early days. (Courtesy of the Freeport Police Department.)

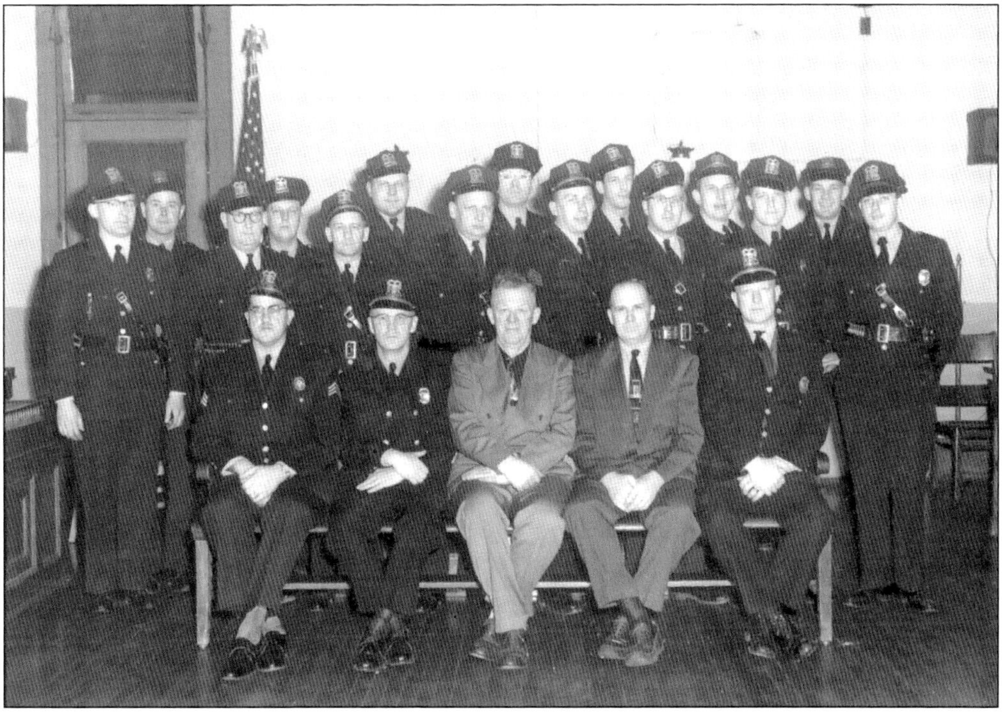

GUARDING THE CITY. Shown are members of the Freeport Police Department in 1954. (Courtesy of the Freeport Police Department.)

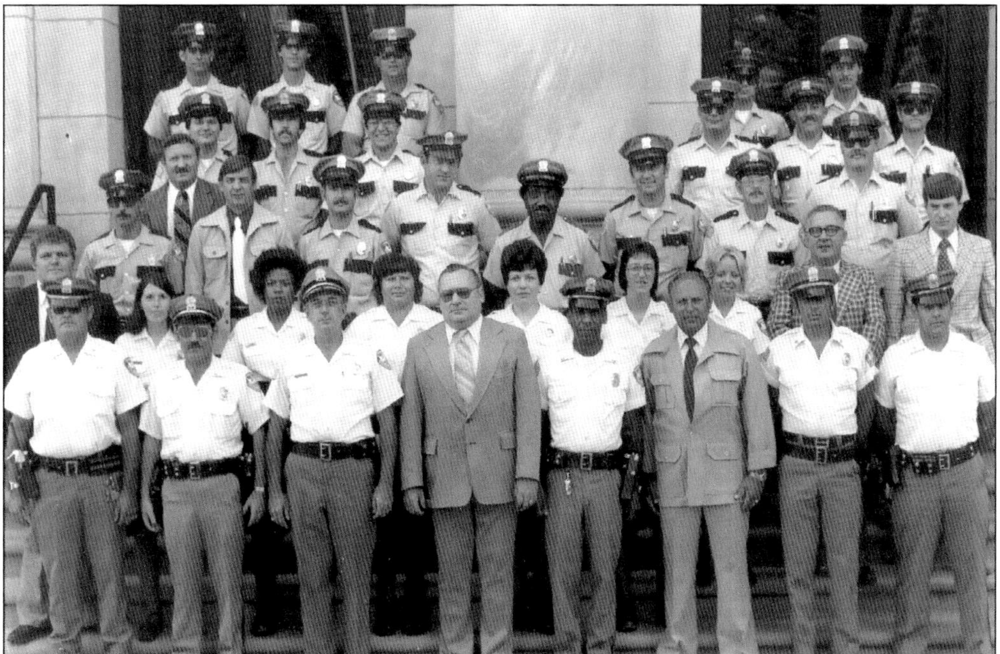

GROWING STRONG. As Freeport's population grew, so did the size of its police force. Members of the Freeport Police Department gather for a group photograph. (Courtesy of the Freeport Police Department.)

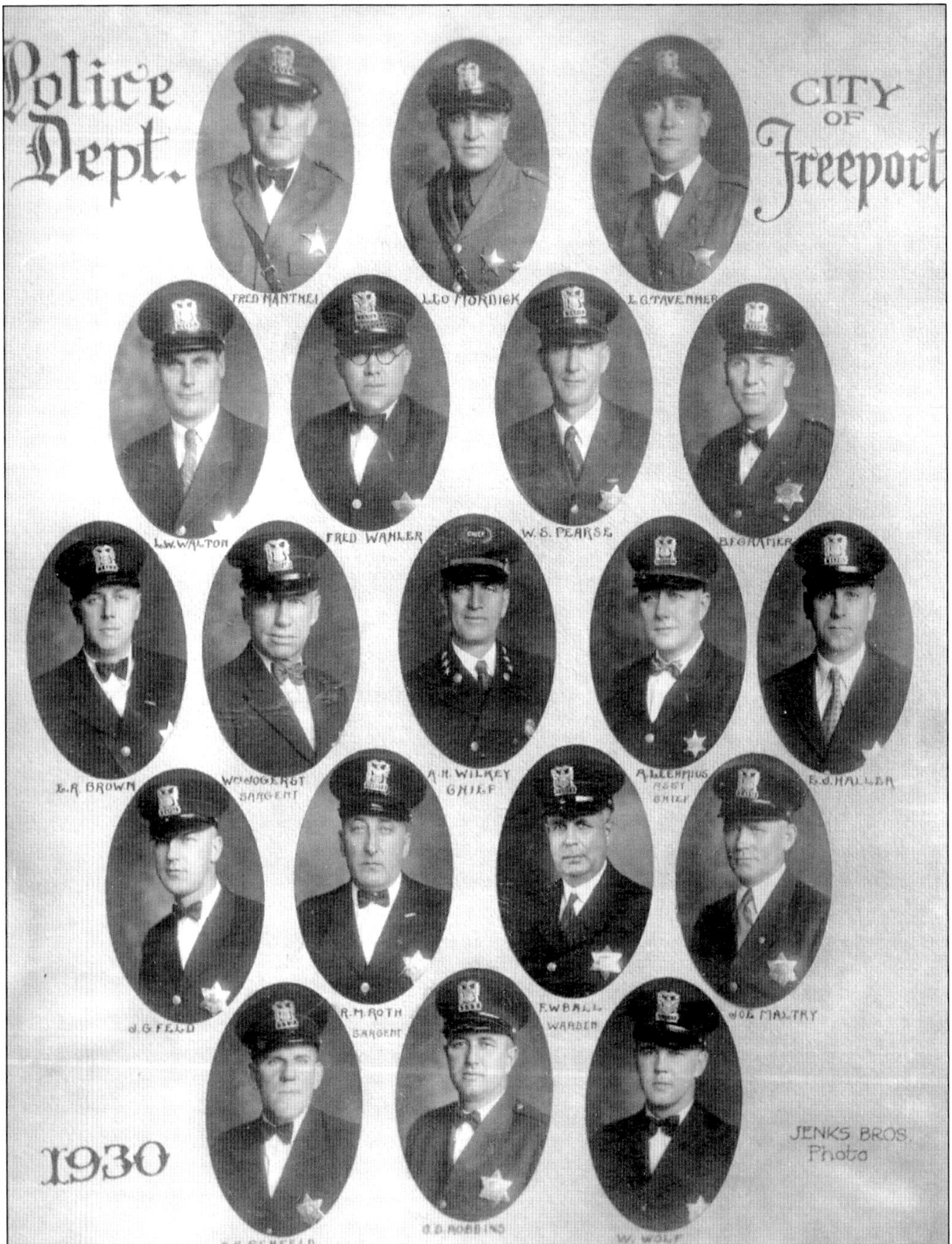

ON DUTY, 1930. This photograph features members of the Freeport Police Department in 1930. (Courtesy of the Freeport Police Department.)

Five

Transportation

Railroads played a major role in the development of Freeport. When the import and export of products were "at the ready," stars glimmered in the eyes of some prosperity-hungered individuals.

The Henney Buggy Works of Cedarville moved here. Before long, ingenious hopefuls like W. T. Rawleigh and Daniel Stover saw the possibilities and began gathering their wits and ways together "to make hay while the sun shone." Soon smoke stacks were pouring forth smoke and steam all over the city, close to the railroads.

The city groaned and grew. Of course, all this necessitated a municipal undergirding, and a government evolved. Running water and plumbing, lights, fuel, gasoline, and transportation came to the city on the Pecatonica River. Necessity brought into place police and fire departments, street improvement and maintenance, sanitation regulation, and care of the elderly and impaired.

Streetcar lines were formed. An interurban line carried folks east to Rockford and beyond. The more venturesome could travel by rail in any direction.

Soon these eager Freeporters, not to be left behind, hankered for air travel. A small but busy airport was carved out of some acres east of town on the Hill farm. Hillcrest Airport had the opportunistic youth of the city haunting the place to learn to fly. It was a small airport with short runways and gained quite a reputation for "daredeviling." However, this apparently turned out to be a blessing in disguise, as Hillcrest Airport gained recognition for the number of skilled aviators it supplied the military during World War II.

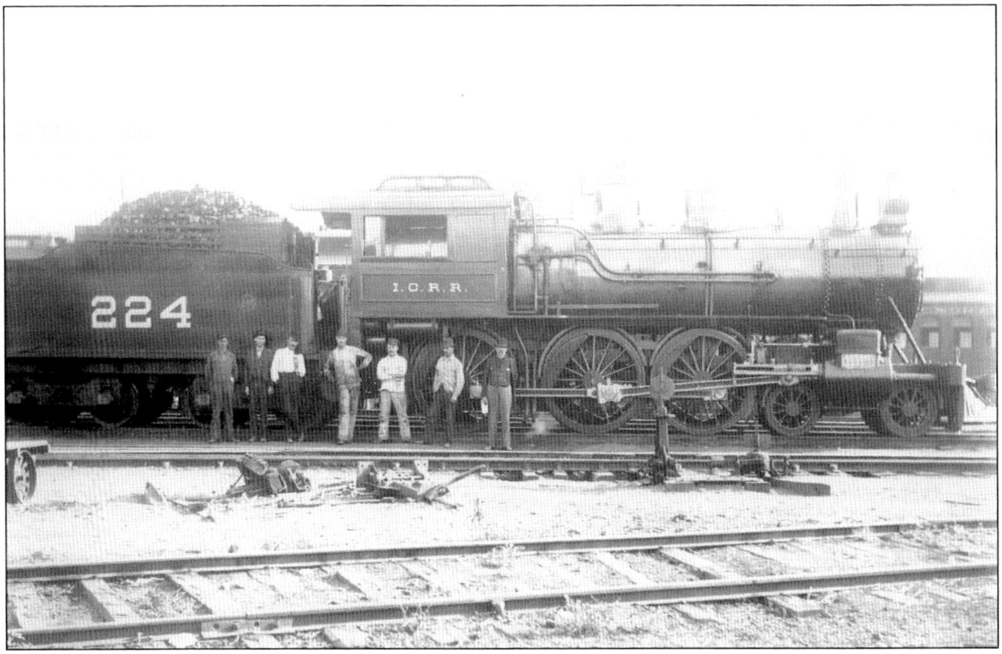

ILLINOIS CENTRAL RAILROAD WAS KING. This scene is believed to have been just south of the Illinois Central Railroad freight house. The track curving toward the foreground went up the alley between Spring and Jackson Streets. It was commonly called the "Manny Switch Track." The Illinois Central Railroad was one of Freeport's primary life-sustaining employers in the city's industrial heyday.

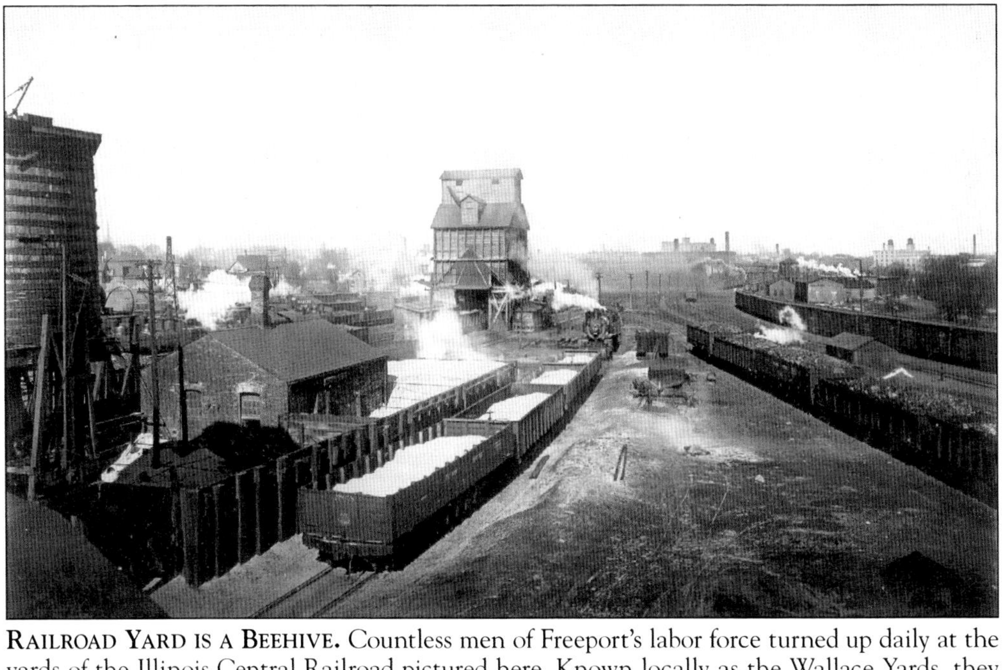

RAILROAD YARD IS A BEEHIVE. Countless men of Freeport's labor force turned up daily at the yards of the Illinois Central Railroad pictured here. Known locally as the Wallace Yards, they were located north of Galena Avenue and west of Illinois 26.

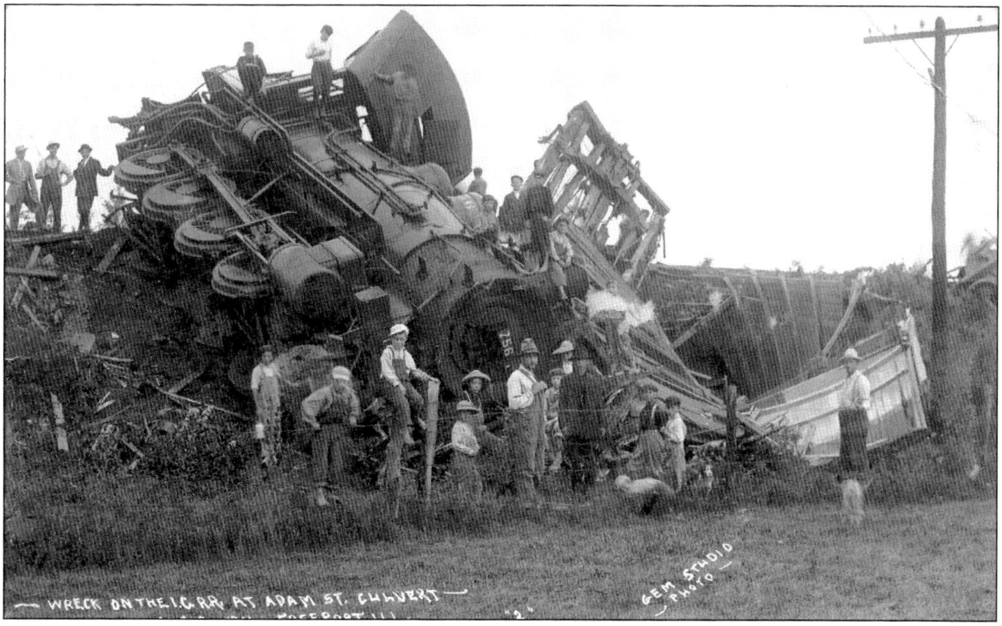

TRAIN WRECK DREW CROWDS. An enormous pileup of the Illinois Central Railroad took place on August 3, 1911, at the Adams Street culvert at the edge of Freeport. It took many expert hands to clean it up.

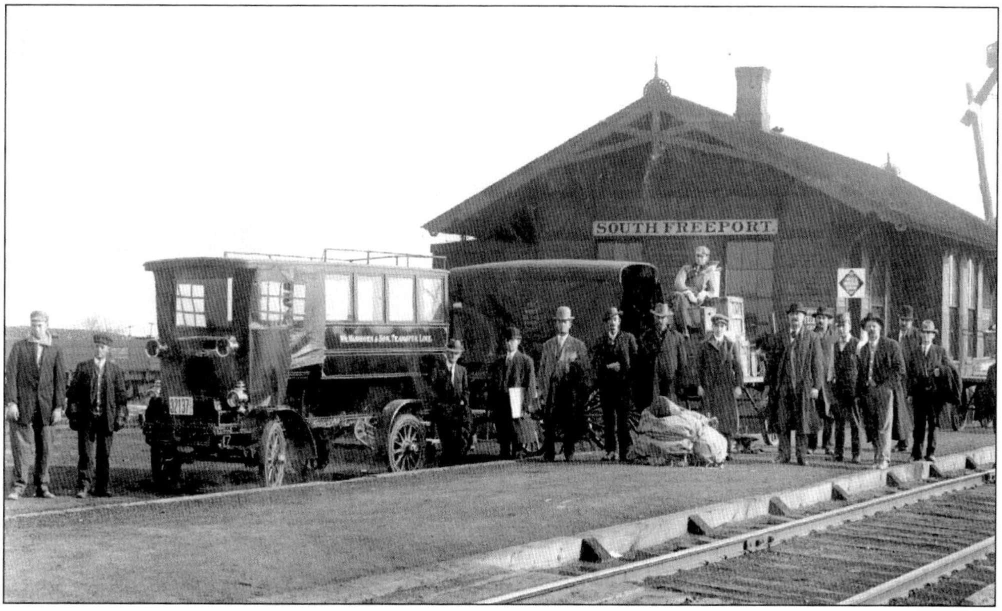

THE SOUTH FREEPORT STATION. Freeport once had a railroad depot south of the city. The vehicle at the left of the depot is a bus for transporting passengers into town. Dignitaries of some sort stopped to pose for the picture.

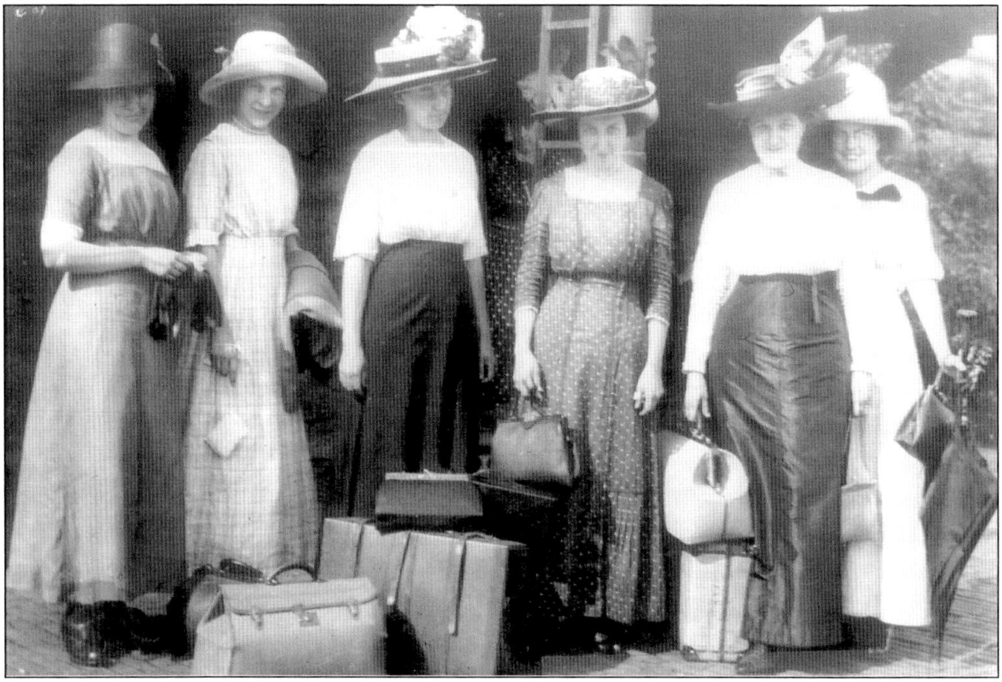

BIG TOPPERS ON THE GALS. These Gay Nineties travelers were all for the independence ladies were beginning to exert in those days. They are shown in their fine, oversized millinery with their luggage waiting for a train.

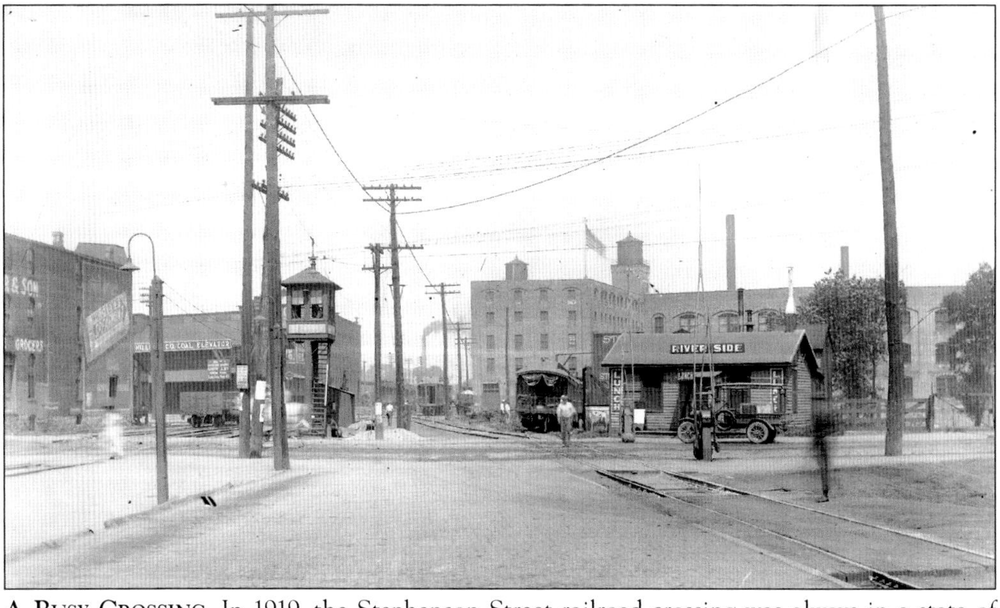

A BUSY CROSSING. In 1919, the Stephenson Street railroad crossing was always in a state of caution. This view is from the Illinois Central Railroad–Chicago and Northwestern Railway depot. The tower on the left controlled the crossing gates. The small River Side café was a popular eatery for workmen. The huge factory in the rear is now gone. In its final years it was the home of Burgess Battery Company, which nationally marketed batteries of all sizes. (Courtesy of the Freeport Public Library.)

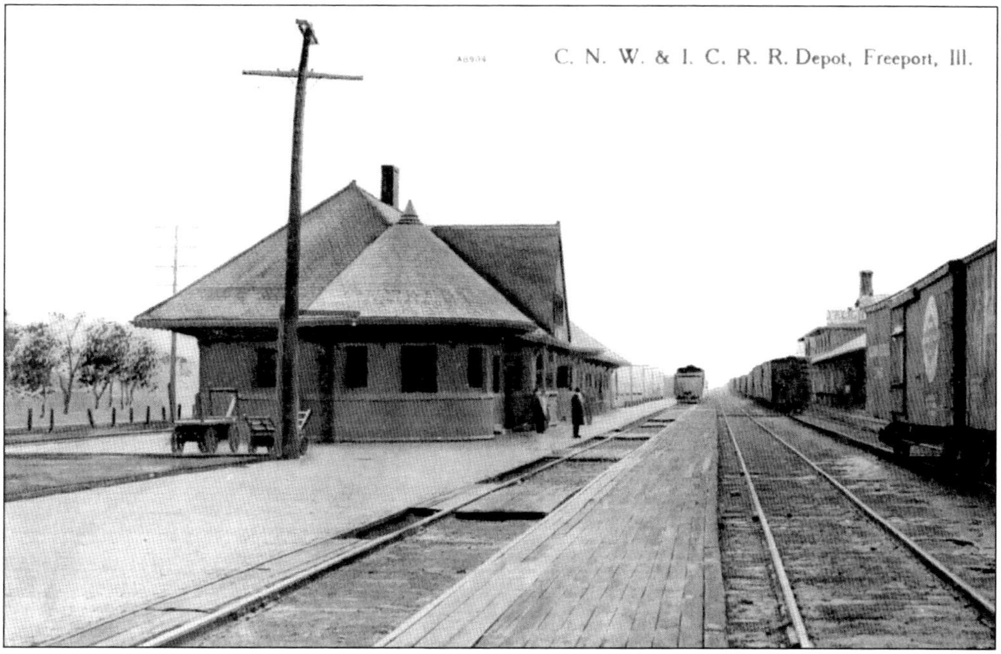

RAILROADS MADE FREEPORT, 1910. The Chicago and North Western Railway–Illinois Central Railroad passenger depot (center left) was a hub of travel at the time. Horse and buggy was still the main mode of local transportation. The railroads were also major components of the industrial scene at that time.

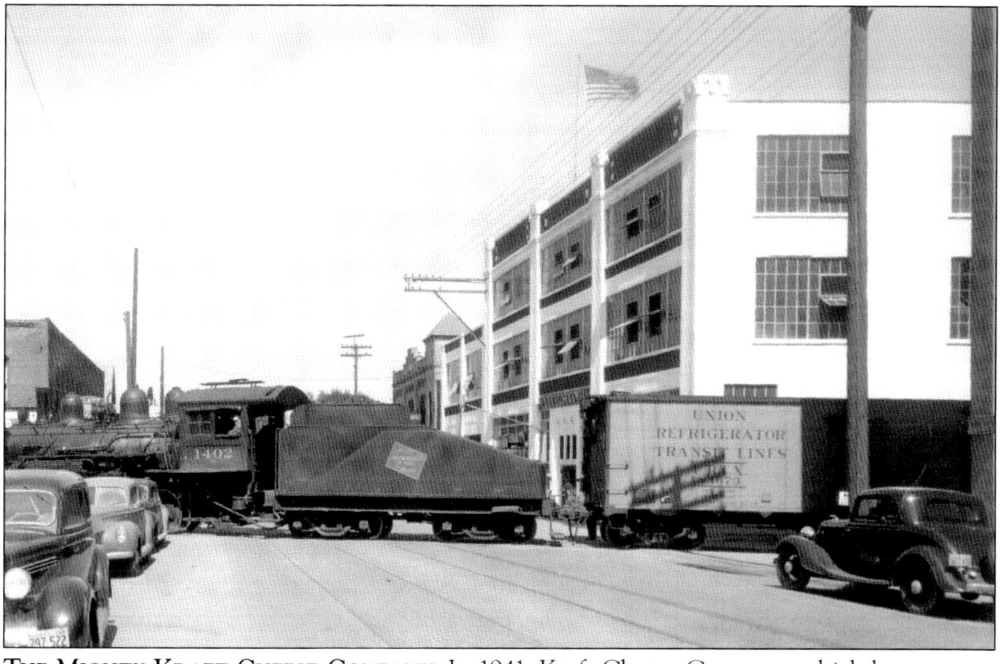

THE MIGHTY KRAFT CHEESE COMPANY. In 1941, Kraft Cheese Company, which became one of America's industrial giants, was going strong in Freeport. The Milwaukee Road steam switch engine shown has long been scrapped. The streetcar tracks in the brick paving are still intact long after the railcars ceased operation here.

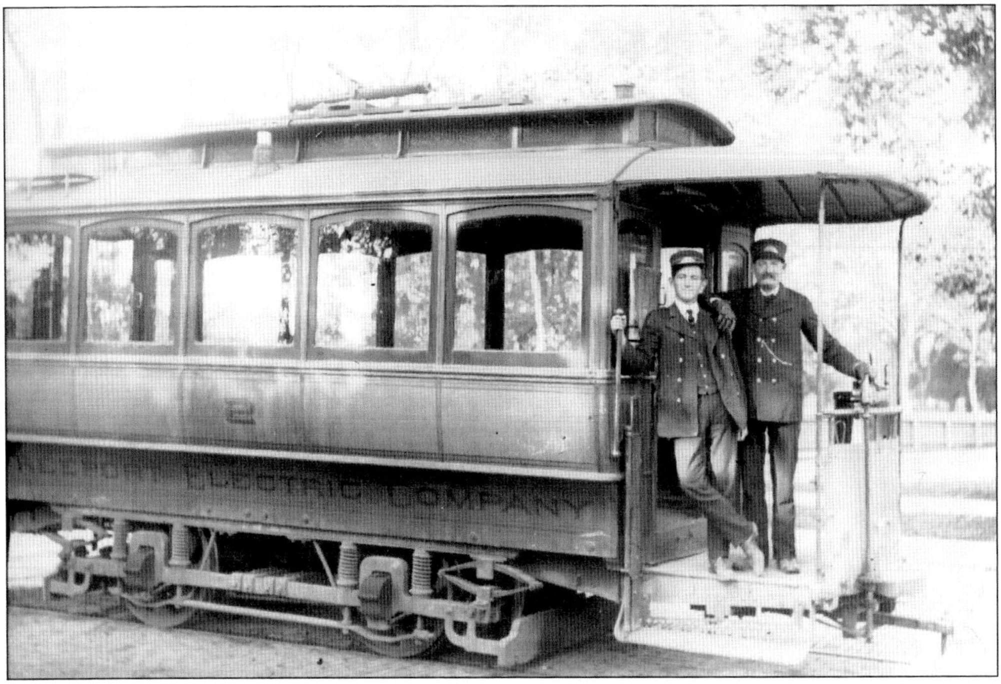

EARLY DAYS OF ELECTRIC TROLLEY. This electric trolley streetcar was one of the first in Freeport. The service began in 1894 or 1895. At that time, motormen stood out in the open with no protection from the weather.

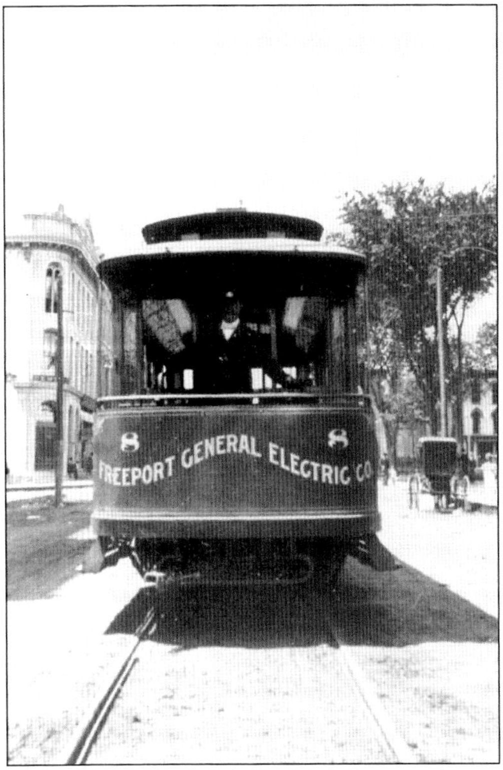

THE STREETCAR ERA. In 1896, during Freeport's street-railway era, open car No. 8 of the Freeport General Electric Company is shown on West Stephenson Street near Van Buren Avenue. The horse and buggy on the right was destined to become an obsolete mode of travel. Service from the electric streetcars apparently ended in Freeport in October 1931 when an increasing number of automobiles decreased patronage.

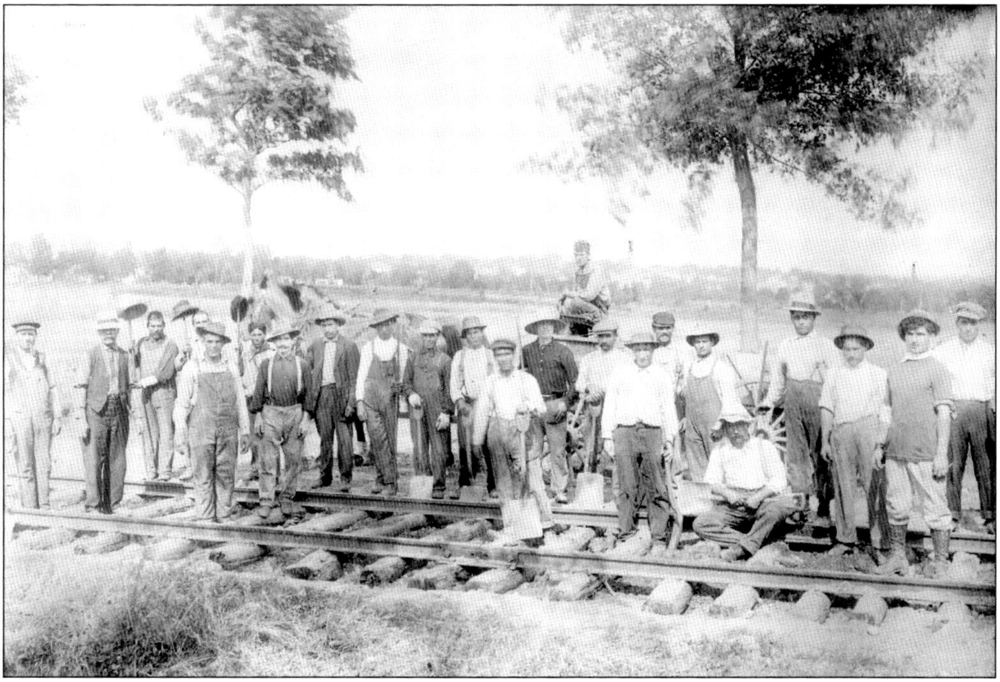

CREW LAYS STREETCAR TRACKS. These hands were laying rails for streetcars to run into Krape Park on August 12, 1913. The track runs adjacent to what was then Globe Avenue, but is now South Park Boulevard. The expanse behind the workers is now an area of upper-class homes near the site of St. John United Church of Christ. W. H. Green (second from left) was superintendent of the crew.

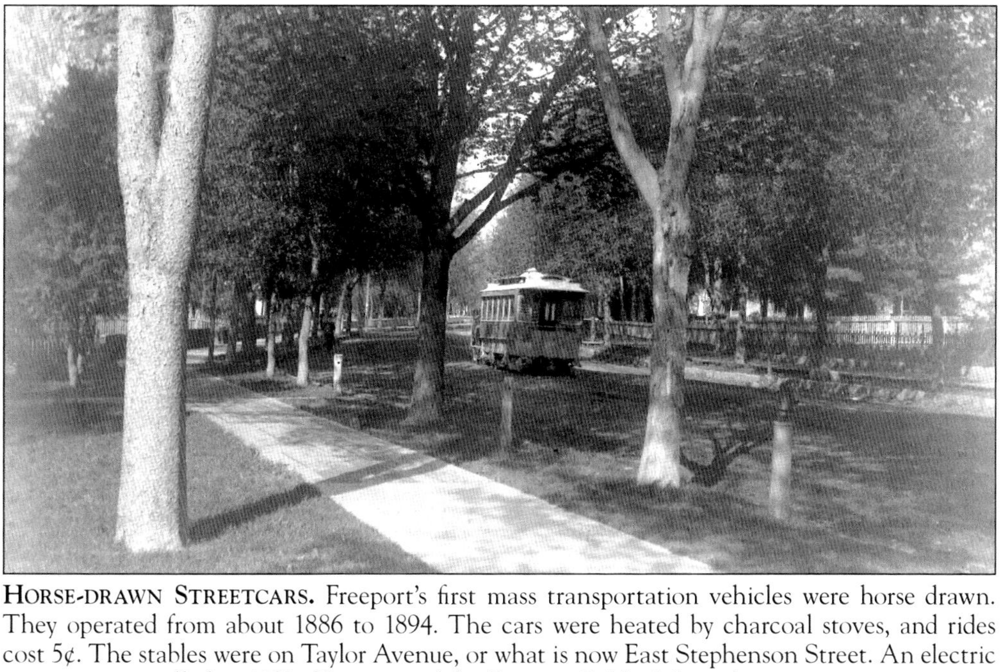

HORSE-DRAWN STREETCARS. Freeport's first mass transportation vehicles were horse drawn. They operated from about 1886 to 1894. The cars were heated by charcoal stoves, and rides cost 5¢. The stables were on Taylor Avenue, or what is now East Stephenson Street. An electric system was installed in 1892. (Courtesy of the Freeport Public Library.)

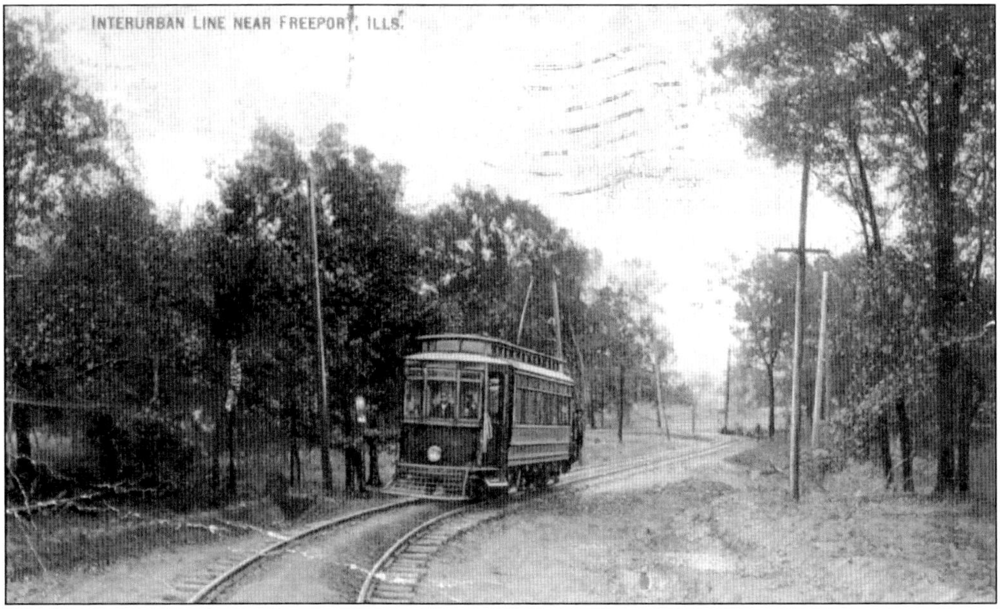

FOLKS TRAVELED ON INTERURBAN. The Interurban Electric Service came to Stephenson County in 1904 with the opening of the Rockford and Freeport Railway. Headquartered in Rockford, a line was completed to Belvidere in 1901, and then built from Rockford to Freeport during 1903. The village of Ridott had a substation, and passenger shelters were built at other points. This scene is east of Freeport.

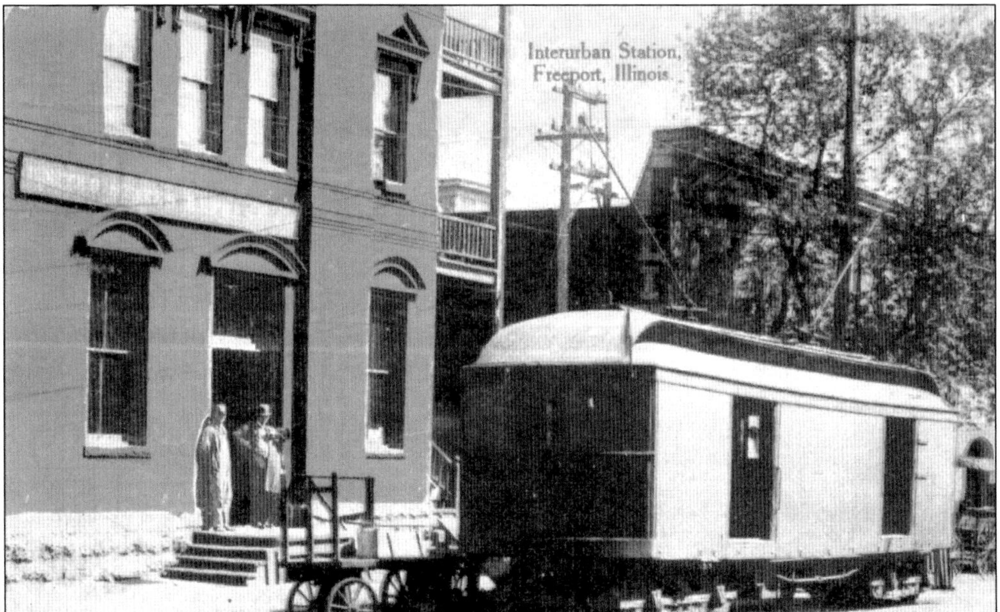

THE INTERURBAN STATION. Folks bought their tickets and boarded and disembarked the interurban cars at the corner of Stephenson and Mechanic Streets. Mechanic Street is now State Avenue, and this site is now a parking lot.

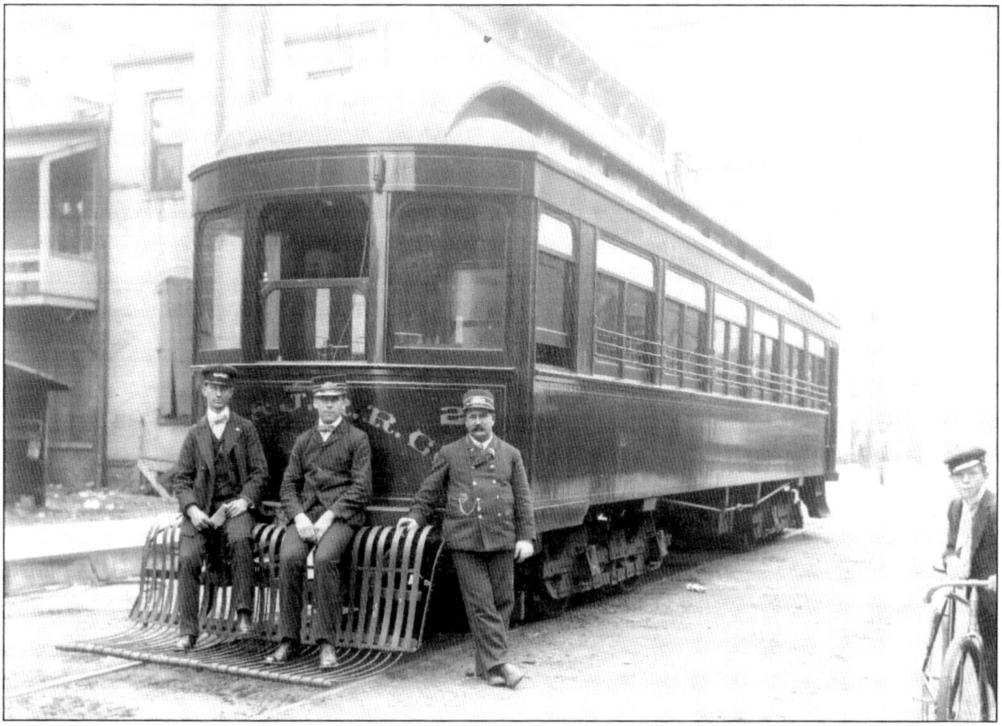

CHEAP TRANSPORTATION. Employees of the Interurban Electric Service posed for this photograph on the streets of Freeport. The service came to Stephenson County in 1904 with the opening of the Rockford and Freeport Railway. Cars ran every hour for years. It was possible to travel by interurban from Freeport to Chicago between 1908 and 1930, changing only at Elgin. Special excursions ran to Chicago for $1.

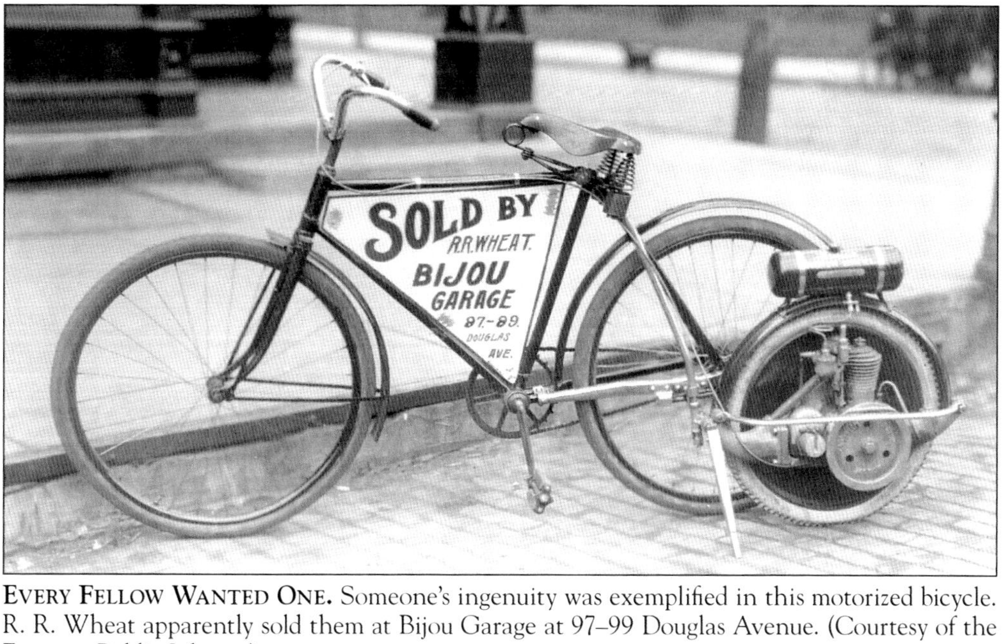

EVERY FELLOW WANTED ONE. Someone's ingenuity was exemplified in this motorized bicycle. R. R. Wheat apparently sold them at Bijou Garage at 97–99 Douglas Avenue. (Courtesy of the Freeport Public Library.)

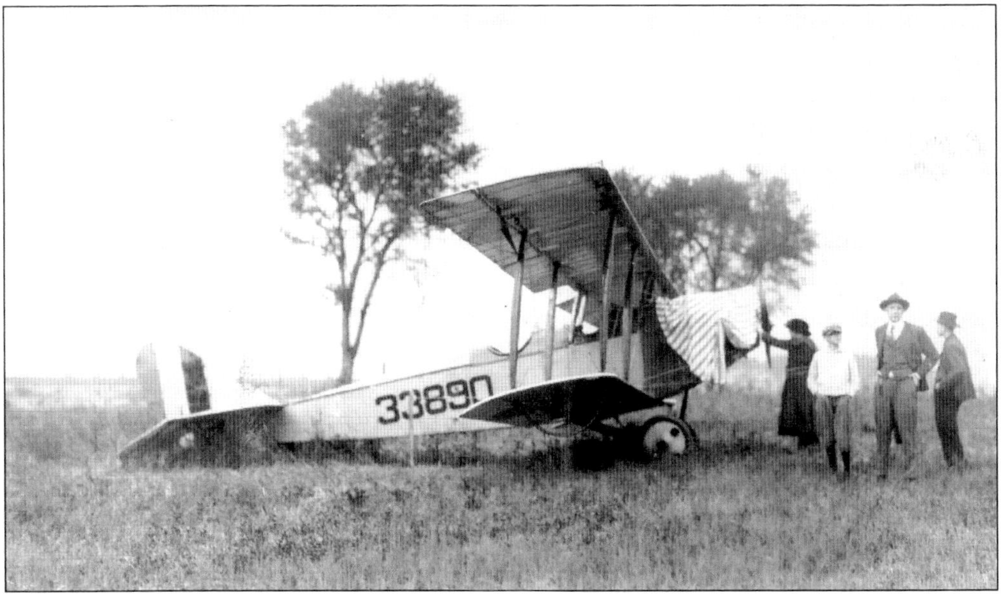

AVIATION COMES TO FREEPORT. This biplane was the first airplane to land in Freeport. In an exhibition flight on August 30, 1911, at Taylor Park, crowds of spectators paid to watch it take off from the horse racing track. The plane crashed immediately near the crowd from a 30-feet elevation, resulting in only minor injury to the pilot. In the photograph below from the same day, a pilot named Simon performed aerial stunts. Freeport soon had the small Hillcrest Airport on the Hill farm east of the city. Flight training there produced many ace pilots who served during World War II. Big names in early Freeport aviation were I. C. Wallace and Wes Brubaker.

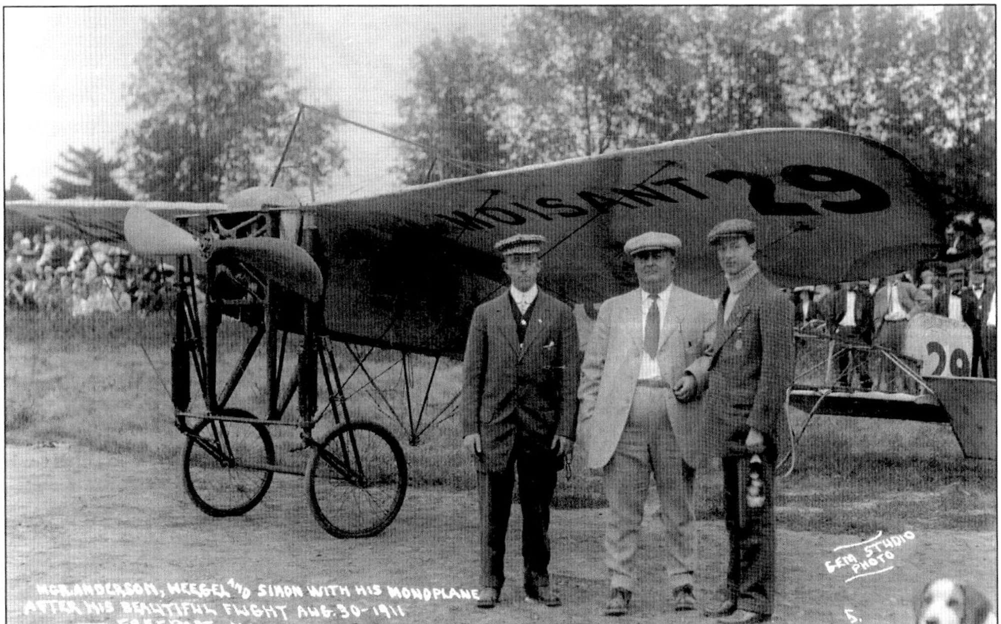

Six

INDUSTRY

It did not take long for the anxious, ambitious minds here to get the wheels of industry turning. The current of the Pecatonica River turned wheels for flour and lumber mills. Fathers, sons, and brothers pooled expertise and engineered new agricultural equipment. All kinds of bolts and belts were whirring for every conceivable kind of shrewd, but perhaps crude, operation to ease the labor-ridden lives of the settlers. Clever entrepreneurs made a lot of money.

Trains chugged in and out, hauling both raw materials and finished goods. Again, those energetic, ambitious settlers plied their trades and talents and put out the necessary products. There were those who built wagons, buggies, and carriages to transport their waiting constituency to town to the factories, stores, churches, and public meetinghouses. The town grew in sophistication, hearing of the finer life from the East and wanting more.

As the years flew by and the steam- and fuel-powered vehicles appeared, the yen for them infected the growing village, and buggy making converted to automobile making. Several automobile manufacturers opened for business in Freeport, but the most successful, prolific, and glamorous was the Henney Buggy Company, eventually maturing to the Henney Motor Company.

The gamut of Freeport industries encompassed a toy-making industry that invaded the world market with both the Arcade Manufacturing Company and the Structo Company here. Collectors today vie for well-preserved products from those lines.

Freeport has made Woodmanse and Stover windmills; W. T. Rawleigh and Furst-McNess food, medical, and animal feed products; Newell window furnishings; Stover engines, tanks, and bicycles; Henney hearses, ambulances, and limousines; Burgess batteries; Honeywell switches; Goodyear tires; and endless other human needs. The labor force was also at work during those earlier eras putting out beers, reed (parlor) organs, canned vegetables, tanks, shoes, clothing, caskets, cigars, and vinegar.

Perhaps the city's greatest blessing has been its willing and able labor force. Many other homespun industries came and went, but the ones shown are representative of Freeport's momentum.

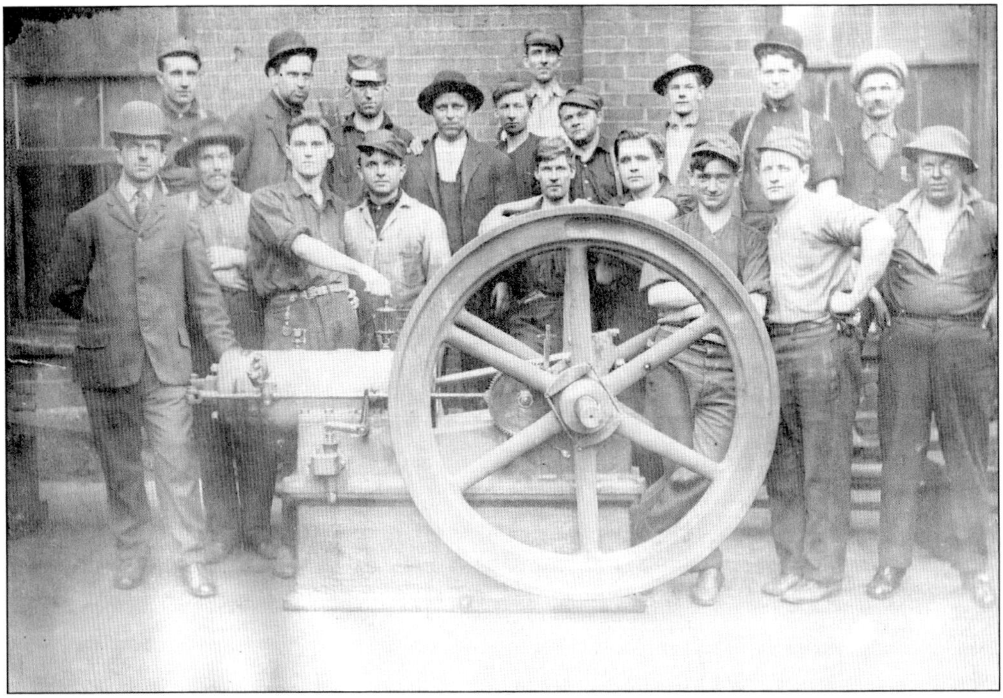

STOVER ENGINE WORKS. These employees at Stover Engine Works built this large gasoline engine in 1911. D. C. Stover's inventions such as a corn cultivator and windmill were used the world over. He became "Freeport's richest man," with factories that manufactured gasoline engines, bicycles, towers, tanks, and assorted farm implements and hardware. Stover Engine Works, shown below, was located on Stephenson Street just east of the Pecatonica River bridge.

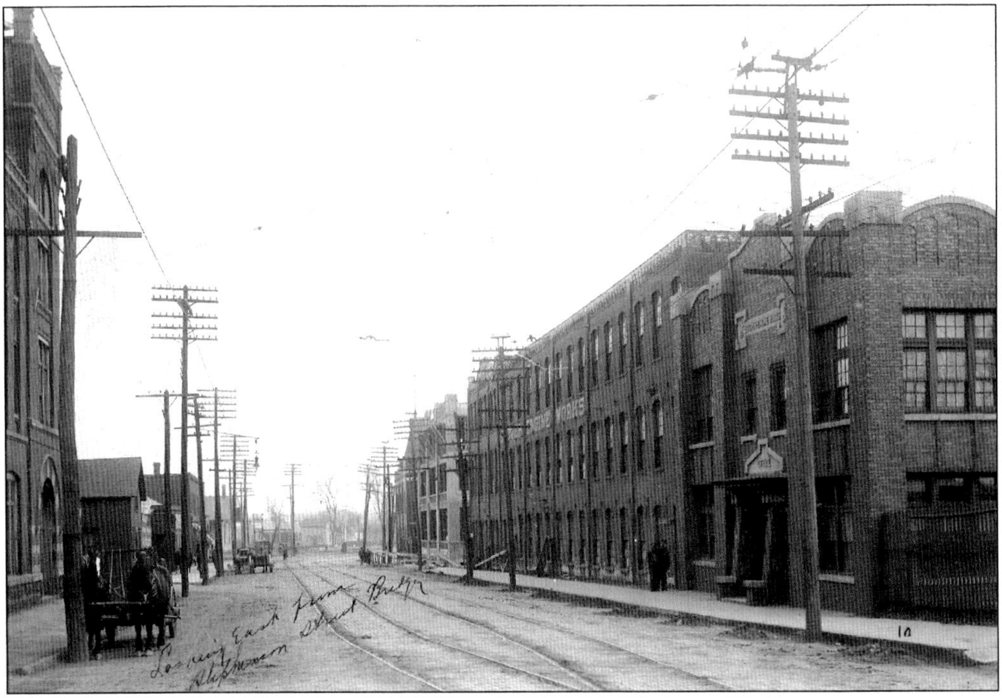

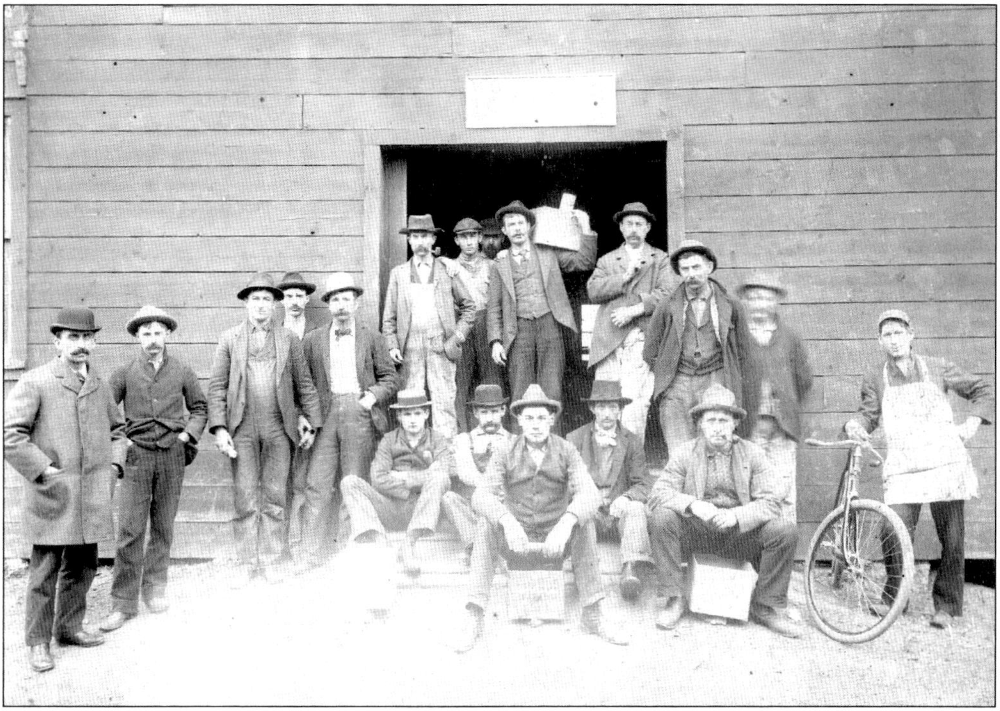

A CANNING COMPANY CREW. William Emery and J. D. Williams started a small vegetable-canning factory in Freeport in 1886. It soon merged with another started in 1887 by Fremont Keene and a Mr. Diffenbaugh. The Keene Canning Company, built in 1888 on Monterey Street, was closed in 1953 by Albion Keene. It sat on the former burial grounds of the Winnebago Indians.

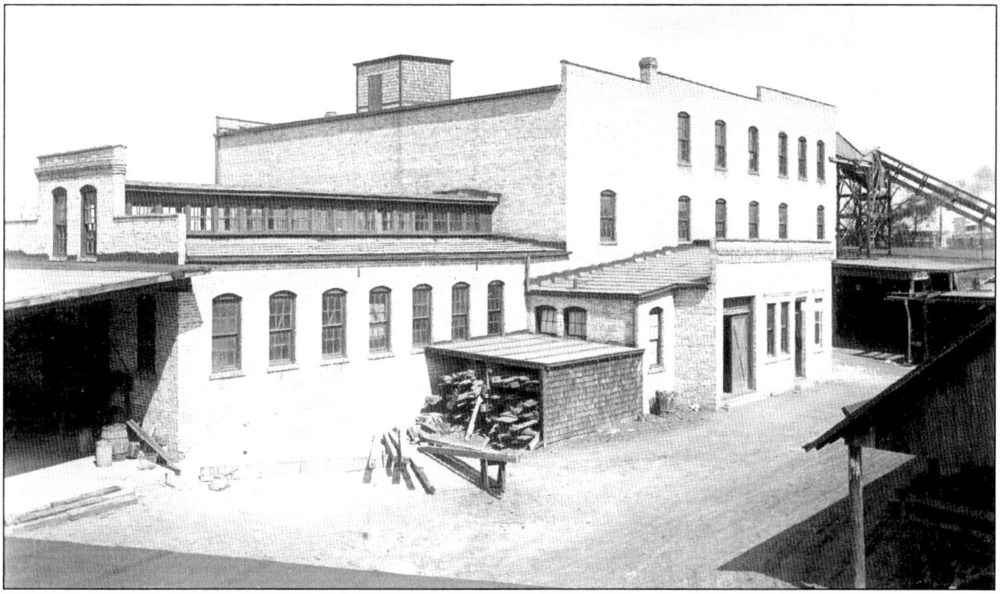

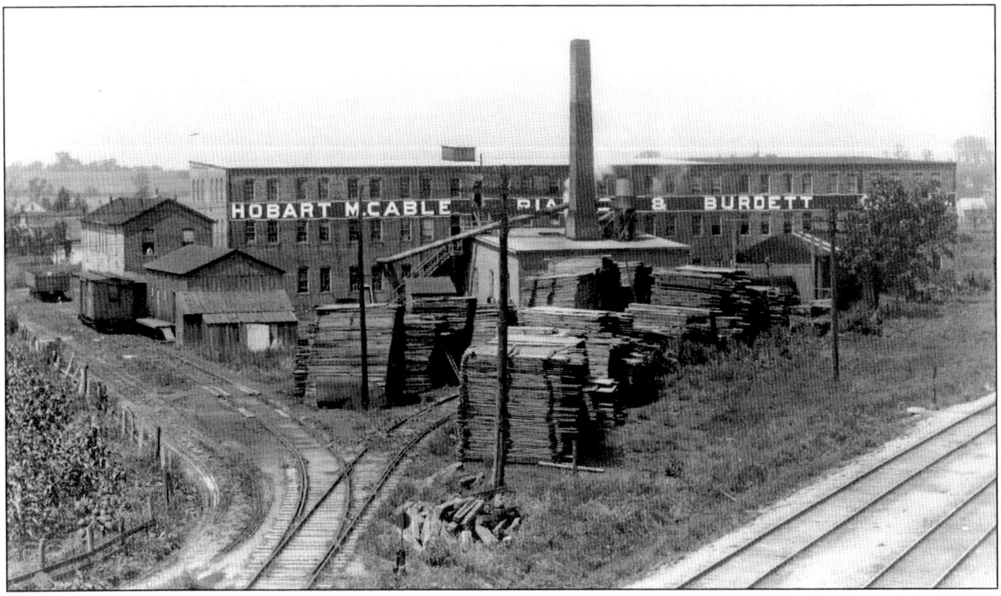

Pianos and Organs Made Here. Note the side tracks that served the Hobart M. Cable Piano factory and Burdette Organ Company in northwest Freeport. Stacks of lumber lay in wait for transformation into fine products. The Burdette Organ Company moved from Erie, Pennsylvania, to Freeport in 1894. After first occupying a factory in Freeport's man-made Manufacturer's Island, the operation was moved to this site in 1898. Cable bought the firm and changed its name in 1901.

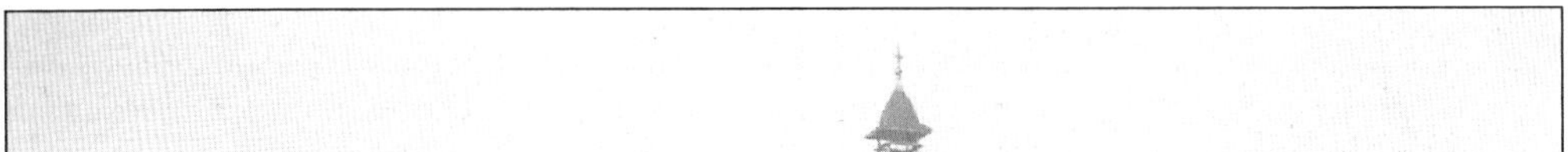

A Bustling Brewing Entity. Schmich Brothers brewery moved to this new building near the Pecatonica River on East Stephenson Street in 1896. Matthew Schmich was a partner with William Huber in a brewery on West Galena Avenue. Schmich's brother George bought Huber's share in 1887, and the name was changed. Brewing was a major part of the Freeport economy until squelched in 1920 by Prohibition. (Courtesy of Harvey Wilhelms.)

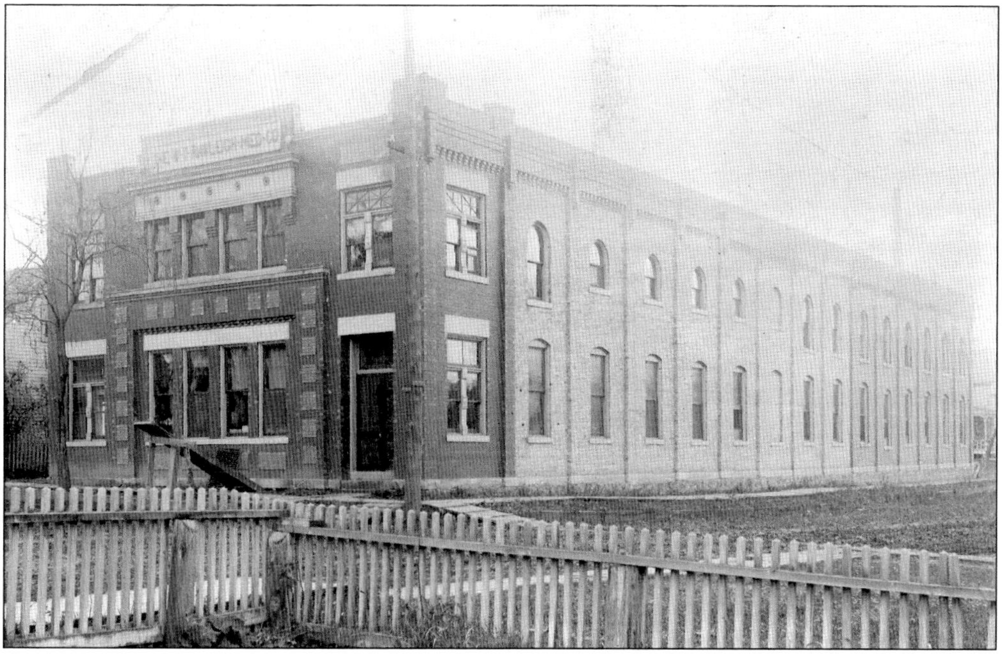

A Large Presence in Freeport. The W. T. Rawleigh Company occupied this building in 1890. Manufacturer of a popular salve, the company also was famous for its vanilla, pepper, and other food flavorings. The plant grew to become one of Freeport's largest employers, oftentimes providing income for three generations of families.

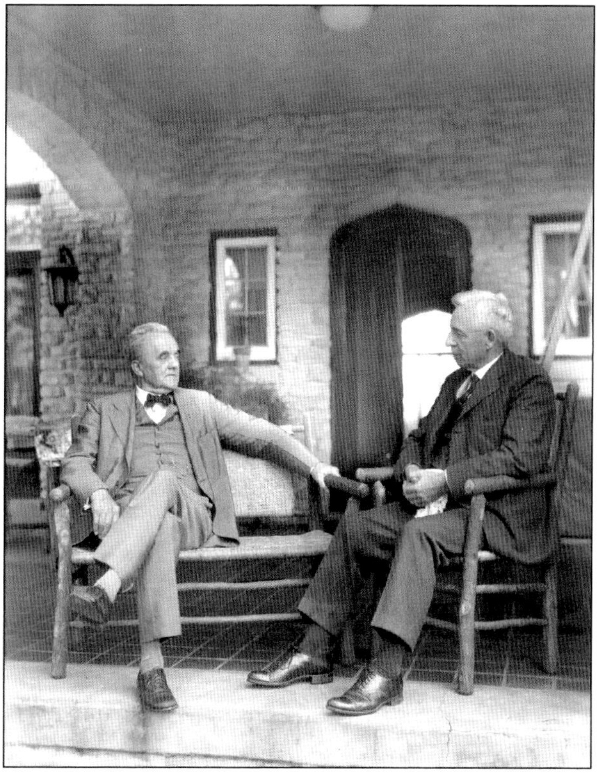

Rawleigh Hobnobs with Senator. Industrialist W. T. Rawleigh, right, perhaps Freeport's most well-known citizen of all time, visits at his mansion with famous U.S. senator William Burah. The senator toured the country speaking against the Treaty of Versailles and establishing of the League of Nations.

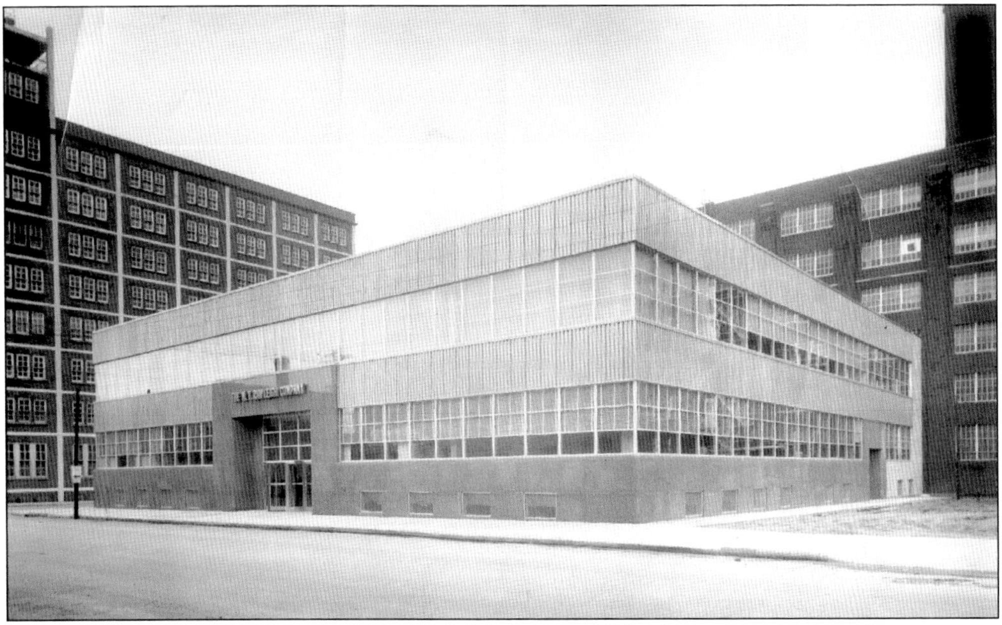

W. T. RAWLEIGH COMPANY. Industrially, the W. T. Rawleigh Company reigned supreme in Freeport with its many innovations in manufacturing and marketing. Rawleigh traveled worldwide purchasing the best of raw materials for his extracts and spices. The building in the foreground housed the offices while those behind had the laboratories, production, and printing facilities. Rawleigh's company made its own bottles and printed its own labels and advertising.

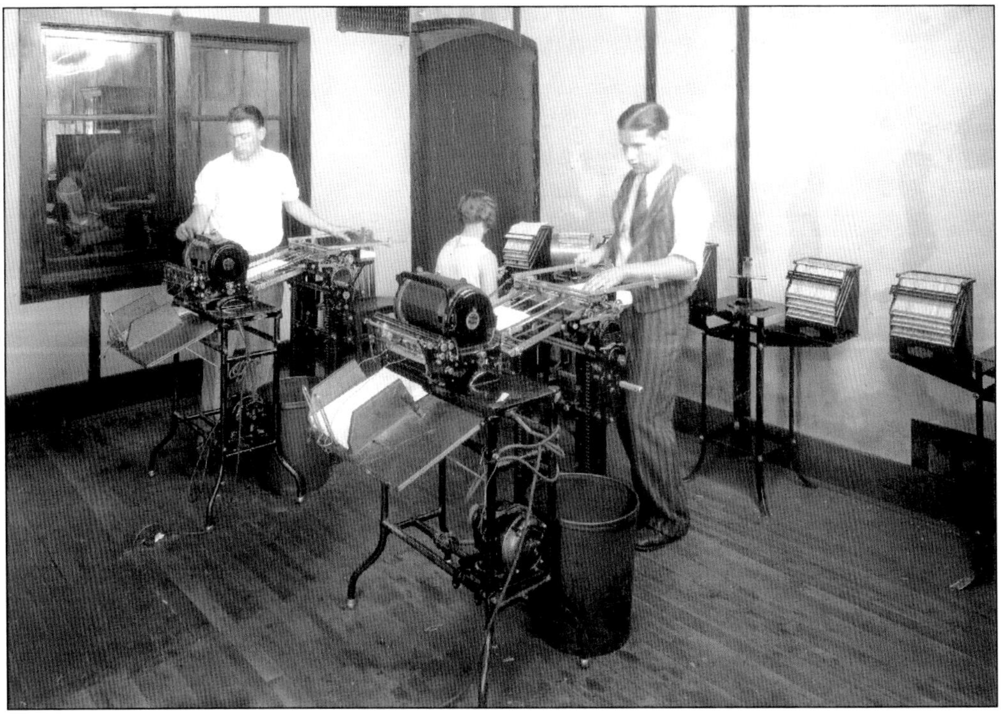

THE LATEST IN OFFICE EQUIPMENT. These printers were up-to-date for their day. They were located in the W. T. Rawleigh Company offices.

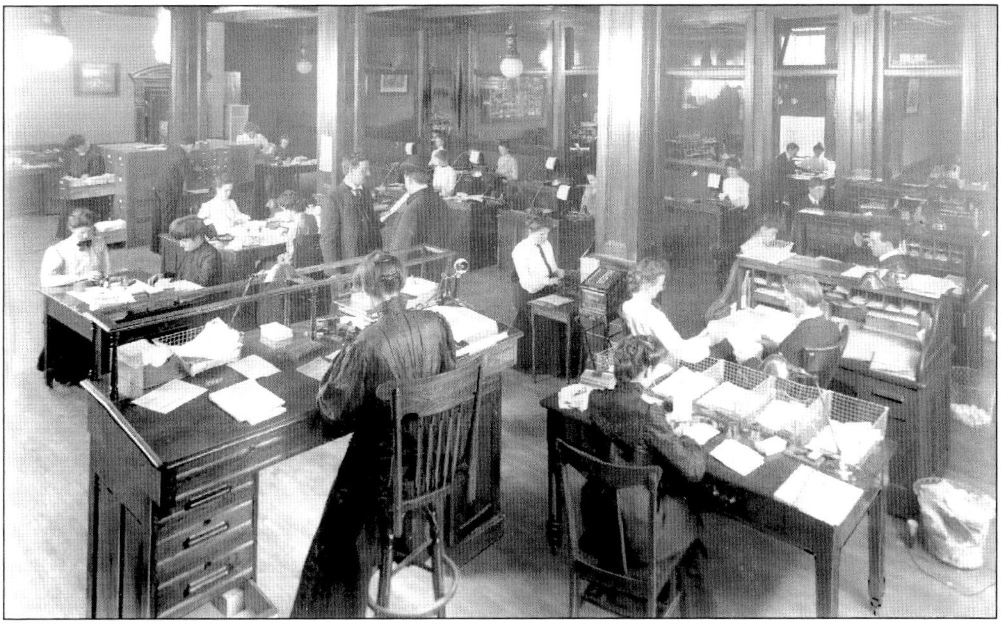

A State-of-the-Art Office. W. T. Rawleigh Company always was at the vanguard of new business and industrial practices. In 1910, modern office equipment was coming into use. A telephone is seen on the desk at the front left, and a stenographer by the center post appears to be using a typewriter. Rawleigh is the man standing in the center of the room. The office was in the plant's building at the corner of Liberty and Main Streets.

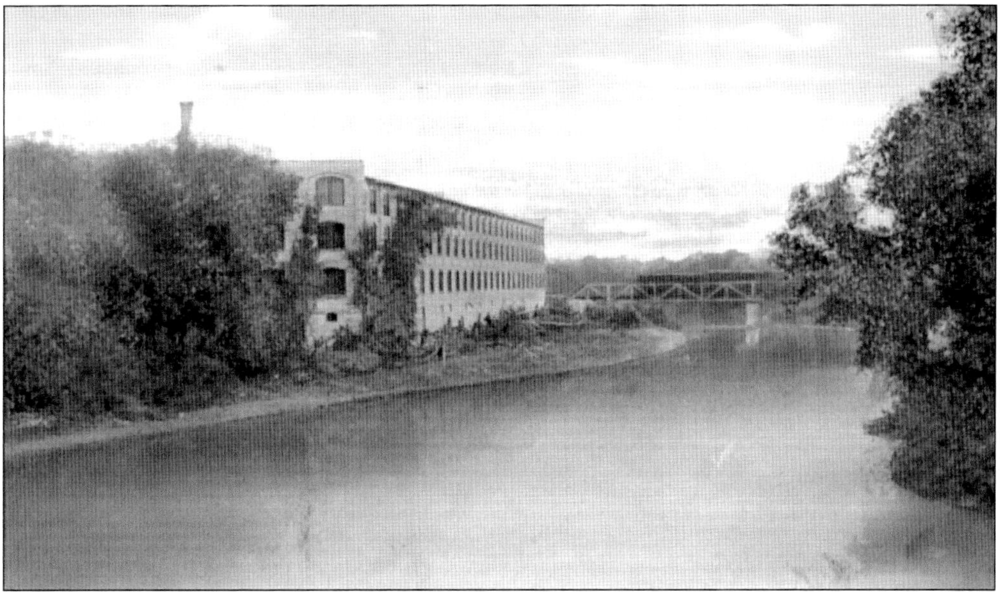

Carriages Made Here. Robinson's Novelty Carriage Works sat on Freeport's Manufacturer's Island. The island, man-made to harness the power of the Pecatonica River, had a number of industries on it, including the manufacturing of the Stephens Salient Six, a sleek automobile for its day. The building eventually housed Freeport's Burgess Battery Company, which furnished the country with batteries of all sizes and utility. In 2009, both the building and island are gone. (Courtesy of the Freeport Public Library.)

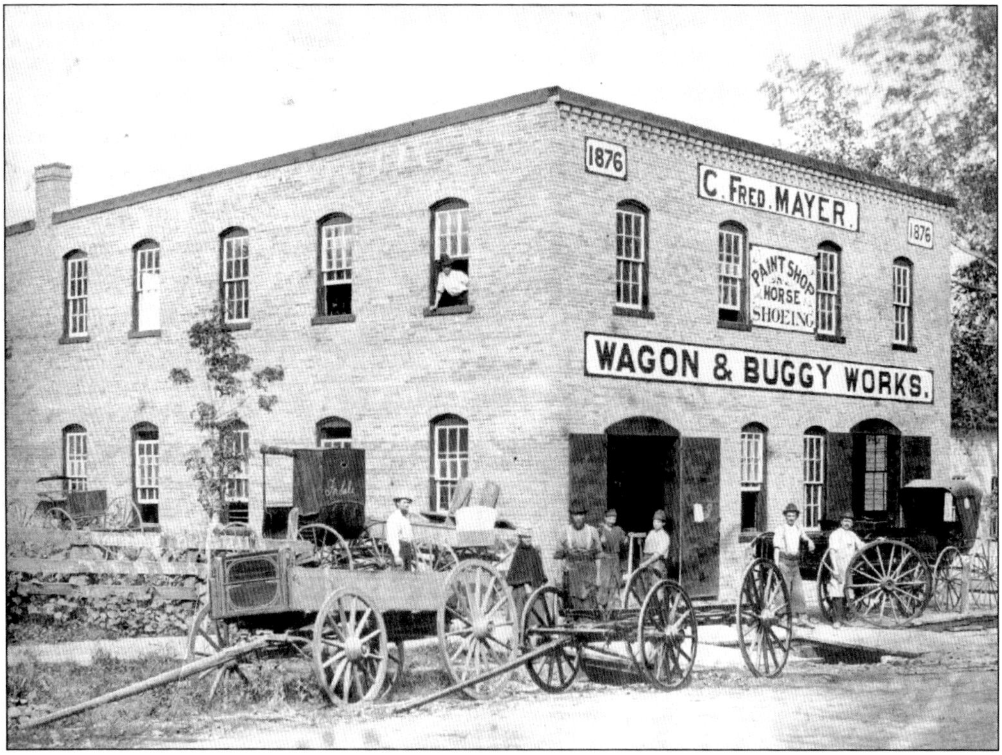

THE WAGON WORKS. The C. Fred Mayer Wagon and Buggy Works in 1880 stood on the west side of the 200 block of South Galena Avenue. Most vehicles were still built in small shops at that time.

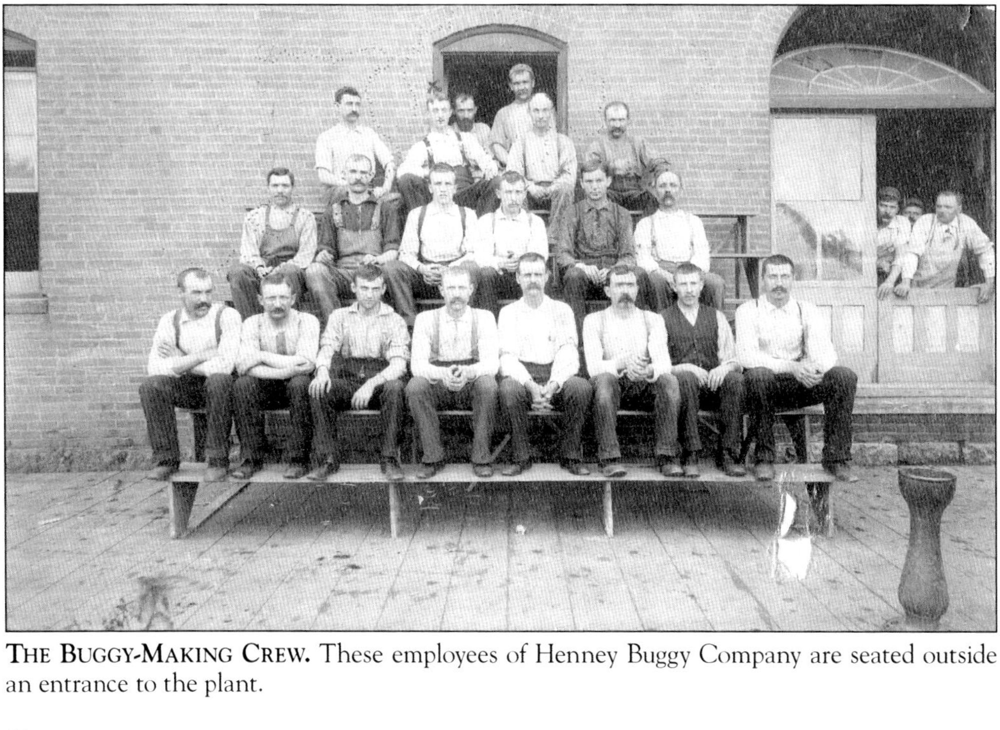

THE BUGGY-MAKING CREW. These employees of Henney Buggy Company are seated outside an entrance to the plant.

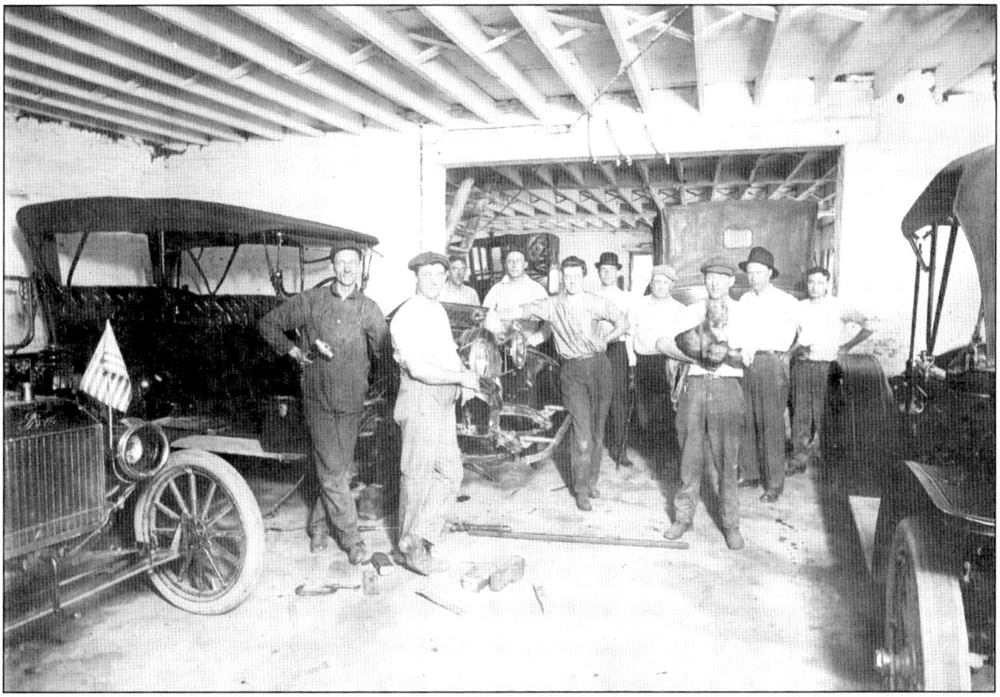

THE STEPHENS CAR FACTORY. Employees at Stephens Motor Works pose for this photograph. The vehicle at the left rear gives a sampling of the finished product.

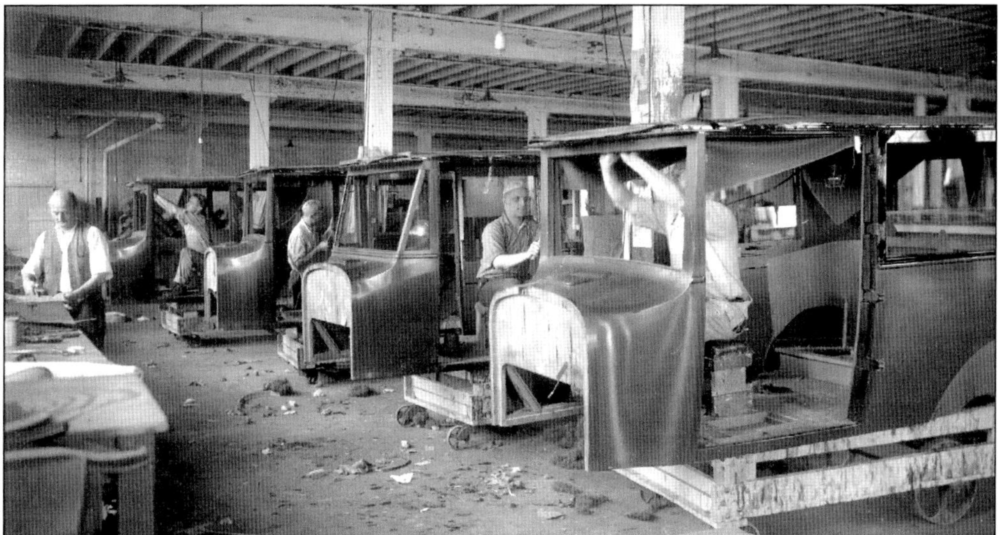

STEPHENS MOTOR WORKS. Skilled workers are building automobiles at Stephens Motor Works. In 1903, Moline Plow Company had purchased the Henney wagon, buggy, and bicycle company, retaining the Henney name. A second factory was purchased on Freeport's man-made Manufacturer's Island where commercial bodies for Ford chassis were built with production of the Stephens Salient Six automobile beginning in 1916. A five-passenger touring car and a three-passenger roadster were among the products. The wheels had wooden spokes and frames covered with metal. The company closed in 1924, ending the Stephens car production.

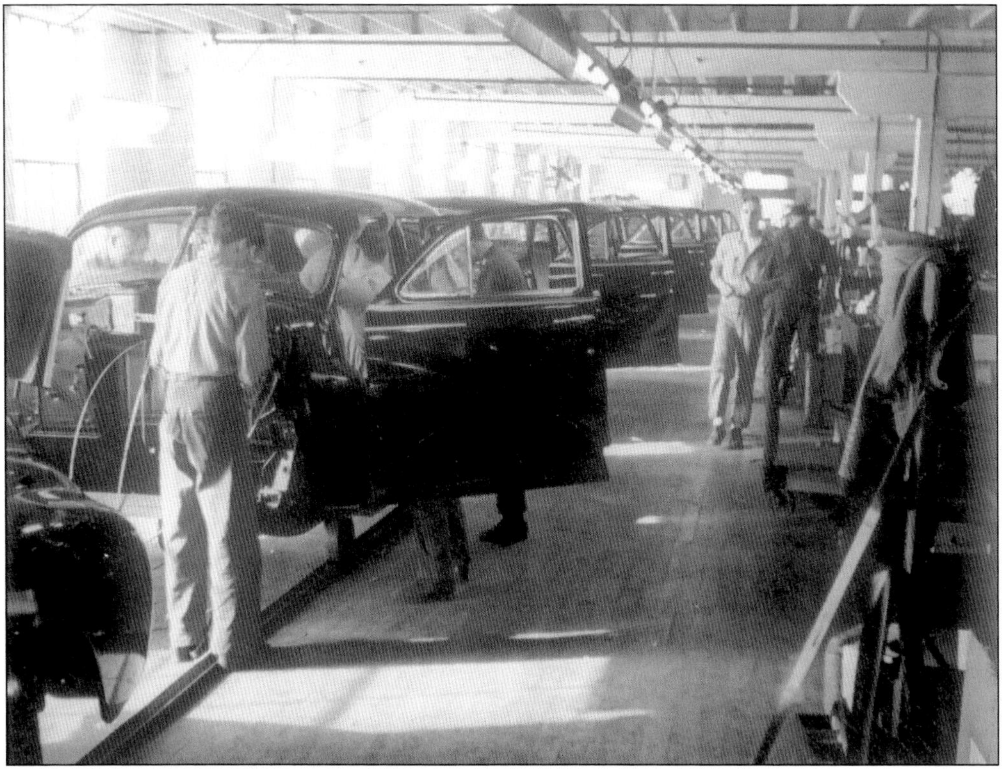

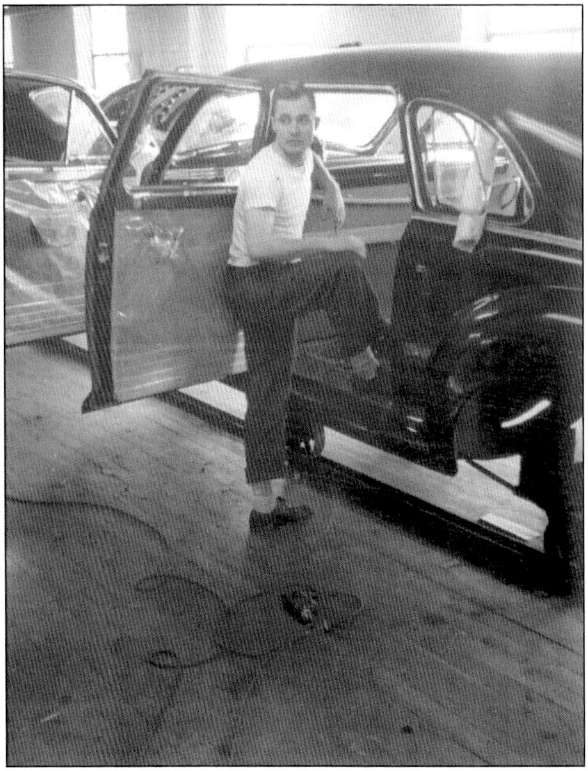

A LINE OF SHINY CARS. In 1947, Henney Motor Company workers were still rolling the sleek, finished hearses and limousines out the door. Production began on the top floor of the massive building between Spring and Jackson Streets and VanBuren and Chicago Avenues, with the finished product ready for test driving and delivery to dealers. A few years later as the giant automobile makers garnered the market, the company was sold only to close in the mid-1950s.

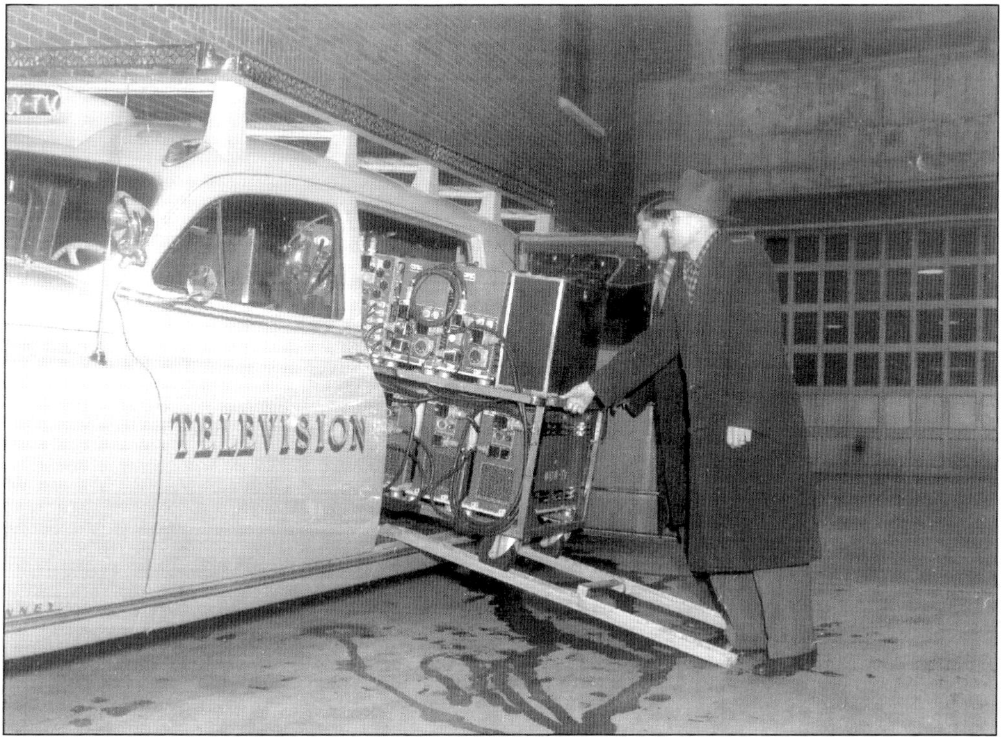

FIRST ONE MADE IN FREEPORT. Henney Motor Company claimed a first in the nation for its 1948 production of the television field car. The car, shown with all the technology of that era, was outfitted with equipment for an Omaha television station. It took 90 days to build the sleek, complex vehicle. It contained a two-way telephone and a working deck on top. The company promoted it as having the capability of broadcasting for 60 miles in any direction.

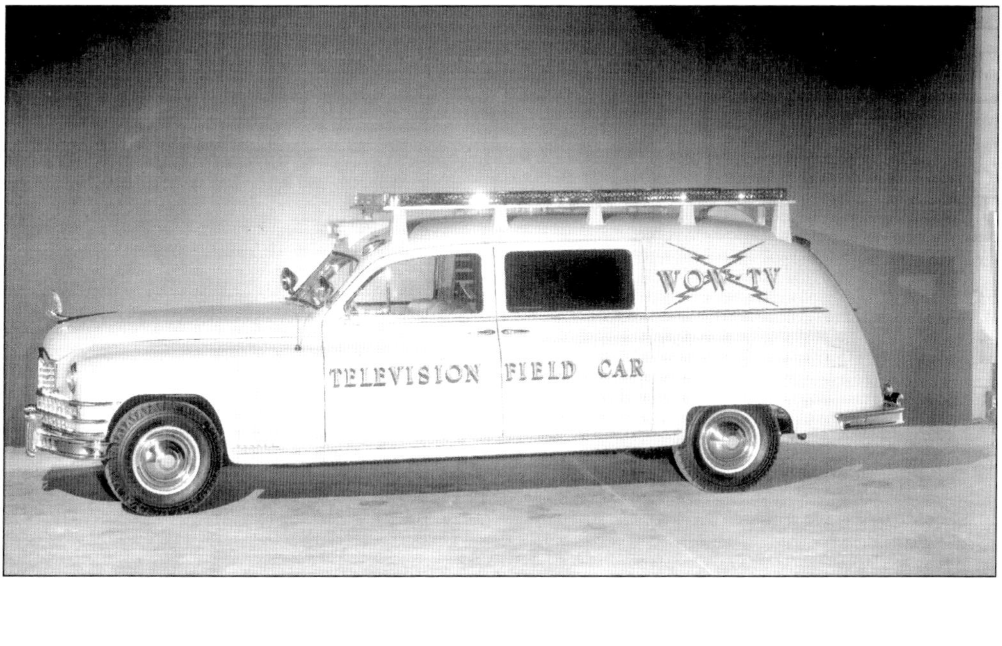

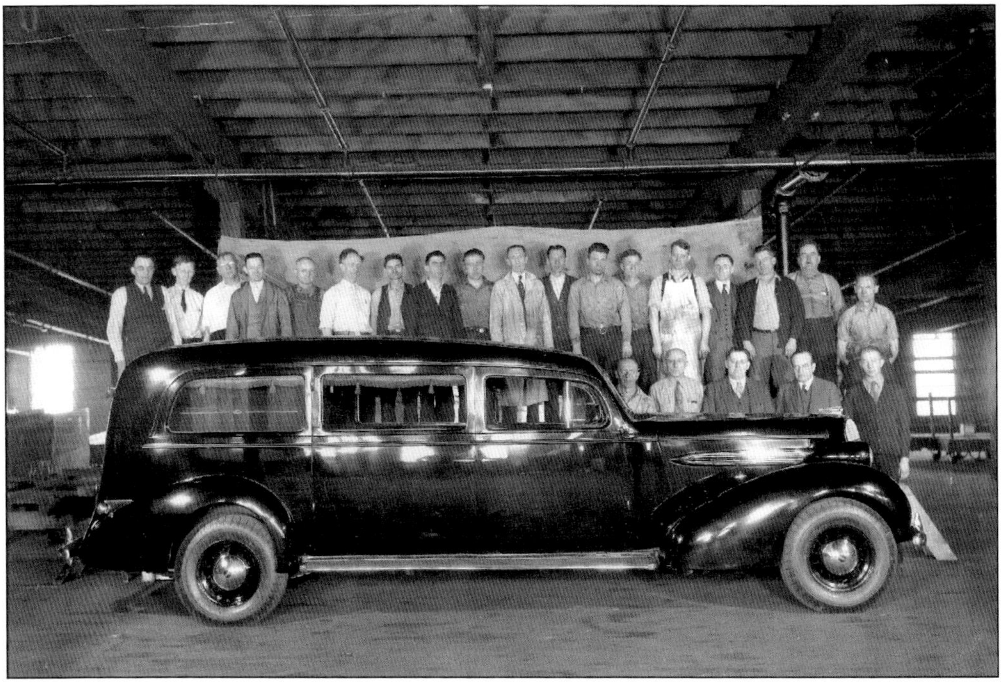

PRIDE AND JOY. These men were skilled craftsmen at Freeport's Henney Motor Company, proud of this Oldsmobile hearse that they had just turned out in about 1936. John Henney Jr., the boss, is the man second from right in the first row.

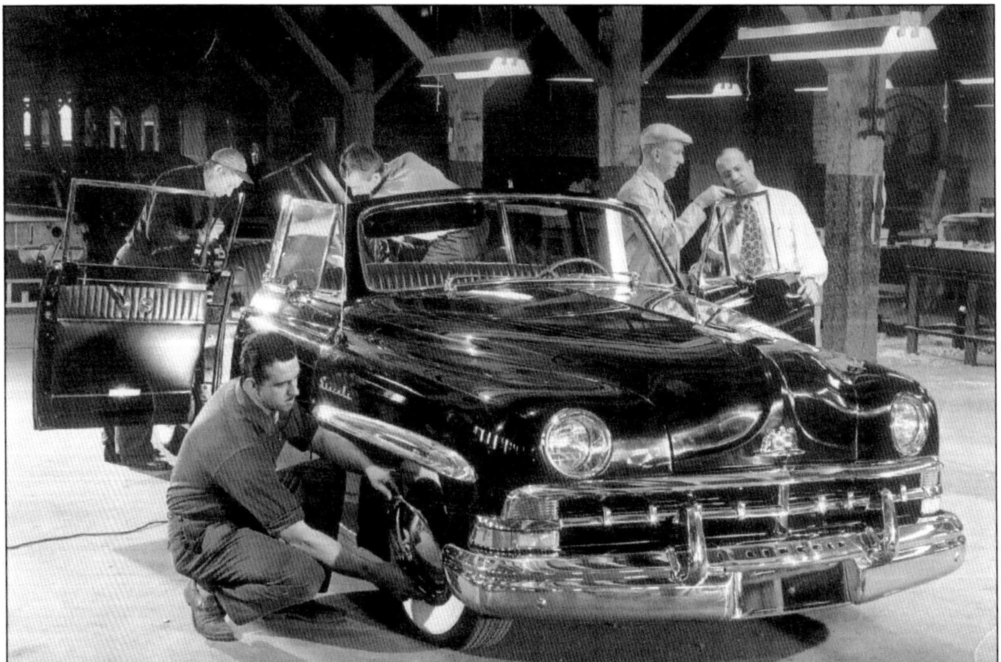

PRESIDENTIAL VEHICLE. This sleek vehicle is believed to have been one of the eight limousines made by the Henney Motor Company in Freeport for the White House fleet while Harry Truman was president. The one for the president was armored and equipped with a telephone.

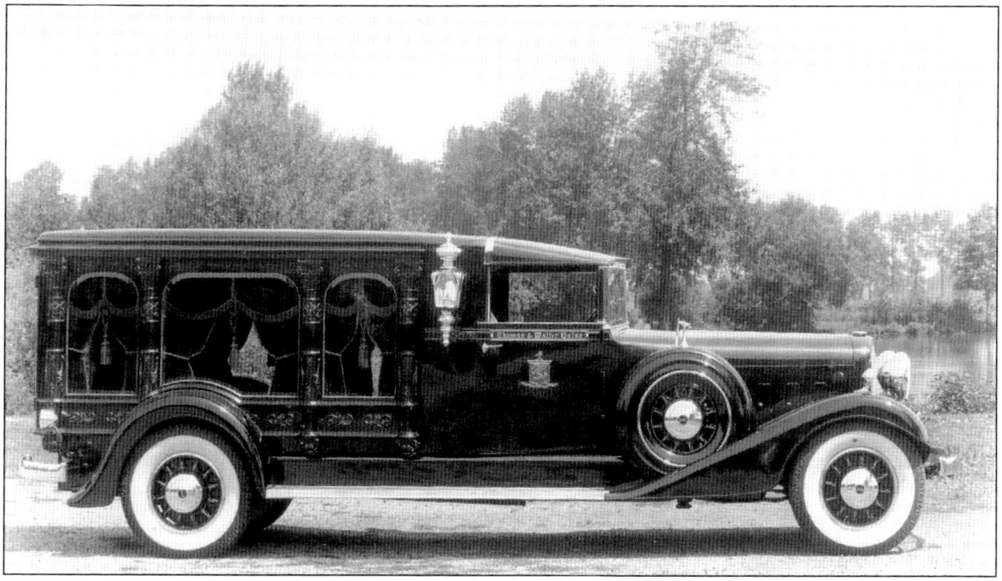

SINGING CHAPEL ON WHEELS. A *Journal-Standard* newspaper story in 1940 told of a Henney-made hearse created to be a "singing chapel on wheels [with] suitable music for funerals at cemeteries." The story said, "It was gaining popularity in the field." These photographs illustrate the ornate decor of the vehicle from inside and out. Below, the interior of this long and low hearse was embellished as a chapel, complete with altar and drapery. Speakers were added to provide sacred music at the graveside.

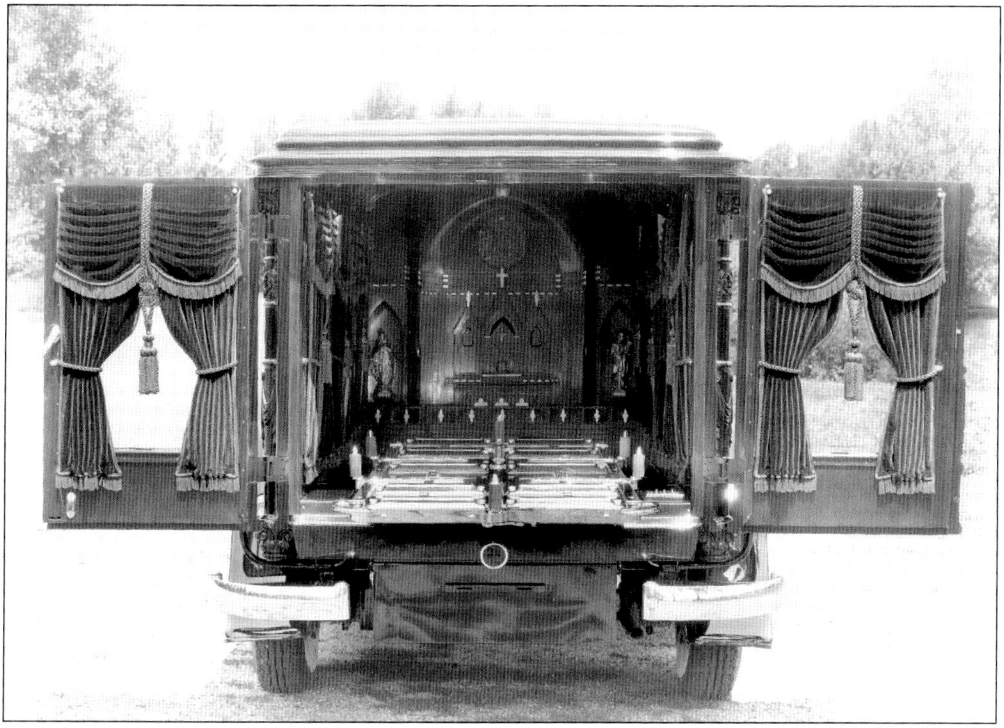

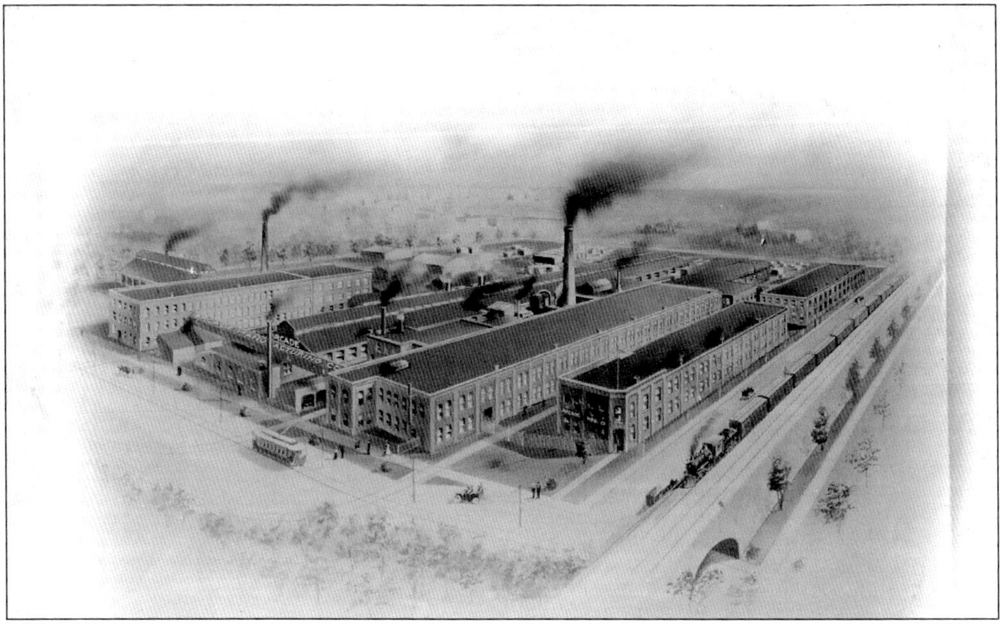

ARCADE-MADE TOYS. The Arcade Manufacturing Company in southeastern Freeport, after producing hardware, turned to making the toys now coveted by collectors. The company, founded in 1885 by Albert Baumgarten, Cyrus Tobias, and Edward Morgan, remained in production through 1953.

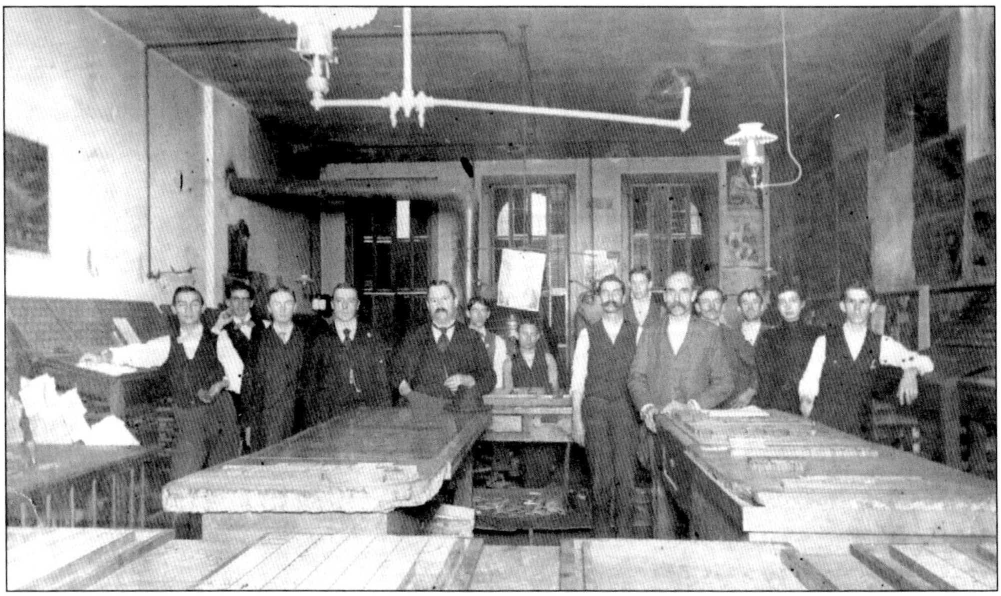

A PIONEER NEWSPAPER. The interior of the *Freeport Journal* was snug in 1900. It appears that 13 men and one woman were at the helm at the building in the unit block of South Chicago Avenue. It was founded in 1848 as a Republican newspaper, published only intermittently. It changed hands several times and in 1913 went under the ownership of the *Standard*. After the two newspapers merged that year, it became known for many years as the politically independent *Freeport Journal-Standard* and ultimately the *Journal-Standard*.

Seven

Historic Businesses

Freeport's downtown was a hub of activity with its many and varied family-owned businesses.

From its first days, enterprising entrepreneurs set up shop to cater to the growing whims of the fast-growing village. Shops of every kind emerged in the buildings that were coming to life downtown.

There was a hunger for news right from the start, and that hunger was fed early on by the establishment of a number of competing weekly vessels. Two of them, the *Journal* and the *Standard* eventually merged into what is known today as the *Journal-Standard*.

There were those businesses that catered to the well-dressed house frau as well as to her gentleman husband and their offspring. The farm families drove to town on Saturday nights to trade their eggs and garden produce for a week's provisions. There were banks, general stores, groceries, apothecaries, and confectioneries. Cigar stores and saloons, stationers and bookstores, furniture, and hardware stores were also open, along with harness shops, blacksmiths, feed stores, and lumber yards. When a need was discovered, someone devised a way to meet it. There also were professional offices, including countless lawyers, doctors, dentists, realtors, and insurance agencies.

Freeporters lacked for nothing. The city always met its residents' needs and has always been a self-contained municipality.

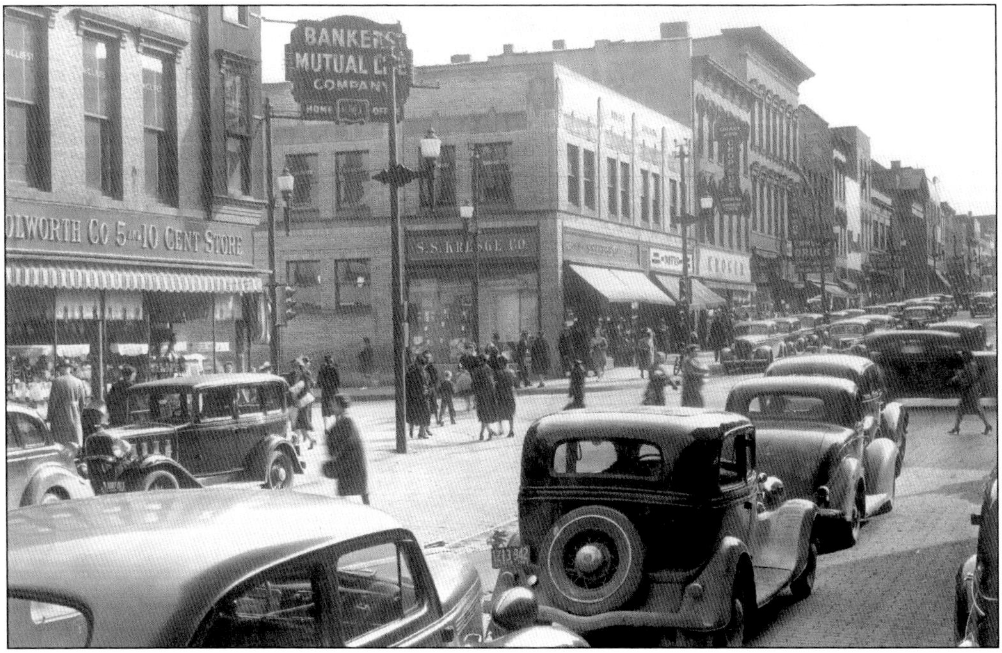

Downtown Streets Teemed, 1940. Taken in late April or early May 1940 just east of Chicago Avenue looking west on Stephenson Street, this picture shows the myriad of businesses in downtown Freeport and how flocks of people patronized them during the years of the reviving prosperity. Two dime stores on one corner drew awed customers to covet their wares.

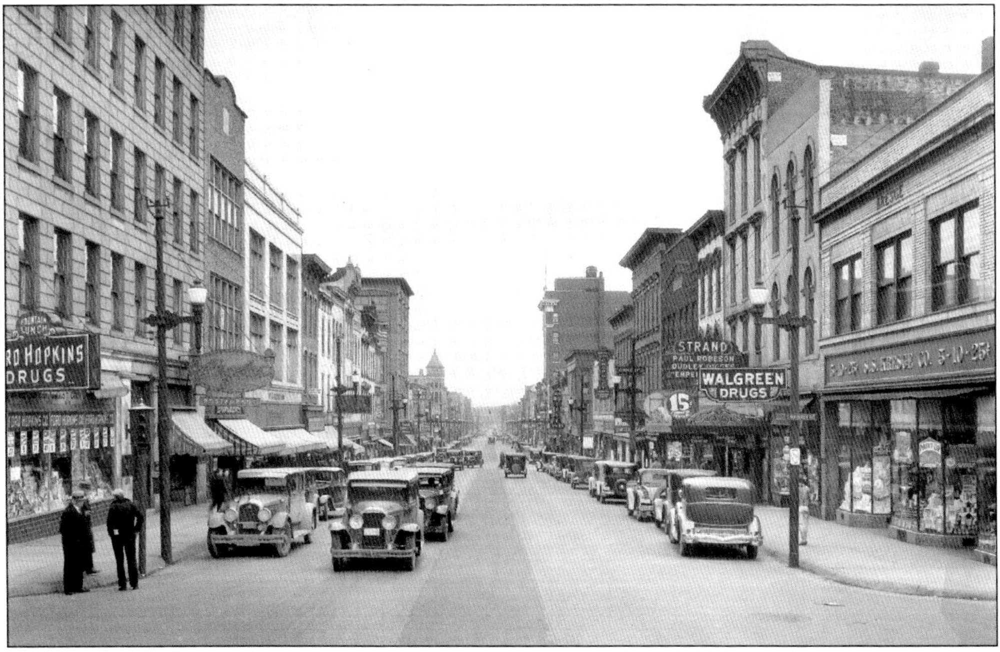

No Sign of Depression Here. For the hard times the country had been experiencing, Freeport's commerce did not appear to be suffering in 1935. This downtown scene looking east on Stephenson Street from Van Buren Avenue shows the Second National Bank building on the left. That building was the former Wilcoxon Opera House.

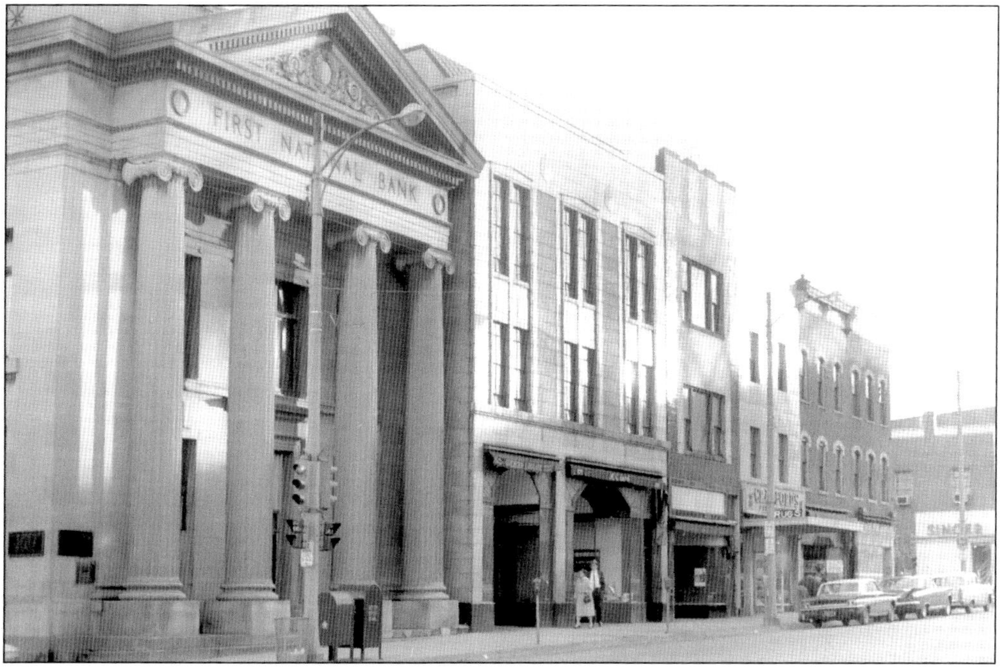

FIRST NATIONAL BANK, COMMUNITY PILLAR. The south side of the 100 block of West Stephenson Street was the hub of downtown Freeport, as shown in the mid-1900s. The bank, as shown above, had its four-column classical front constructed onto an old building in 1912. The bank and its neighboring businesses were razed that year to allow expansion over the entire square block. It remained there for decades, evolving in later years from one owner to another. That site is now Fifth-Third Bank. Below, the interior of First National Bank in about 1890 was a vision of elegant woods and glass, a typical scene in a bank up through the 1910 era. Orland B. Bidwell, president, is the man seated. His son Addison Bidwell, cashier, is at his side.

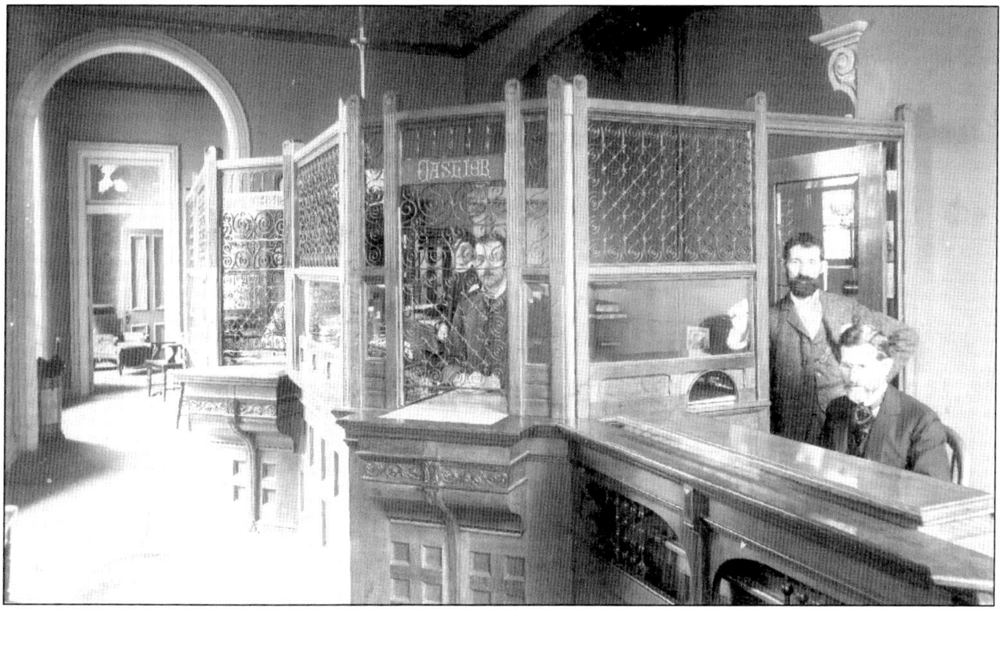

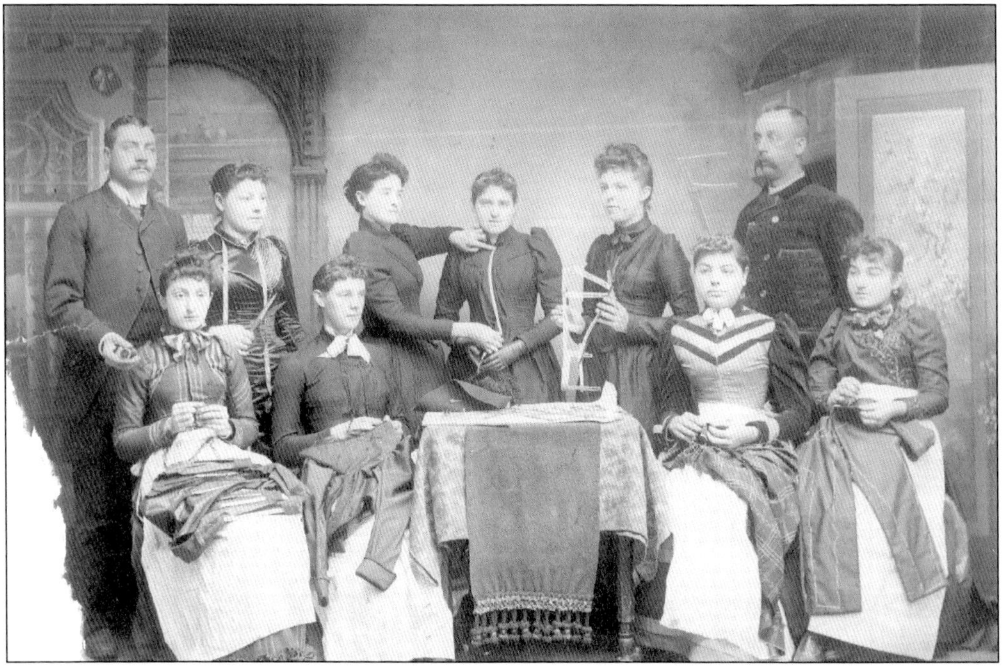

WOMEN BEING TAUGHT TO SEW. Seeley Dry Goods store offered instruction in sewing and other needle crafts for women. The photograph displays the modest high-neck, long-sleeved, fitted-bodice styles so popular with women at the dawn of the 20th century. The women also seem to have the same basic hairstyle.

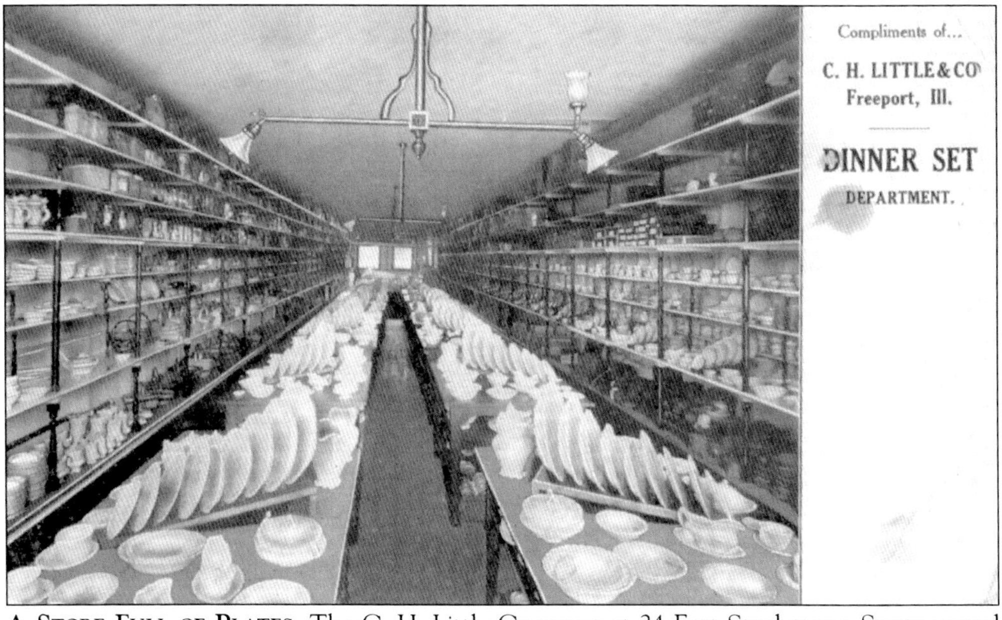

A STORE FULL OF PLATES. The C. H. Little Company at 24 East Stephenson Street served generations of Freeport-area shoppers seeking fine china, silverware, lamps, paintings, and mirrors. In the days before electricity was accessible to residents, kerosene was stocked for lamps. The store's signature landmark was a pillar of white china plates that stood at its front corner.

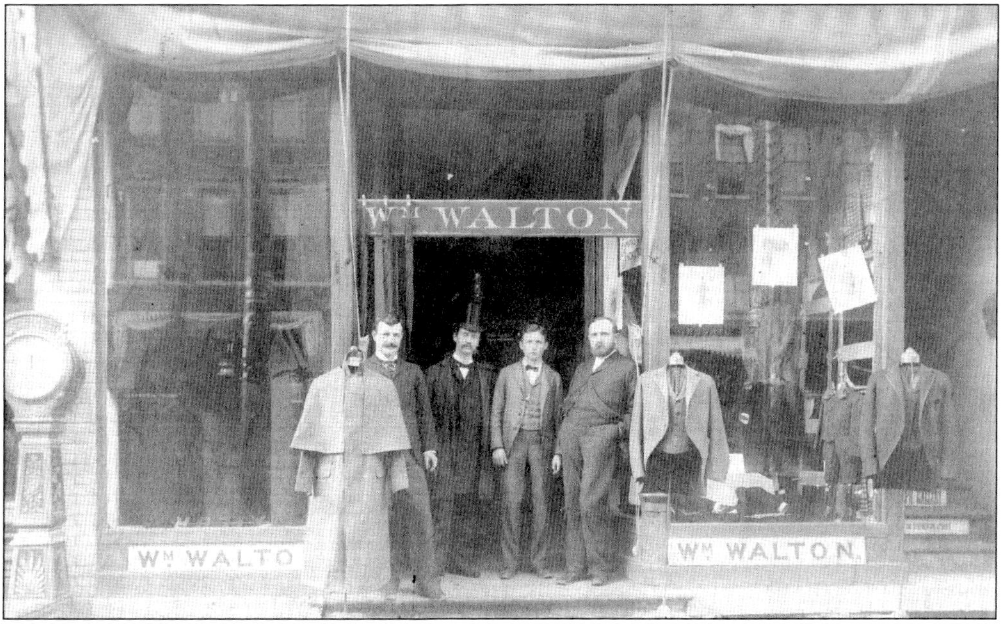

MEN'S DEPARTMENT STORE. This 1890 photograph of the men's department of the William Walton store illustrates what the well-dressed gentleman wore. The dry goods portion of the business was connected, adjoining this one on the right side. The store, Freeport's leading business for many years, was located a few doors east of Chicago Avenue. Walton began his business in 1858.

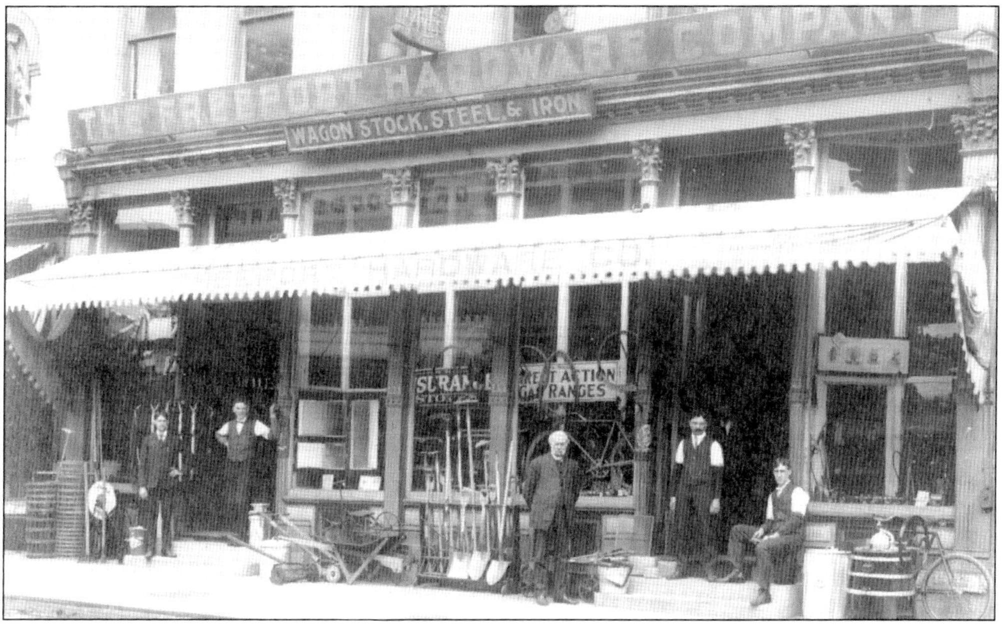

A KEY BUSINESS IN FREEPORT. In about 1910, anything one could possibly want in the hardware line could be found at the venerable Freeport Hardware Company at 16 and 18 West Main Street. Its proprietor at the time was Anton Billerbeck, seen standing in the doorway at left. Later the hardware store moved a block west, and the vacated building became various businesses over the years.

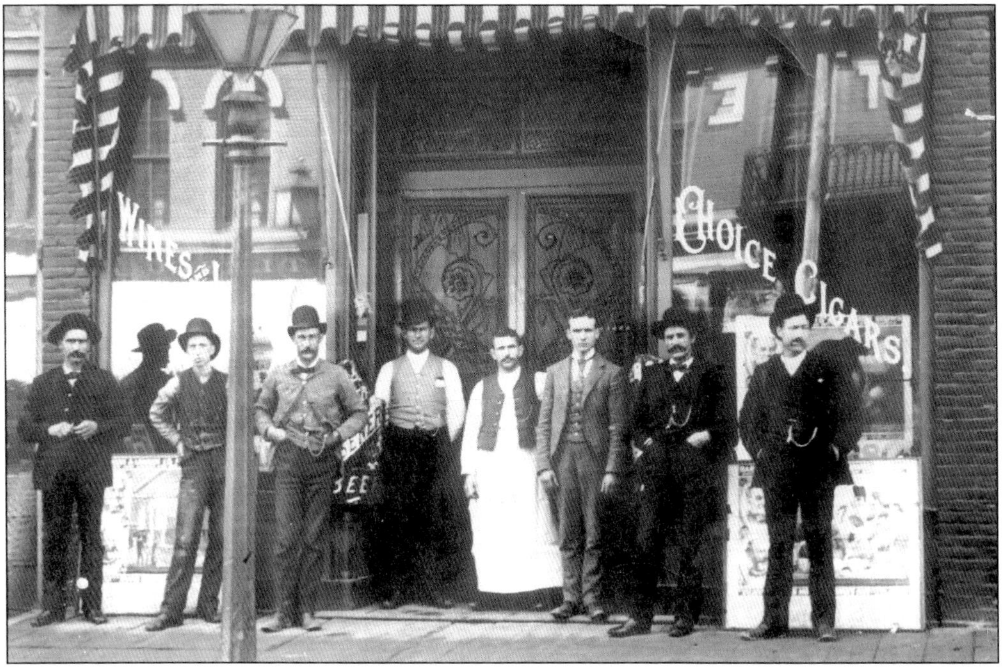

FREEPORT'S SINFUL SIDE. There was a time when Freeport had nary a block in its downtown that lacked a saloon. These gentlemen must have known their way around in such a setting. The handlebar mustaches, the bowler hats, the three-piece suits, and the boardwalks suggest this photograph is from the early 1900s.

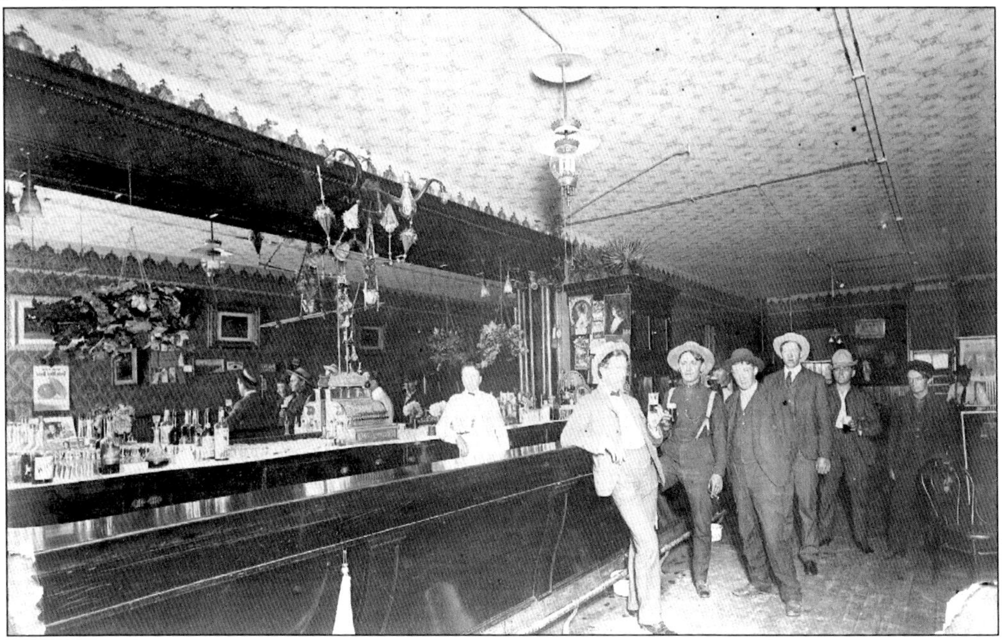

THE AFTER-WORK CROWD. Freeport is a beer and pretzel town. The strong German ethnicity made both products popular and substantiated many saloons. At one time, disgruntled wives submitted a list of their imbibing husbands' names so barkeepers would be inspired to refuse their admittance.

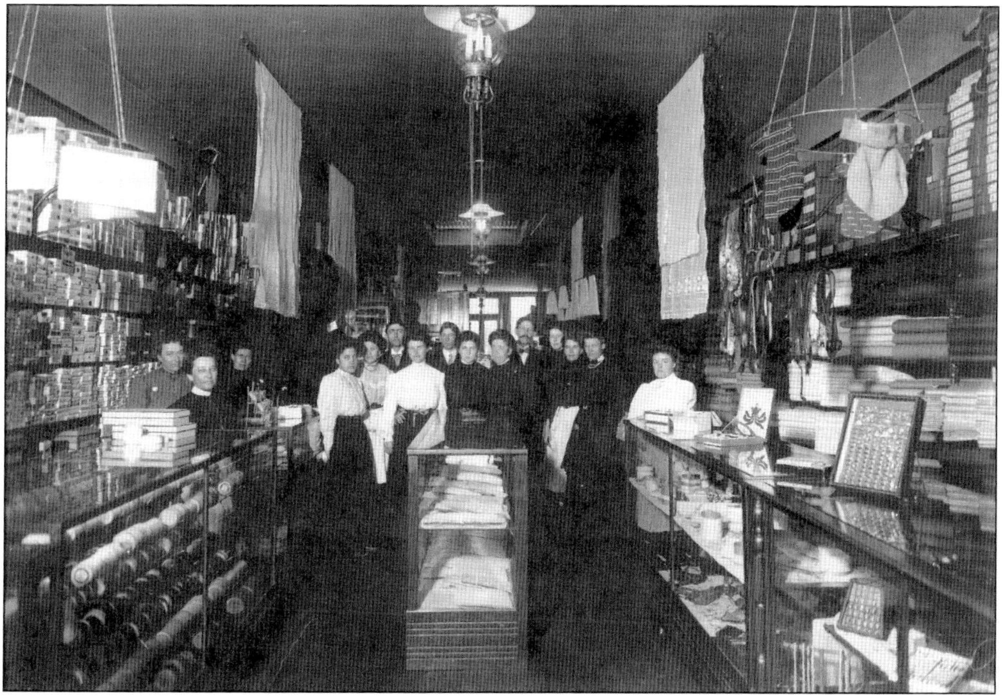

BIG STAFF, LITTLE STORE. It appears as if a little bit of everything was offered in the Williams-Beckmire store, and there were plenty of workers to assist shoppers.

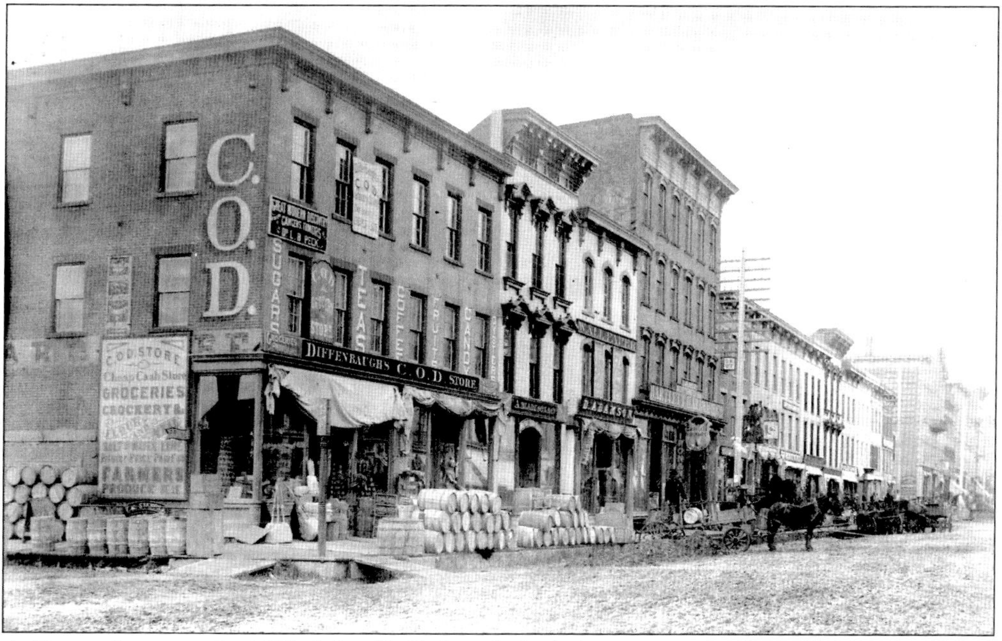

A BUSY CORNER. In 1885, John Diffenbaugh had this grocery and crockery store on the southwest corner of East Stephenson Street and State Avenue, and later on Mechanic Street. The building there now houses offices of Newell Companies, but originally housed State Bank. The dark, four-story building in the center was Bartlett Hardware, with a padlock as its sign. (Courtesy of the Freeport Public Library.)

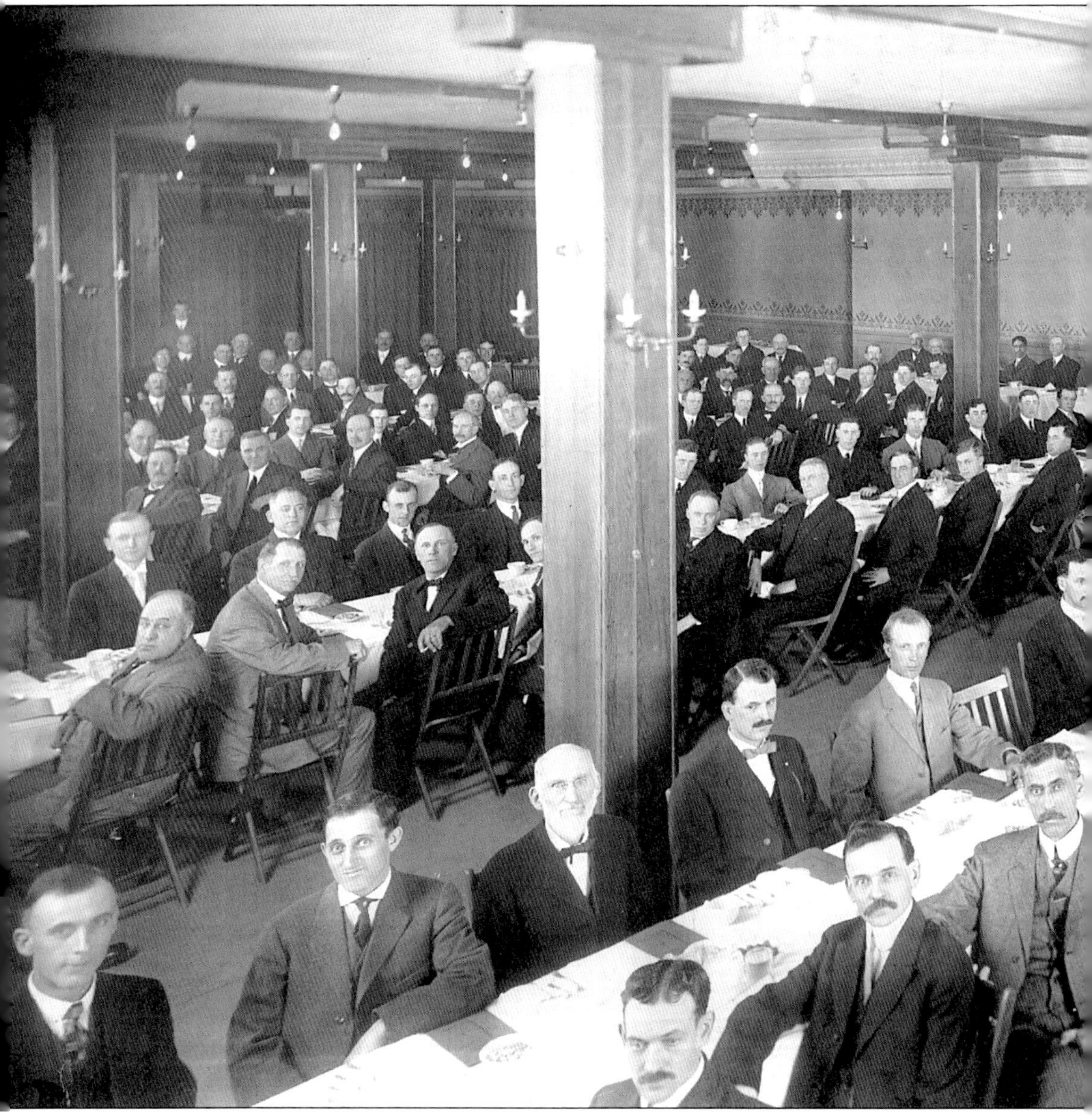

DINNER MEETING. More than 100 Freeport businessmen gather for a dinner in the early 1900s. It was held on May 12, but the year is not known. Speculation is that the event was an early

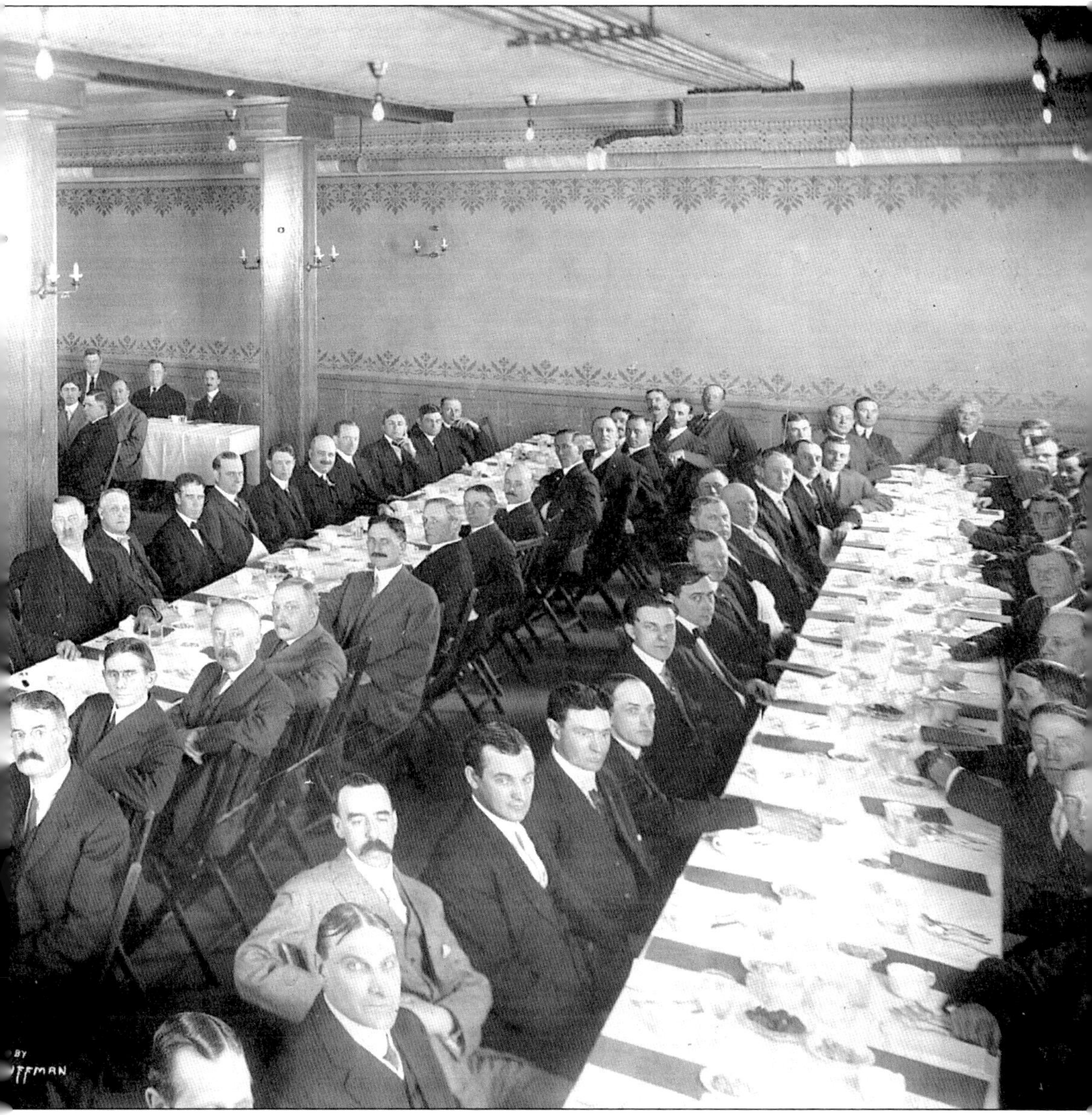

chamber of commerce dinner held on the lower level of the Freeport Hotel. The smaller table in the upper left may have been for the speakers.

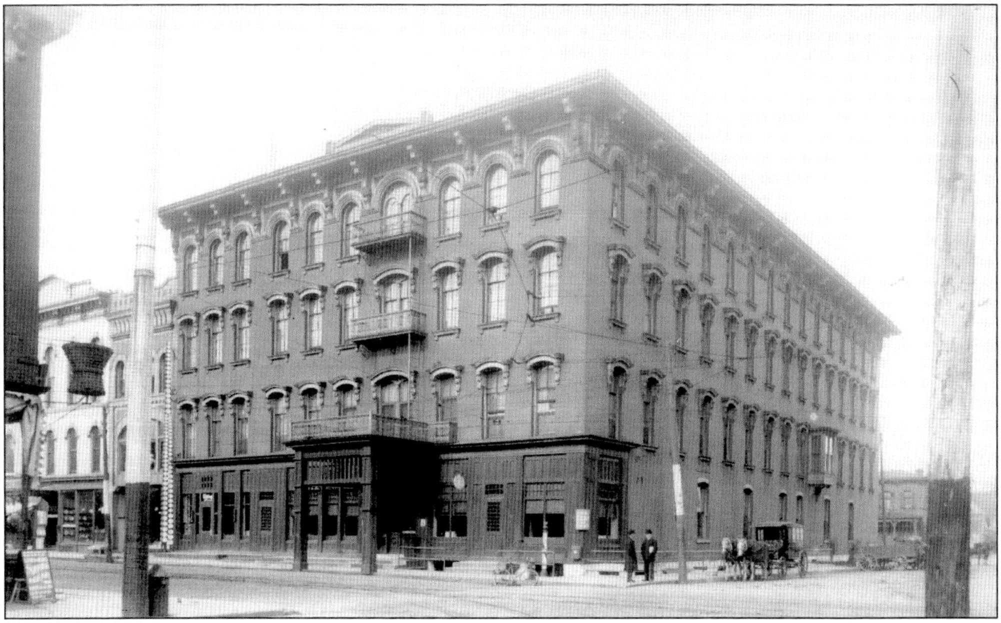

ABRAHAM LINCOLN SLEPT HERE. The Brewster House on the north side of Stephenson Street at the corner of State Avenue was a vibrant hotel in Freeport for decades. Built in 1856, its most famous tenants were Abraham Lincoln and Stephen A. Douglas, candidates for the United States Senate. They were here for their history-shaping debate in 1858. The hotel was razed in 1939.

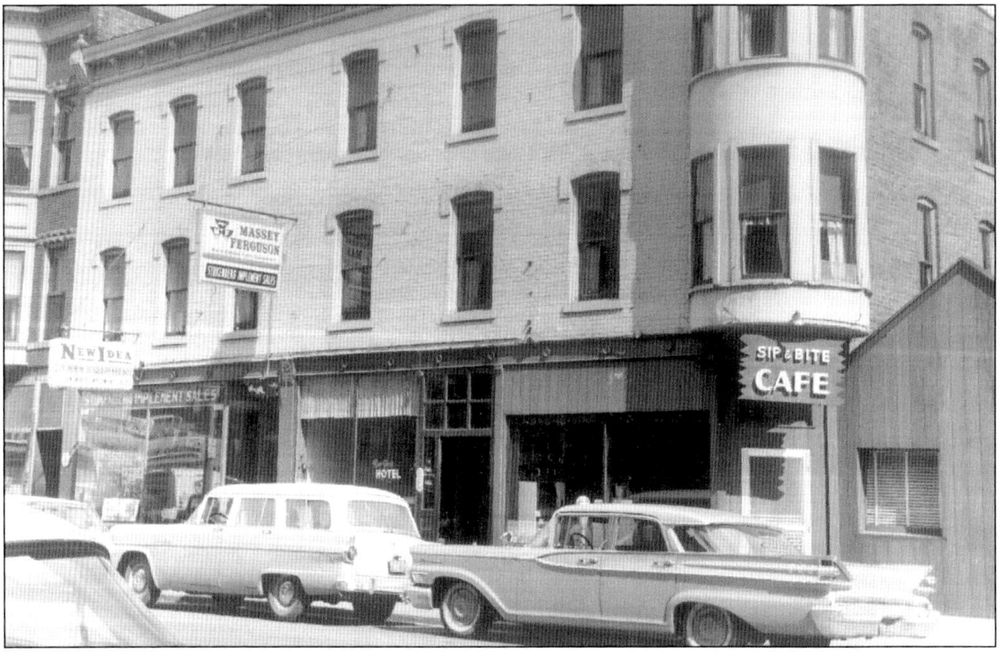

MAIN STREET DREW THE CROWDS. The Sip and Bite Cafe was adjacent to the lobby of the New York Hotel. The hotel was one of Freeport's earlier establishments when the city was a railroad center, and many of the smaller inns catered to the men who worked the trains. That corner is still home to a family-style restaurant.

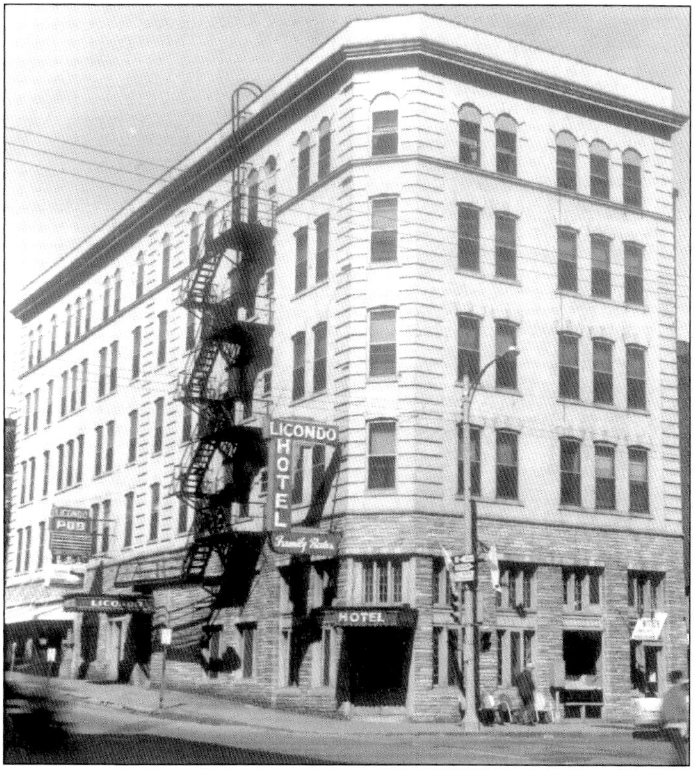

A Tragic End. The Licondo Hotel was a haunt for the night crowd with its attached restaurant and pub. It sat at the corner of Main Street and Galena Avenue until May 2, 1962, when it was destroyed by a fire that took the lives of five elderly people. The location was eventually sold and became the drive-through facility of an expanded First National Bank. The Licondo name derived from a combination of Freeport's two famous visitors, Abraham Lincoln and Stephen A. Douglas.

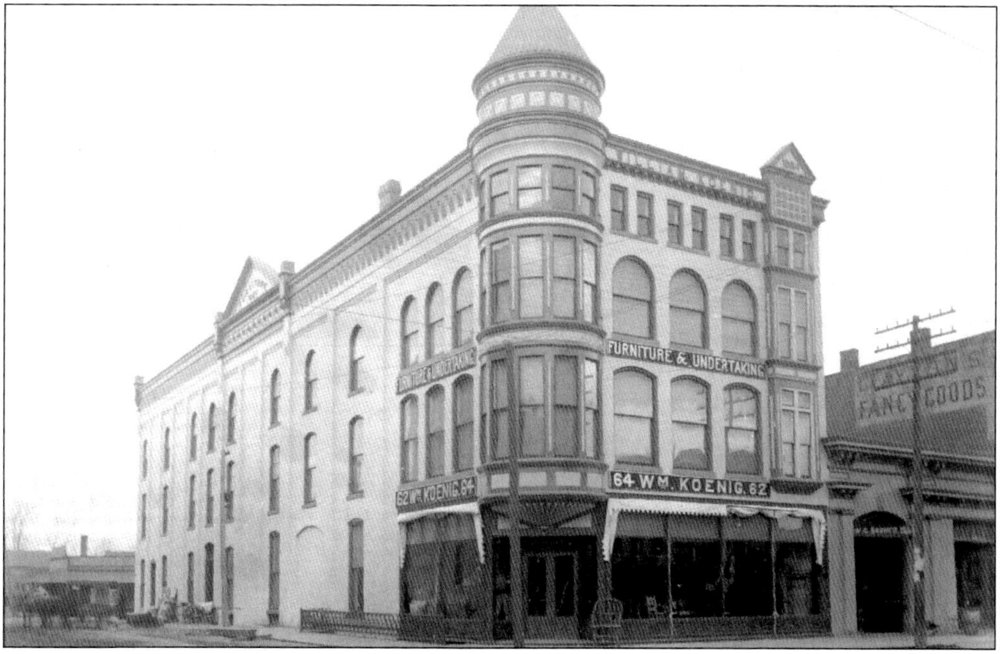

Furniture and Undertaking Went Together. Common in the 19th and early 20th century was the combining of undertaking businesses with furniture stores. William Koenig opened his business in 1878 on the northeast side of the Stephenson Street and State Street intersection, across from the historic Brewster House. (Courtesy of the Freeport Public Library.)

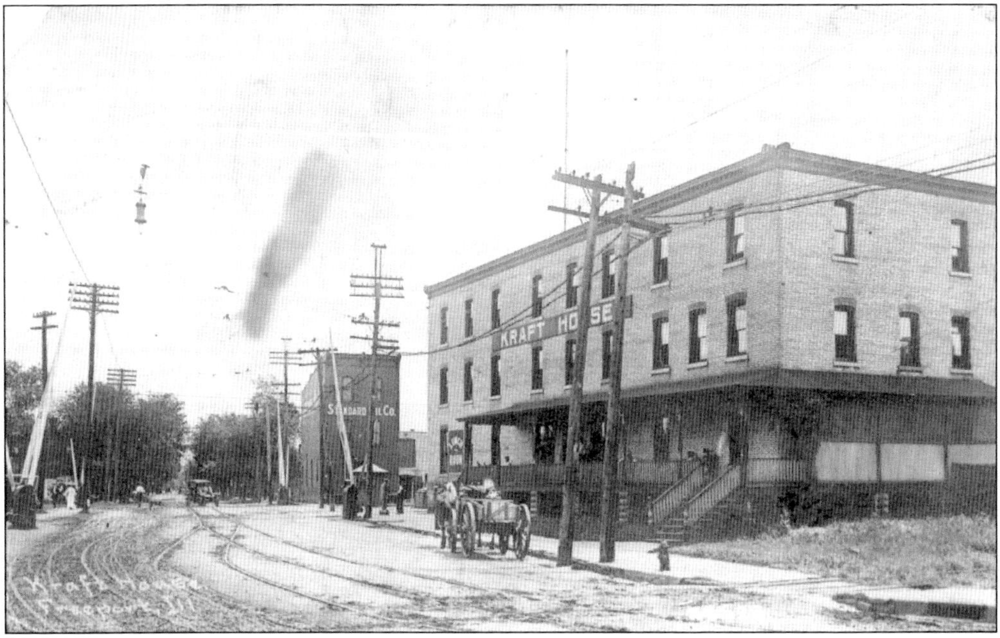

RAILROADERS LODGED AT KRAFT HOUSE. The Kraft House hotel, a favorite lodging for railroad employees, stood near the Chicago, Milwaukee and St. Paul Railroad depot, shown on East Stephenson Street in Freeport about 1910.

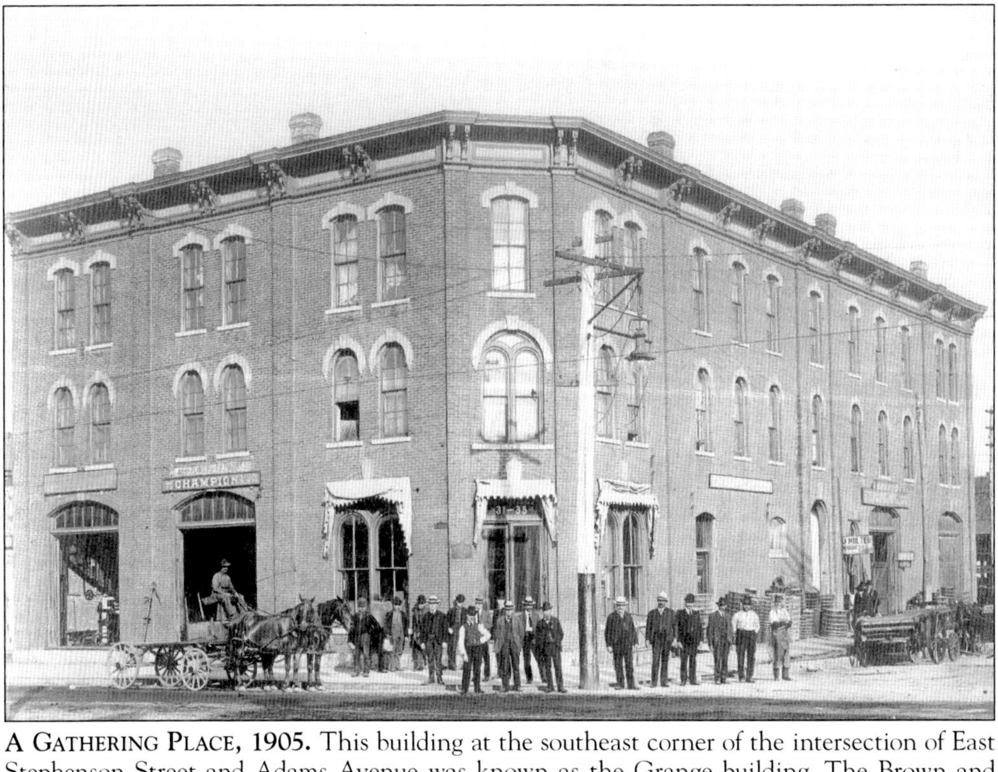

A GATHERING PLACE, 1905. This building at the southeast corner of the intersection of East Stephenson Street and Adams Avenue was known as the Grange building. The Brown and Shouer farm implement business also occupied the building for many years.

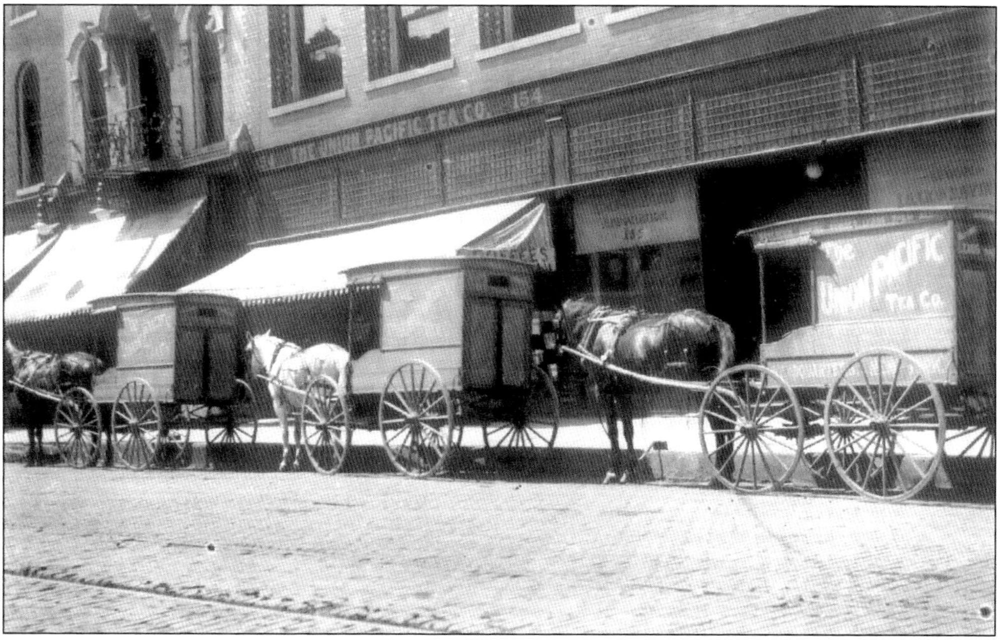

Horsepower was Plentiful. What is now 208–212 West Stephenson Street in downtown Freeport was once the hub of horse-drawn delivery wagons. The Union Pacific Tea Company must have had a good business, with three rigs ready and waiting to go. Note the streetcar tracks that left ruts in the brick paving.

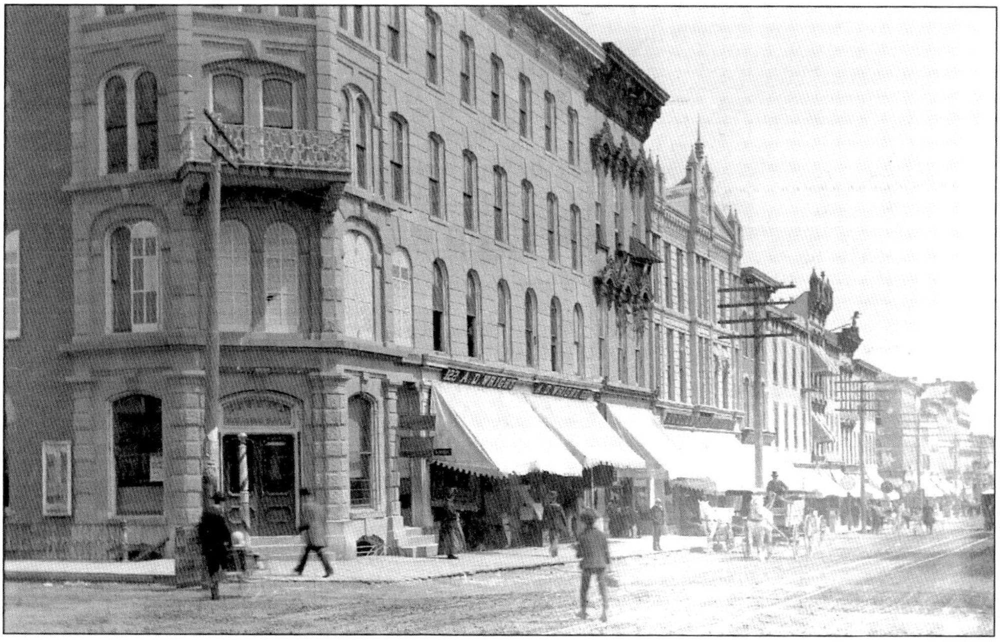

A Revered Opera House. The Wilcoxon Opera House, erected in 1869 at the northeast corner of Stephenson and Van Buren Streets, served many years as both an opera house and public meeting place. Entertainment of all kinds drew the crowds. There were plays, minstrel shows, speakers, and according to the *History of Stephenson County, 1970*, an equestrian show was featured with 15 horses clomping up the stairs. (Courtesy of the Freeport Public Library.)

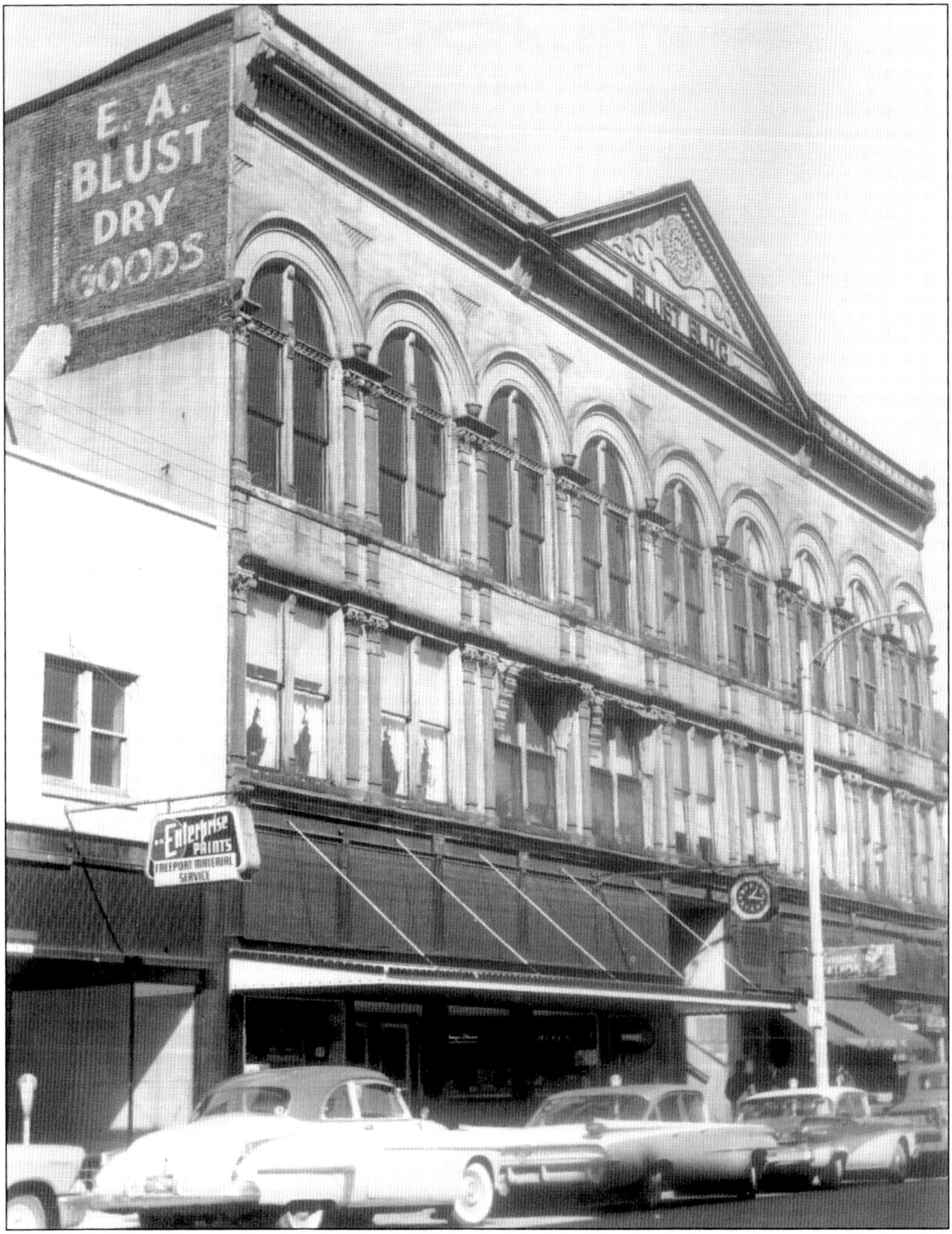

HISTORIC DEPARTMENT STORE. The E. A. Blust sign remains on this historic fortress at 10 East Main Street even though the Blust business closed in 1956. E. A. Blust opened his business in 1893. He built this three-story structure in 1892, where he maintained a stock of quality merchandise in dry goods and notions. His son-in-law Robert Luecke, who operated a jewelry store in one side, expanded his business in the building where it has remained under succeeding generations of Lueckes ever since.

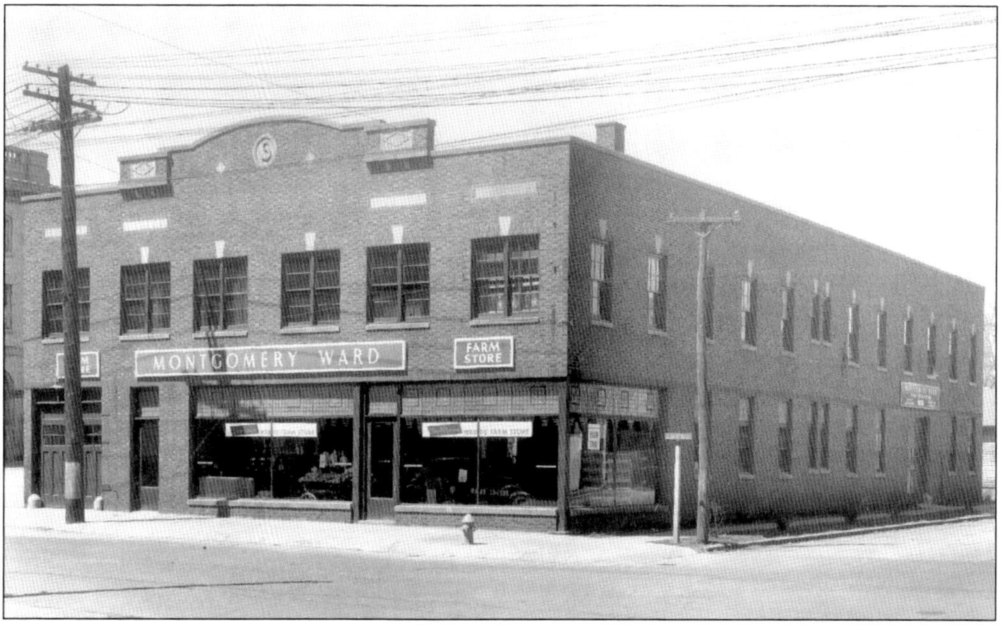

AN EARLY AUTOMOBILE SALES BUSINESS. This building, which once housed Montgomery Ward, still stands at the northwest corner of Exchange Street and State Avenue. It was first used as an automobile sales and repair shop, owned by Marshall Miller. A large, square, brick house occupied the lot prior to the building's construction. Mike Herold, a blacksmith, lived there. His shop was down the street at the southwest corner of Exchange Street and Adams Avenue.

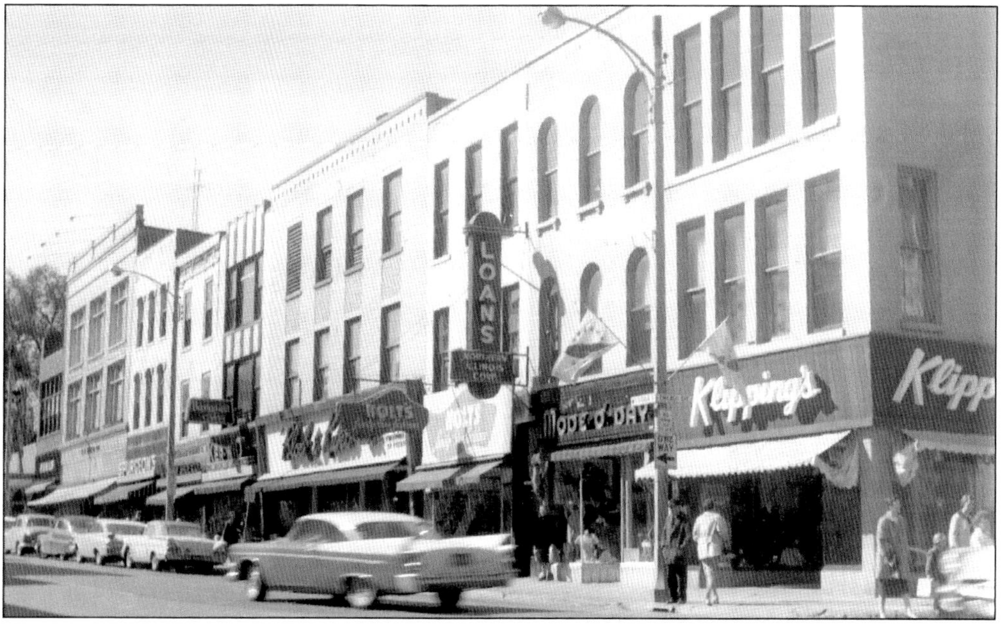

OLD, FAMILIAR HAUNTS. Shoppers around Freeport will recognize these stores from the affluent 1950s. The scene looks west in the unit block of Stephenson Street in the city's downtown. Four of the stores served Freeport for decades, including Ruhl's, F. A. Read Company, Spurgeon's, and Winslow's. F. A. Read's and Spurgeon's were department stores.

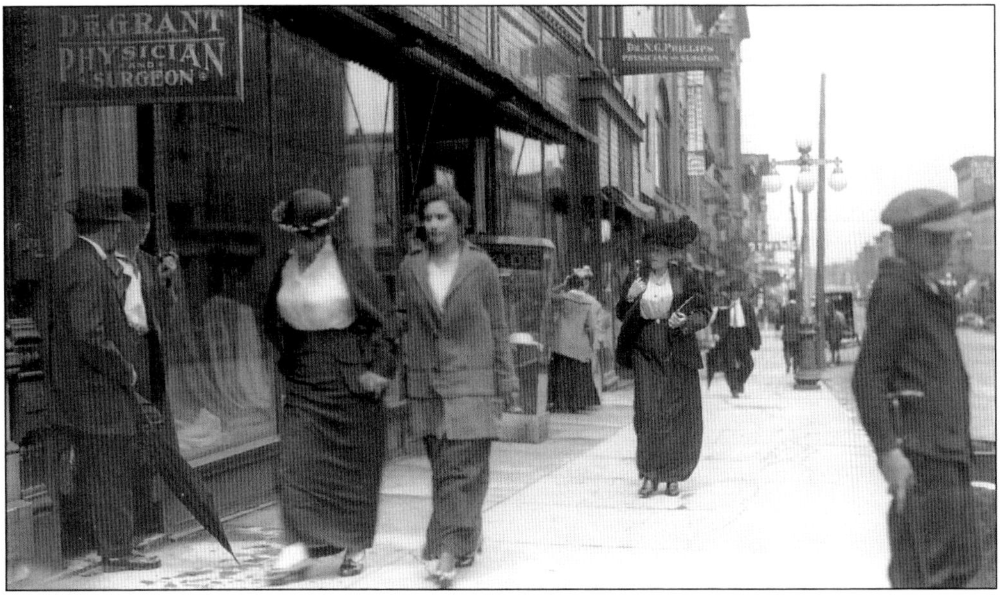

HOBBLE SKIRTS, SMART FASHION. The hobble skirt on the woman in the center foreground denotes the picture's era. She hobbled down Stephenson Street in a skirt so tight below the knees that it hampered walking. Hobble skirts were in fashion between 1910 and 1914. The scenes in both photographs show the F. A. Read Company, Freeport's longest-lived department store (left foreground), which opened in 1877 and closed as a Bergner's store in the early 1980s, retaining the Read name for most of that time. (Courtesy of the Freeport Public Library.)

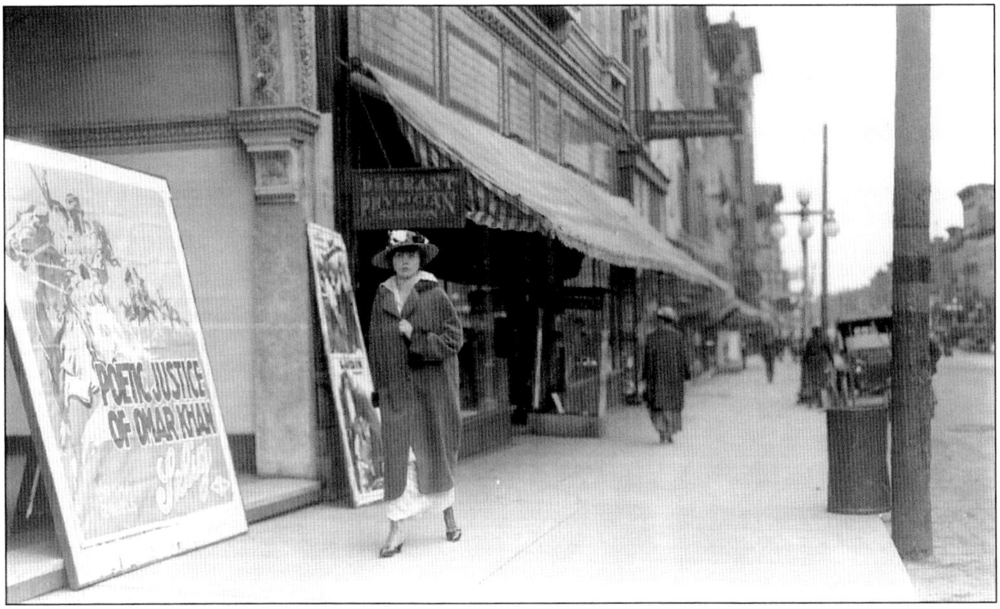

A Modern Movie Theater. In 1925, the Lindo Theater on South Chicago Avenue in downtown Freeport was the city's first modern movie theater. The theater went through a series of ownership and name changes, but is now once again the historic Lindo, enlarged and glamorized with offerings for every taste in its nine theaters. (Courtesy of the Freeport Public Library.)

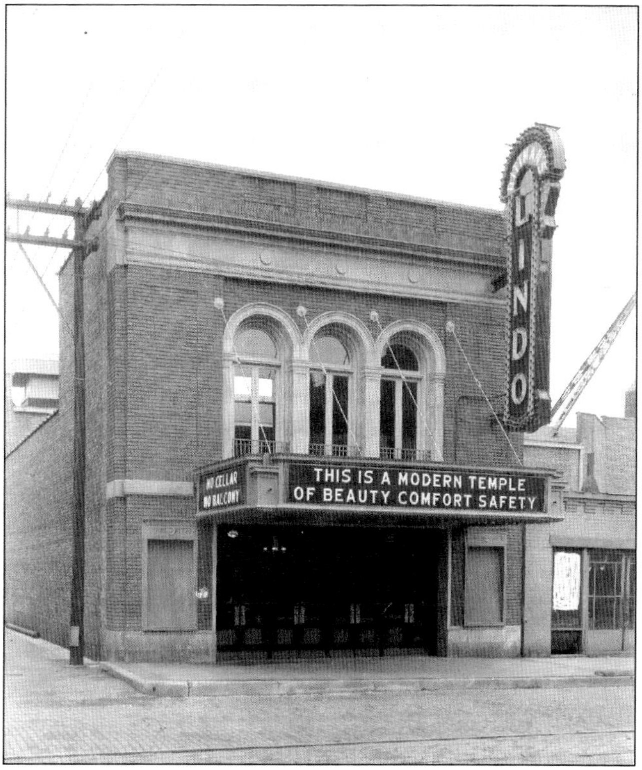

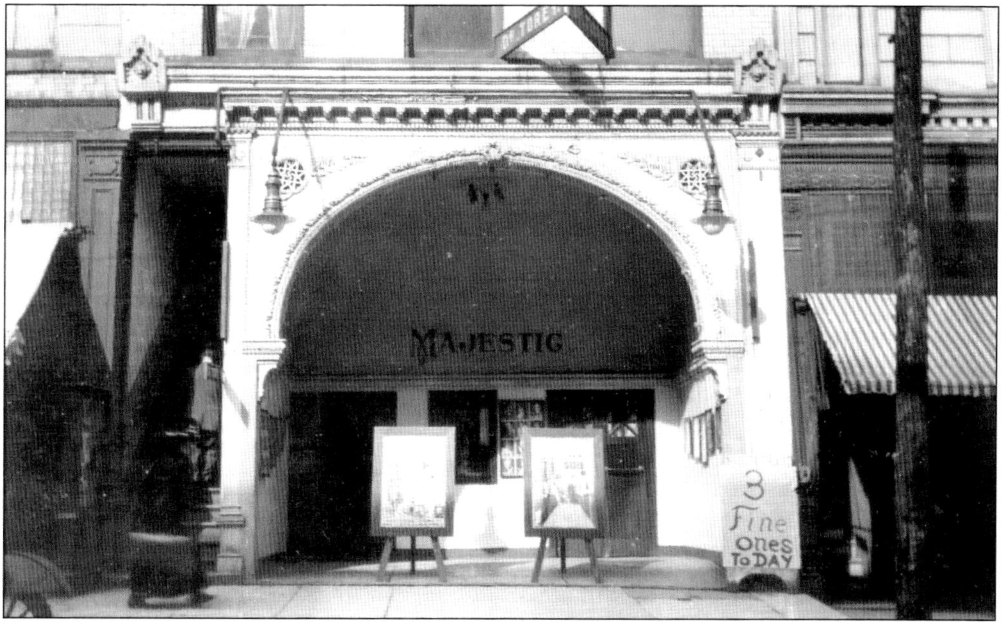

This Theater was Majestic. Freeport's first movie house was the Majestic Theater at 24 West Stephenson Street just off of Van Buren Avenue. It opened in about 1908. Its first showing was *The March of the Teddy Bears*. Admission at first was 5¢. Like most movie houses of its day, it was located in a long, narrow converted store with a center aisle. Musical accompaniment to the pictures was supplied by a phonograph placed in a small pit below the screen.

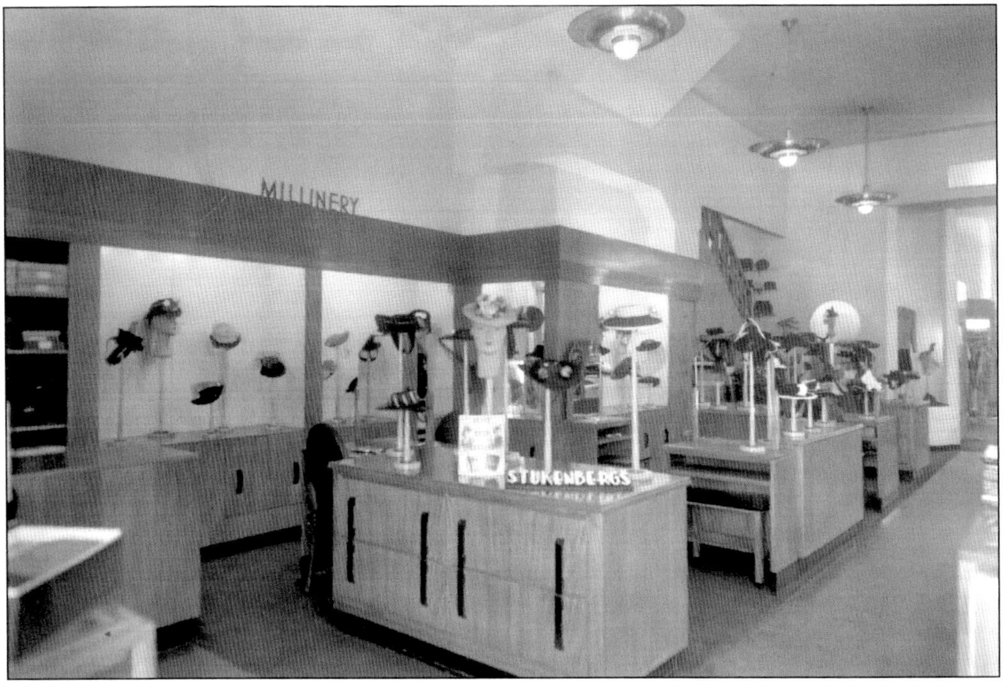

A. J. STUKENBERG DRY GOODS STORE. The Stukenberg store was popular among women when it was still vogue to wear hats to church and other social functions. Note its extensive millinery department.

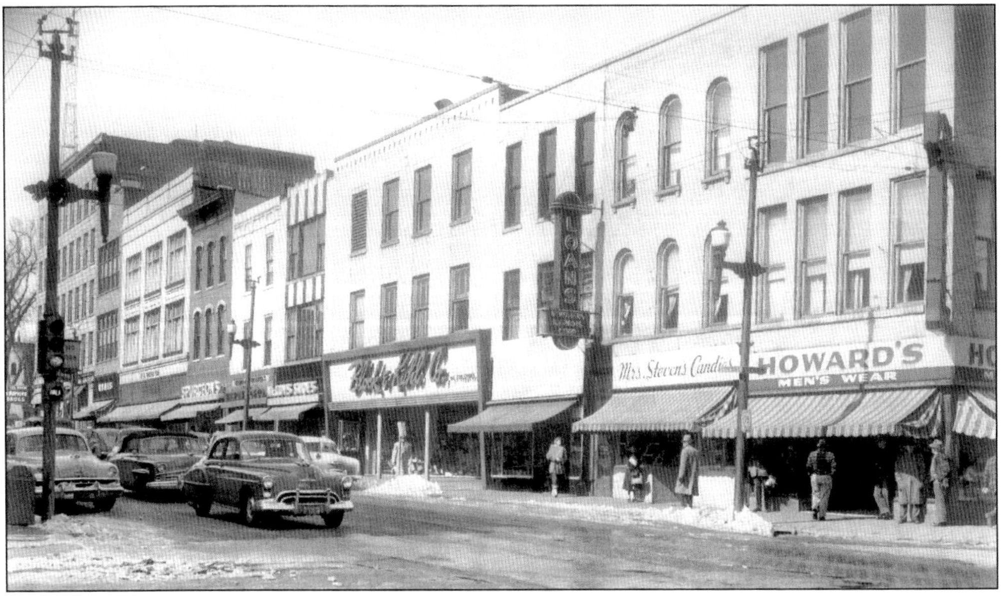

A TWO-WAY STEPHENSON STREET. Snow-blotched streets and sidewalks marked this early-1950s scene at the corner of Chicago and Stephenson Streets in downtown Freeport. Favorite shopping places there at that time were the F. A. Read Company, Spurgeon's, and the Block and Kuhl Company department stores. Note the two-way traffic that changed to one-way when the landscaped parkway was built to divide the street into a traffic-free plaza for approximately 30 years. The striped canvas awnings were also characteristic of the times.

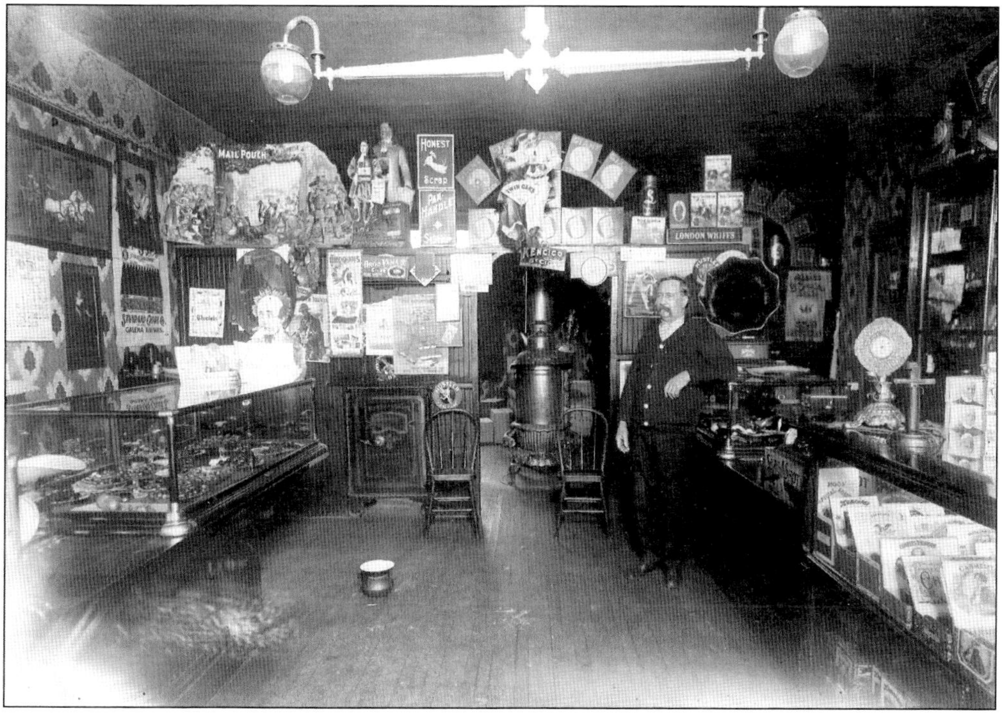

JAEGER'S STORE HAD PERSONALITY. Henry Jaeger's cigar store featured more than cigars. Note the potbellied stove in the rear with handy chairs for those who gathered around it. A spittoon is placed strategically in the middle of the floor. The glass case on the left is laden with sweet treats. Below, a Native American statue outside the store garnered a lot of attention. Customers were invited to "chew and smoke." (Courtesy of the Ted Luecke family.)

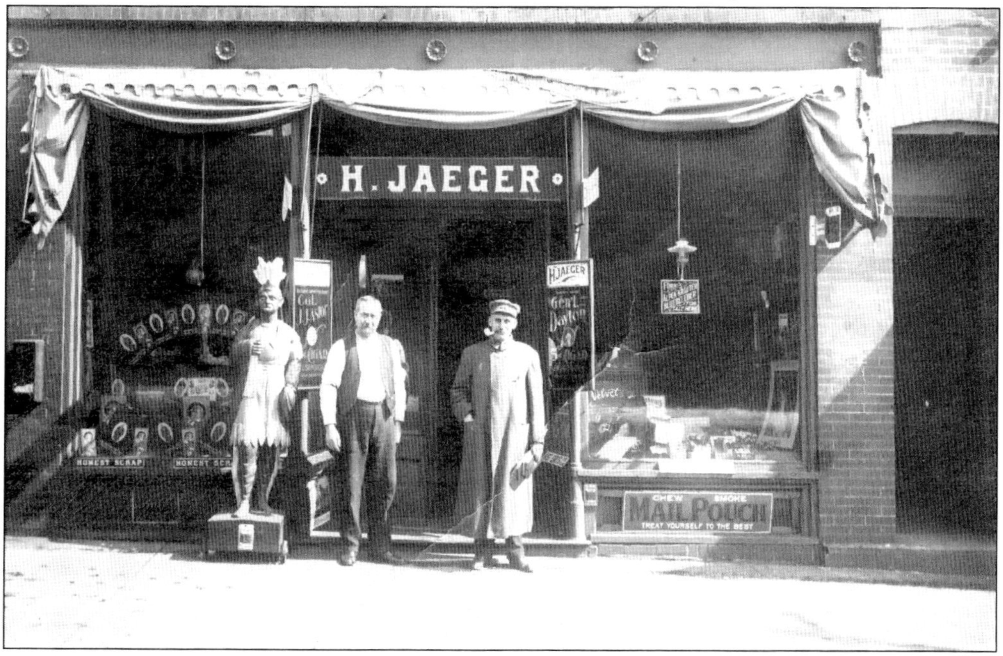

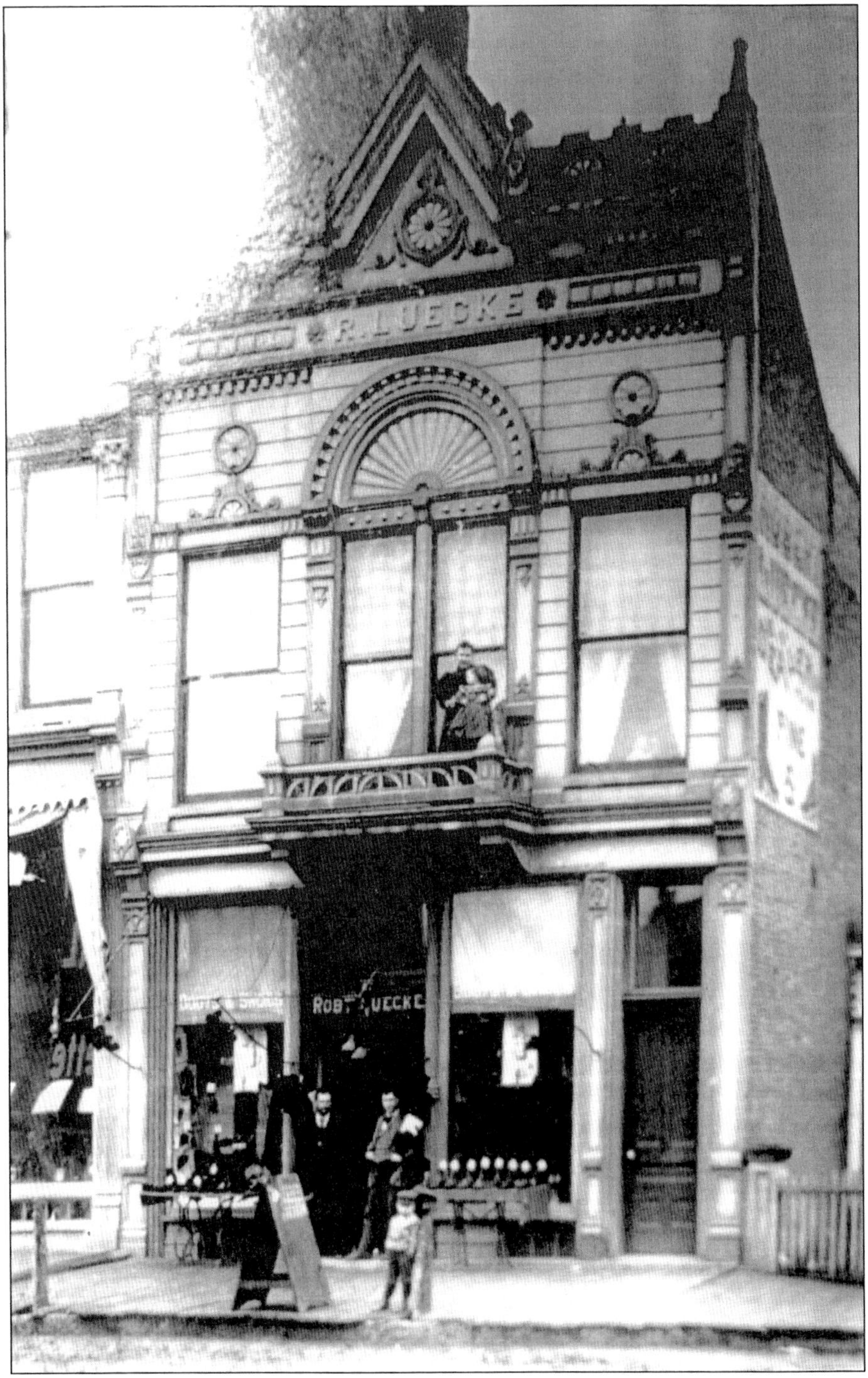

GENERATIONS HOLD ON. The Luecke family lived upstairs in the building that housed their men's clothing store at 10 East Main Street. Robert's wife, Elizabeth, is seen on the balcony in 1895 holding their daughter, Loretta. Later in life, Loretta wed Doug Grant, a one-time sports editor at the *Journal-Standard*. Today the location is the home of Two Eagles Family Restaurant, but much of the building's gingerbread is gone. (Courtesy of the Ted Luecke family.)

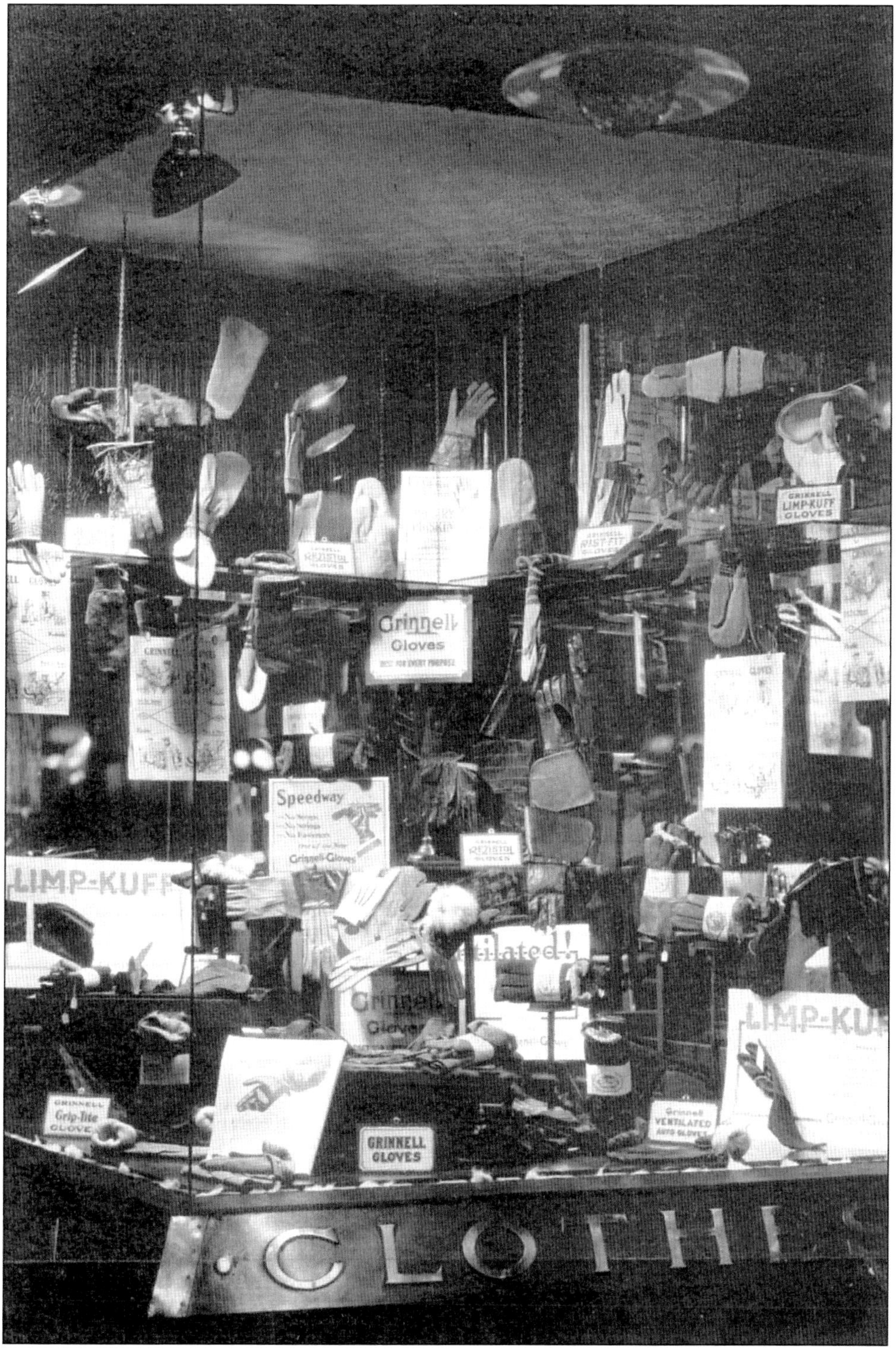

UNUSUAL ITEMS OFFERED. Both the early-day E. A. Blust business and Luecke's store kept their inventories of high-quality goods, even if it was not the most up-to-date. This window in Luecke's business displayed a wide assortment of merchandise. (Courtesy of the Ted Luecke family.)

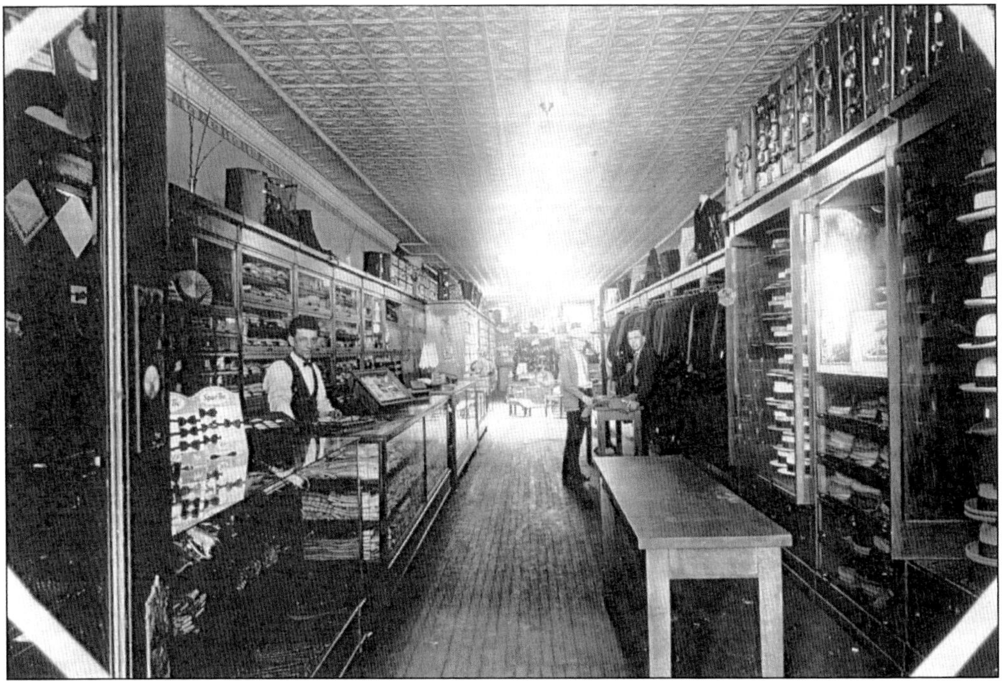

ROBERT LUECKE'S STORE. The Lueckes operated a clothing store from 1867 to 1956 on East Main Street. The business, first known as Robert Luecke's, became Robert Luecke's Sons' store in 1913 when his sons Leo and Henry took over. (Courtesy of the Ted Luecke family.)

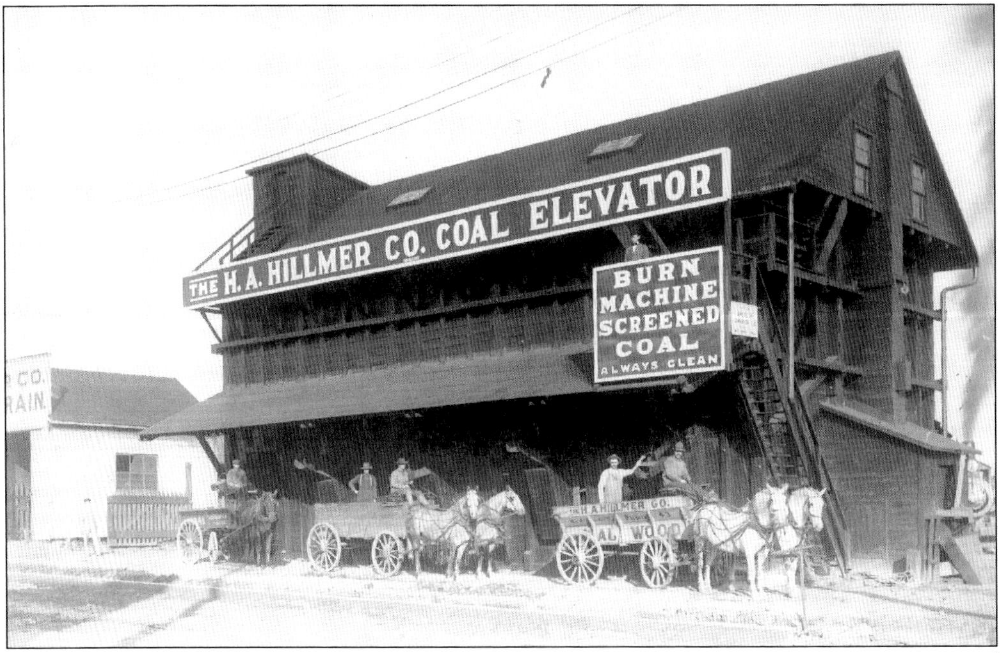

COAL WAS BIG BUSINESS. The H. A. Hillmer Coal Elevator, shown as it was in 1910, was one of the larger local coal yards. It was at the east end of Exchange Street not far from the Pecatonica River. Most homes were heated by coal until 1950, and many of them had chutes where the coal could be unloaded directly into the cellars.

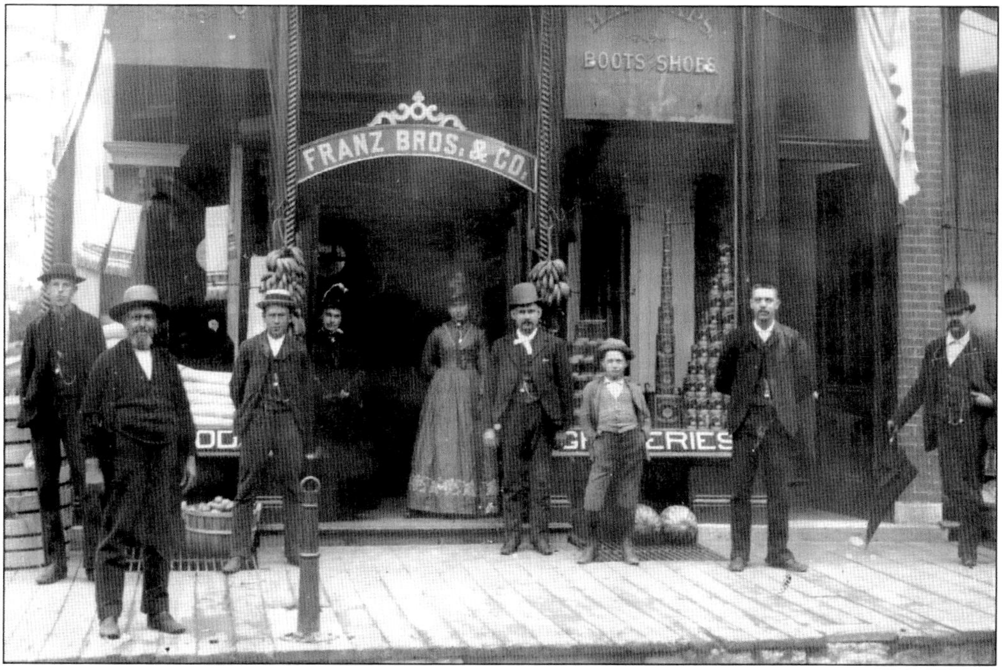

AN EARLY-DAY SHOPPING CENTER. Franz was a prominent name in Freeport at the dawn of the 20th century, especially in the mercantile business. Here posing in front of the Franz Brothers and Company dry goods store are dapper gentlemen, two ladies, and a lad in his knickers. The store dealt in groceries, millinery, linens, shoes, and boots. (Courtesy of the Ted Luecke family.)

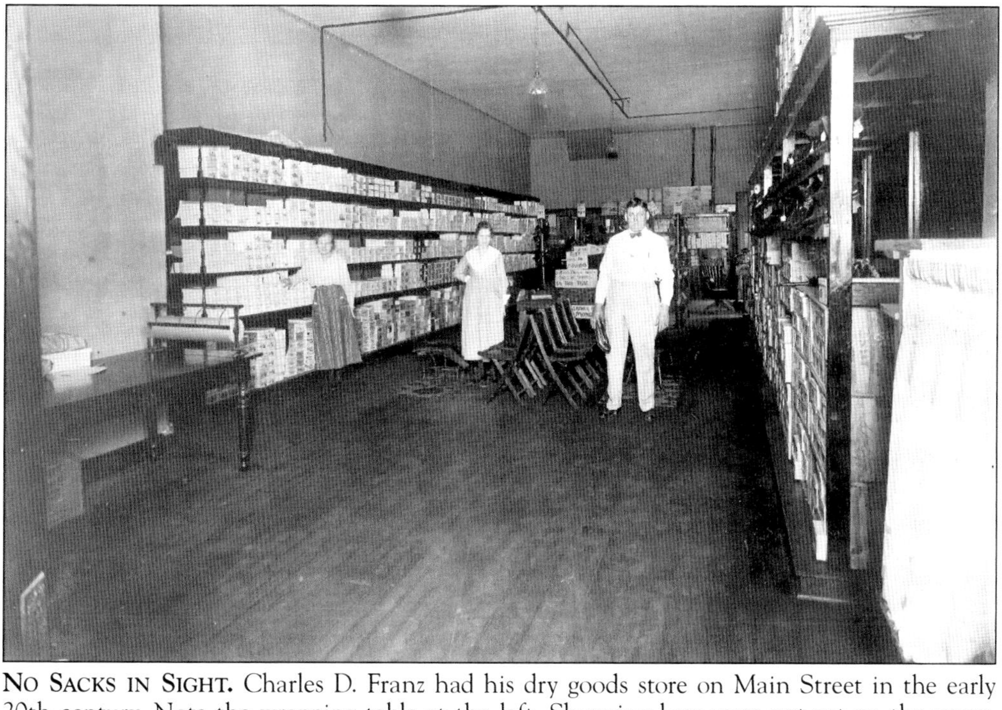

NO SACKS IN SIGHT. Charles D. Franz had his dry goods store on Main Street in the early 20th century. Note the wrapping table at the left. Shopping bags were not yet on the scene. (Courtesy of the Ted Luecke family.)

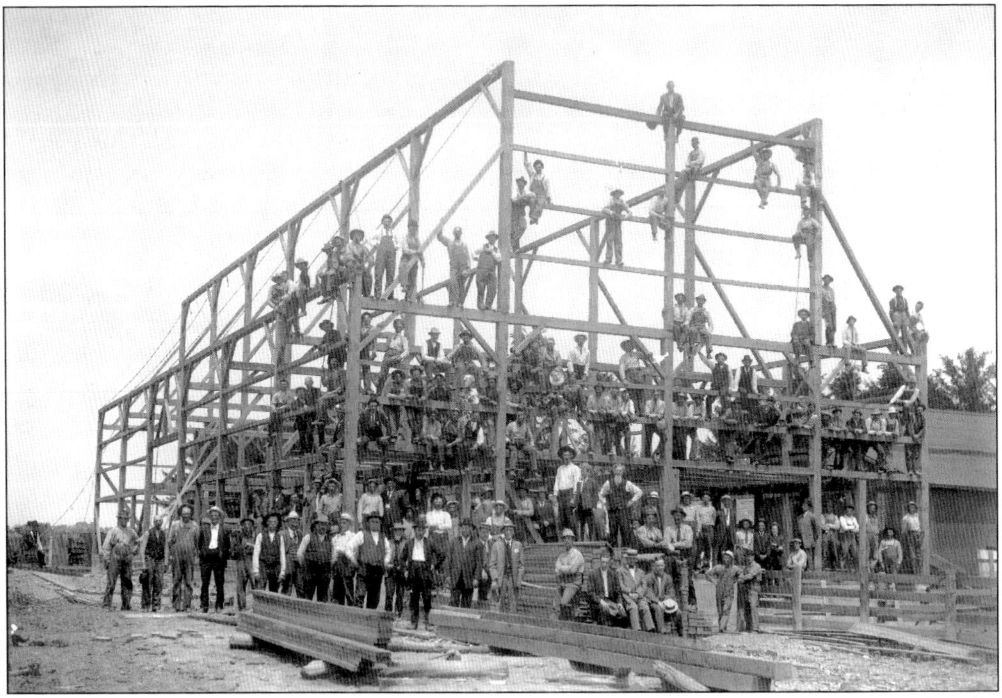

Many Hands Make Light Work. It did not take long to raise a barn with this much help. This took place on the William Amendt farm in Harlem Township.

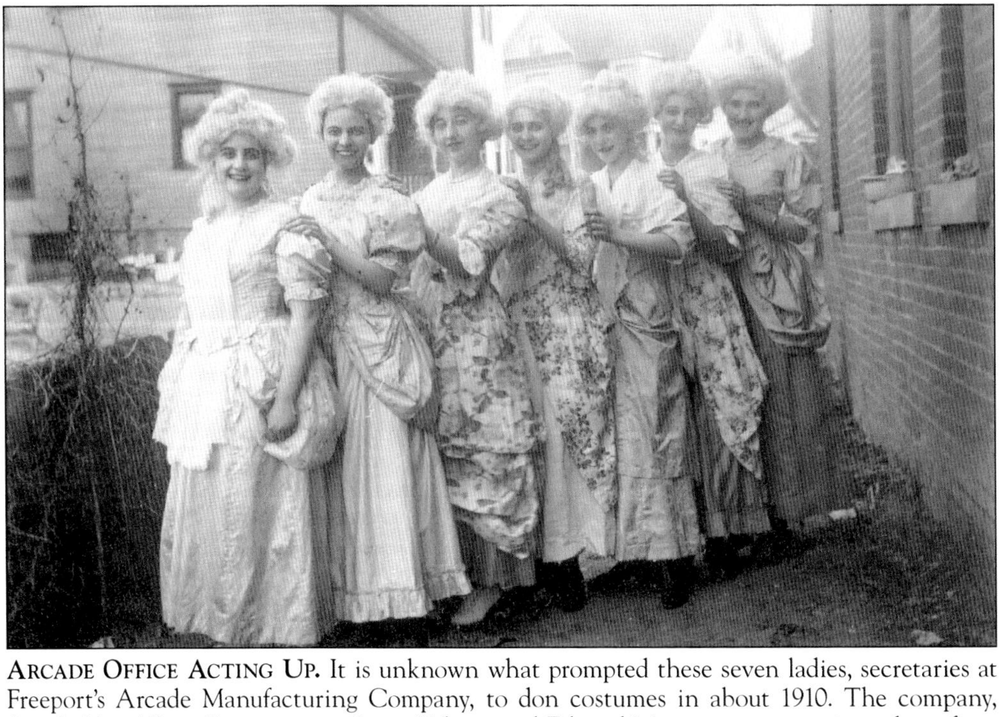

Arcade Office Acting Up. It is unknown what prompted these seven ladies, secretaries at Freeport's Arcade Manufacturing Company, to don costumes in about 1910. The company, founded by Albert Baumgarten, Cyrus Tobias, and Edward Morgan, was prominent here from 1885 to 1953. (Courtesy of the Ted Luecke family.)

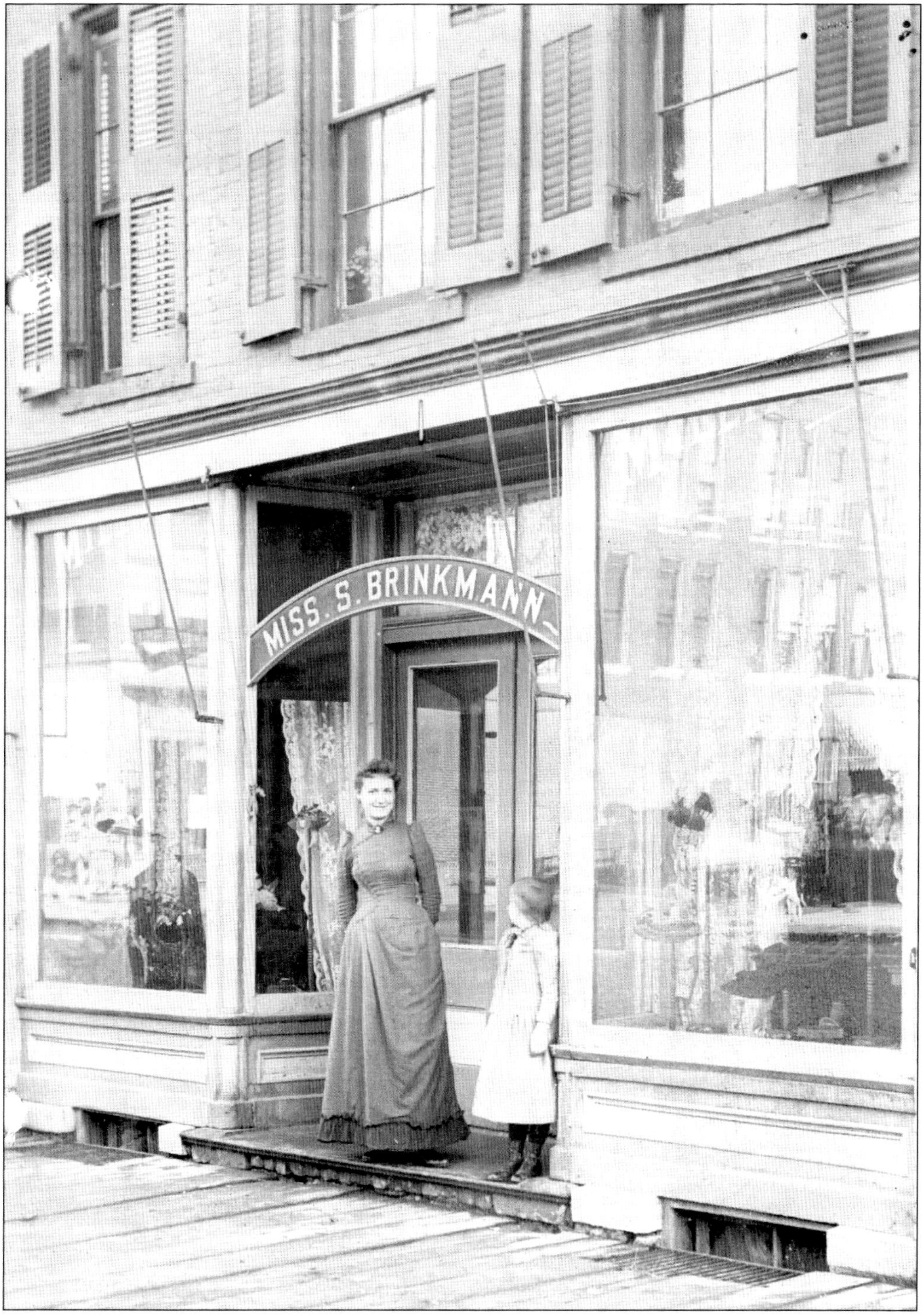

MILLINERY BUSINESS BIG, 1880S. Sophie Brinkman had her hat-making business at 103 West Main Street for many years. Note the plank sidewalk and the shutters on the second-story windows in this 1880s photograph. Millinery was a legitimate trade and thriving business well into the 20th century.

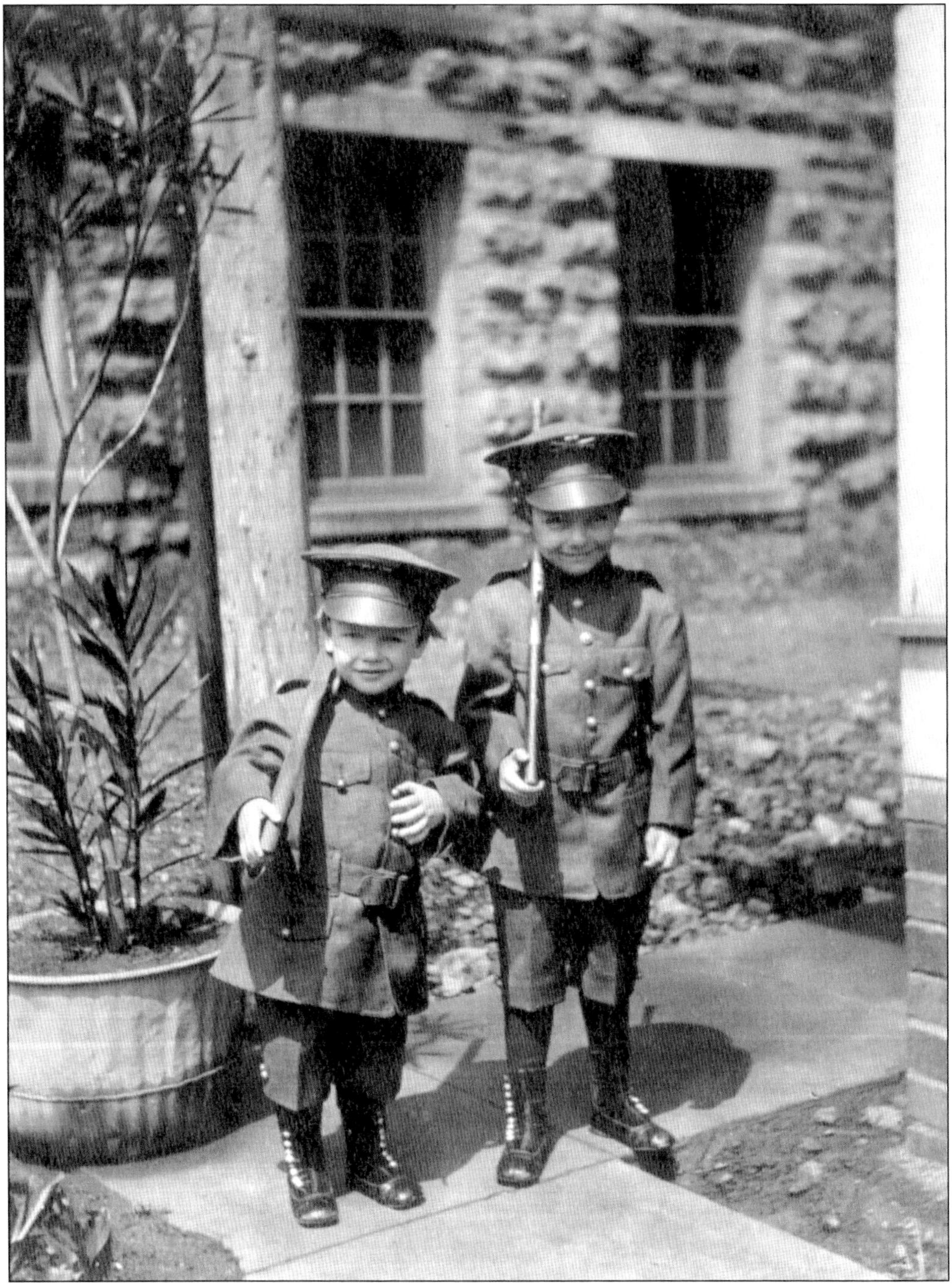

MEN IN UNIFORM. Fred and John Luecke wore uniforms at a tender age. These brothers were members of a prominent Freeport clan. John (right) served 18 years on the Freeport Park District board and was employed in administration at Micro-Switch, a key Freeport industry now called Honeywell Sensing and Control. (Courtesy of the Ted Luecke family.)

About the Organizations

The Stephenson County Historical Society, with the assistance of the Freeport Park District, maintains a museum complex at 1440 South Carroll Avenue. The 150-year-old mansion, which is the museum proper, was the home of two leading citizens of early Freeport, Oscar and Malvina Taylor. It is decorated richly in Victorian fashion, using some of the original Taylor pieces. The facility is maintained by the park district and volunteers. Ed Finch is the society's executive director.

Judy Birdsell and Crystal Haddad, board members, work together planning and arranging displays. Other volunteers help with special events. Harvey Wilhelms is society president.

In addition to the mansion, the complex includes a log cabin, a country school, and a farm/industrial museum. A carriage house serves as the office and storage area. A gift shop is maintained in the mansion.

Some of the trees in the society's arboretum are rare species planted by the Taylors 150 years ago. The grounds are landscaped with a gazebo, decorative shrubs, and beds of foliage and florals.

The society's aim is to preserve records and artifacts carefully by documenting their origin and donors. Its further aim is to make the facilities attractive and enjoyable for the patrons' education and enjoyment.

Hours are noon to 4:00 p.m. Friday through Sunday. Tours may be arranged in advance. The number to call for arrangements is (815) 232-8419.

The Frances Woodhouse Local History Room at Freeport Public Library is an excellent resource for historical research. There is a wide selection of books on local history and other documents available for genealogical research, as well as microfilmed area newspapers arranged by date. The history room has equipment for reading and printing articles from the newspapers.

The facility has a complete set of Freeport city directories, Freeport High School annuals, and Stephenson County plat books. There are assorted family genealogies and published histories of area towns.

The staff at Freeport Public Library, including Cheryl Bronkema and Cheryl Gleason, is there to assist patrons in research. Volunteers are also available weekdays to assist patrons.